WOMEN AND WORK IN PRE-INDUSTRIAL ENGLAND

THE OXFORD WOMEN'S SERIES

WOMEN AND WORK IN PRE-INDUSTRIAL ENGLAND

Edited by
Lindsey Charles and Lorna Duffin

CROOM HELM
London • Sydney • Dover, New Hampshire

©1985 Lindsey Charles and Lorna Duffin
Croom Helm Ltd, Provident House, Burrell Row,
Beckenham, Kent BR3 1AT

Croom Helm Australia Pty Ltd, Suite 4, 6th Floor,
64-76 Kippax Street, Surry Hills, NSW 2010, Australia

British Library Cataloguing in Publication Data
Women and work in pre-industrial England.
 1. Women – Employment – England – History
 I. Charles, Lindsey II. Duffin, Lorna
 331.4'0941   HD6136
  ISBN 0-7099-0814-8
  ISBN 0-7099-0856-3 pbk

Croom Helm, 51 Washington Street, Dover,
New Hampshire 03820, USA

Library of Congress Cataloging in Publication Data
Main entry under title:

Women and work in pre-industrial England.

  Includes index.
  1. Women – Employment – England – History – Addresses,
essays, lectures. 2. Women – England – Economic
conditions – Addresses, essays, lectures. 3. Home
labor – England – History – Addresses, essays, lectures.
I. Charles, Lindsey. II. Duffin, Lorna.
HD6136.W66 1985   331.4'0942   85-14950
ISBN 0-7099-0814-8
ISBN 0-7099-0856-3 (pbk.)

Printed and bound in Great Britain by
Biddles Ltd, Guildford and King's Lynn

CONTENTS

PREFACE

Lorna Duffin

This collection of papers originated as a series of
seminars convened under the auspices and with the
financial support of Oxford University Women's Studies
Committee. The editors are most grateful to the members
of the committee for their support, to all those who
attended the seminars and contributed to the discussions,
and to Queen Elizabeth House for providing the venue.
The work of the contributors in first presenting the
seminar papers and subsequently revising them for
publication deserves our generous thanks.

Lindsey Charles had the main responsibility for
organising the seminars, and took on the task of
academic editor. Lorna Duffin prepared the manuscripts
for publication and was given substantial and much
appreciated assistance by John Corlett.

This book is the eighth in the Oxford Women's Studies
series.

INTRODUCTION[1]

Lindsey Charles

'To the Victorians', it has been said, 'belongs the discovery of the woman worker as an object of pity'.[2] This goes far towards explaining why the bulk of historical research on women's work concentrates on the nineteenth and twentieth centuries. To begin with, the extensive investigation and legislation which arose from this concern for women workers engendered considerable material for use by historians. In addition, the position of the woman worker in modern industrial society is the subject of continuing historical and sociological debate, thus the nineteenth century woman worker is a natural object of attention and interest.

By contrast, women's work in earlier periods has been relatively neglected and described by one historian as the 'least well-explored area of women's studies.'[3] The reasons are not hard to find: empirical data is scarce and what there is presents considerable problems of interpretation and methodology. While some important pioneering work has been done in this field, most notably Alice Clark's *Working Life of Women in the Seventeenth Century*, there has until recently been little subsequent debate.[4] This volume is intended to contribute to this growing debate. Its concern is with English society before its transition to industrial capitalism in the eighteenth and nineteenth centuries. This period of economic transition has been chosen as an end point because it is often argued to have radically changed female work patterns and established the norms of women's work today. Whether it was industrialization or pre-existent capitalist organization which affected such changes is not always clear, and one of the points made here by Chris Middleton is that the analytical framework within which such arguments are formulated requires critical scrutiny. Whichever is the case, we hope that the time span of this volume will prove long enough to allow useful comparisons of women's work patterns across

1

several phases of economic and social organization. The starting point for our period was more difficult to determine. 'Pre-industrial', it has been pointed out, is a 'somewhat negative label'[5] which can subsume many different eras and forms of economic organization. The choice of a starting date of 1300 is largely pragmatic since the late thirteenth and fourteenth centuries mark the appearance of more adequate written sources and records through which women's work can be explored. Thus the collection straddles the two customary historical categories of medieval and early modern and encompasses fundamental and far-reaching social and economic change.

Some brief outline of these changes might be useful here.[6] English society at the turn of the fourteenth century could still be called feudal in that there was still a large body of unfree labour rendering dues in kind or labour service to the seignurial class, and that manorial organization and jurisdiction continued to be strong, even over the towns. But money rents were becoming increasingly common. This was partly due to land hunger caused by a rising population which led to the reclamation of new land without the attachment of customary dues and the sale of old land at an inflated value requiring cash payments as well as traditional dues. As a result, by the time of the Black Death (1348) 'the whole situation was extremely fluid ... The scramble for land, together with commutation had somewhat blurred social status, villein and freeman often working side by side on land for which they paid a money rent.'[7] Taking advantage of the rising prices often associated with population pressure many lords took to farming their demesne lands for profit, selling their surplus to other parts of the country and, in many cases, abroad, where it formed part of the swelling tide of English exports. Trade in general had increased during what is often seen as the economic expansion of the twelfth and thirteenth centuries, and with it towns had grown in number and size. As their economic strength grew they began to slough off the social and political control exerted by the baronage.

Over the following 200 years the manorial system suffered increasing dislocation and although the vestiges of villeinage lingered until the seventeenth century (when the last legal bondman died) the society in which it had flourished had long since disappeared. By 1600 many of the descendants of medieval barons were still holding very large estates, but their tenantry was free and usually paying money rent, and their legal jurisdiction over the locality had dwindled to nothing. Nor were they the only group of substantial landowners as, with the exception of the church, they had been in the fourteenth century. The gentry class was now an affluent and influential social group, and had acquired an importance, local and national, in the countryside almost equal to that of the aristocracy. Below the gentry there was the nearest thing England ever seems to have had to an independent, prosperous peasantry [8] in the shape of the yeoman class – small scale, largely owner occupying farmers, rivalling, at their wealthiest end, the poorer gentry. Alongside these were cottagers with more precarious leasing arrangements over their land and wage labourers who were often either landless or supplementing the products of an inadequate land holding.

Several reasons have been adduced for these changes. There was, to begin with, the dramatic disruption of the Black Death and subsequent plague outbreaks which reversed the population rise of the previous two centuries and in so doing may well have had some far reaching social consequences. There was now a land surplus and labour shortage and this is frequently argued to have been to the advantage of the smallholder who could get better terms of hiring and service and cheaper land. Town dwellers also invested increasingly in land. During the fifteenth century the baronage further weakened their position as a class in the prolonged internecine strife of the Wars of the Roses. This reduced their numbers, stretched their purses and considerably reduced their political power when the Crown eventually succeeded in asserting more control than ever before over its great peers. Their control over the local countryside was also quietly undermined by lesser sorts buying up the land of impoverished barons or gaining influence in local affairs during the prolonged absences of warring lords. The final major factor in the change in the balance of landed power was the sixteenth century English Reformation and the accompanying sale of monastery land. The purchase of such land by prosperous middle class families, urban and rural, helped to create the solid gentry class which was politically so much in evidence in the seventeenth century.

Changes in the trading and manufacturing sectors of the economy during this period were also extensive. English trade at the beginning of the fourteenth century, both internal and international, was brisk and expanding. Marketing and exchange took place at all levels: from the local sale of peasant surpluses to raise money for dues or the purchase of commodities not obtainable from land holdings (for example, salt, fish and iron implements), to large landowners selling the produce of their farms and mines to central and southern Europe and Scandinavia. The staple of English exports however, was wool. English wool was in demand throughout Europe, particularly in the northern cloth making centres of Flanders, Brabant and Holland. Its export reached a peak in the early fourteenth century and remained at a high level throughout the 1300s despite the disruption of the Hundred Years War with France. Since it was inevitably a prime target for Crown taxation it was fiscally more convenient to channel exported wool through one centre abroad – the Staple, which became fixed at Calais from 1392. By the mid-fourteenth century this was dominated by a small group of large English merchants known as Merchants of the Staple or Staplers, who by the mid-fifteenth century controlled about four-fifths of the English wool trade. They included, as Kay Lacey shows, at least two women in their numbers in the fifteenth century.

This trade in raw wool was, however, increasingly challenged by the growing export of woollen cloth. This increased thirtyfold between the mid-fourteenth and mid-sixteenth centuries and by the seventeenth century constituted over 92% of all woollen exports and 80-90% of exports as a whole. It retained its importance until outstripped by cotton at the end of the eighteenth century. Behind this expansion in the cloth trade was the development and expansion of the English cloth industry. A cloth industry there had always been, producing for the home market, but it was not until the fifteenth and sixteenth centuries that English cloth started to compete with fine Flemish products in the European markets. This was partly due to influxes of Flemish refugees from the Low Countries who were particularly influential in establishing the 'New Draperies' in East Anglia. Technological change such as the introduction of the fulling mill in the thirteenth and fourteenth centuries, may also have been an important factor. By the seventeenth century the manufacture of cloth was being deliberately encouraged by the government at the expense of raw wool exports since it had greater pay-offs in terms of employment as well as fiscal revenue. On a number of occasions the export of raw wool was banned and in 1617 the Staple was disbanded.

Woollen cloth, then, for much of our period was centrally important to the British economy both as a staple export and as a major manufacturing activity, a fact which explains its prominence in this collection. Many towns and areas were involved in its manufacture at some time and their fortunes waxed and waned with those of the particular types of cloth they made. The cloth industry was both urban and rural. In towns it was usually based on a network of cottager outworkers organized by middle-man clothiers. Sometimes the two interlinked in that urban masters also organized rural work, especially spinning, which was never gild organized and always undertaken by outworkers, whether urban or rural. So, for example, the fourteenth and fifteenth century worsted industry in Norwich was closely integrated with its suppliers of yarn in surrounding villages. But in other regions urban and rural cloth manufacture was unconnected and even, at times, in competition. One of the major early cloth towns, York, was in decline by the fifteenth century while around it the rural West Riding industry was thriving. This largely independent rural cloth industry is often seen as being one of the first industries to experience large scale organization, resting as it did on the employment and coordination of numbers of workers carrying out different and specialized processes: spinning, weaving, fulling, dyeing and so on.

Other industries were also growing in importance, however, as demand for their products increased, both at home and abroad. Iron work of all sorts, pottery and coal were chief amongst these. During the seventeenth century, as English trade networks began their rapid expansion to take in Africa, Asia and the Atlantic, and goods were increasingly carried, with government encouragement, in English ships (as opposed, for example, to Dutch carriers) shipbuilding and fitting also became a major industry. By the end of the century such mercantile activity had become at least as important in English overseas trade as the cloth trade. Cloth still comprised by far the largest export in terms of volume, but other commodities of less bulk sold into new and unpredictable markets had disproportionately large returns. England had also evolved a system of re-export and monopoly supplying with its colonies, particularly in the New World, which proved lucrative until blown apart by the American revolutionaries in the late eighteenth century. Undertaking or investing in risky but potentially profitable ventures overseas became a living in itself, despite the occasional speculative disaster, and London became the commercial capital of the world.

It was perhaps the spoils of this trading empire and the opportunities it offered in terms of raw materials and markets which contributed to the industrial development of the late eighteenth century. Changes in agricultural organization, combined with growing population, have also been singled out as contributory factors. By the end of the seventeenth century 'the movement towards the Great Estate was beginning',[9] at the expense of smaller farmers and landholders. These were increasingly pushed out by dispossession by consolidating and enclosing landlords or neighbours or by overwhelming competition from the great estates which, it is argued, were frequently created and expanded for the very purpose of allowing increased efficiency. By the mid-eighteenth century a widening gap had opened up between substantial farmers and large landowners on the one hand and virtually landless wage labourers on the other. This, combined with accelerated population growth in the later eighteenth century is traditionally argued to have provided the pool of surplus labour required for industrial development. At the same time, capitalist agriculture created surplus capital which could be invested in industrial development and the technological innovations which enabled it to happen. Capitalist organization is frequently argued to have been well established in many sectors of the economy by this time — for most Marxist historians the seventeenth century forms the watershed between feudalism and capitalism. The mix of causes and the weight each should carry in an explanation of eighteenth century industrial change is the subject of prolonged and heated dispute.[10] What is clear is that the last years of the eighteenth century with their large, capital intensive cotton factories (albeit still dependent on wooden machinery and water power) heralded the massive changes in manufacture which by the late nineteenth century had transformed the English economy into an industrial one and the English population to a predominantly urban one, working for wages on an increasingly specialized and mechanized basis.

Such, then, is the general social and economic background to the study of women's work. What picture has emerged from such study to date? For the earlier part of the period, up to the seventeenth century, some common features emerge from the existing literature. It is generally agreed that women, while on the whole virtually excluded from public life, played an extremely active economic role. This was expected by contemporaries: 'husband and wife were then mutually dependent and both supported their children.'[11] The exact nature of this role is difficult to define. There was, it is argued, far more to be done in the way of production for consumption by the household — 'the spinning of thread and weaving of cloth, the making of clothes, and the preparation of foods.'[12] — which was largely undertaken by the women of the household. But women also undertook remunerative work. They appear to have participated to some extent in most craft gilds. Many carried on a craft or trade independently, and a handful, particularly in the upper reaches of society, were successful and prominent in their field. On the whole, however, women's involvement in gild organized crafts was through their participation in their husbands' or fathers' trades. These, it must be remembered, were frequently carried on in the same premises as the household's living quarters, and it is argued that the women of the house assisted in them almost as a matter of course. There was also, however, a range of occupations undertaken by women outside gild organized crafts, many of which were almost exclusively female. The most common of these were spinning, brewing, retailing and general provisioning. Rural women, by far the most numerous but most forgotten group, worked the land and tended livestock. In cloth manufacturing districts, both men and women frequently drew part of their livelihood from out-work for entrepreneur clothiers: spinning generally seemed to fall to women, while men looked after the looms.

It is generally assumed that female activity was largely determined by the demands of the household and the fortunes of its male workers. Hence Eileen Power, a pioneer in the study of medieval women argued that 'it was necessary for the married woman to earn a supplementary wage' [13] in whatever way she could, and designates many wives' occupations as 'bye-industries' — sidelines rather than full time occupations. This view also emerges from more recent literature — Sally Alexander, for example, argues that a woman's work in the home was 'allocated between domestic labour and work in production for sale, according to the family's economic needs.' [14] Further, it is often argued that 'these were often trades which related directly to the work of women in the household because at this stage domestic and industrial life were not clearly separate. Women thus carried on food, drink and clothing production.' [15] For the most part women's work is also seen in the context of marriage and widowhood since it is generally assumed that the demographic balance between the sexes was more even than in the past 200 years and that most women married at some time. [16] Only Power maintains, on somewhat shaky evidence, that there was a 'surplus' of single women who had to support themselves. [17] Overall, women's labour is seen as determined by, and subordinate to, the demands of husband, household and family. On the whole they were also legally subordinate to their husbands and their economic activity was in theory closely confined by legal incapacity, which affected, amongst other things, their right to own and dispose of property. This, however, was not as incapacitating as the legal subordination of women in the nineteenth century, partly due to loopholes arising from conflicting and overlapping jurisdictions which at times allowed even married women considerable legal independence. [18] One further important characteristic of medieval women's work which has been generally identified is the low level of female wages. In examples where these can be compared with those of men — in field labouring or servant, work, they appear to be considerably lower. [19]

The picture of women's work generally presented for the earlier part of this period is a somewhat static one. Few have identified any movements for change in women's work over time.[20]   This is in contrast to the seventeenth century and onwards, which, as described above, is generally seen as a period of radical social and economic transformation and where research focusses on how this affected women's labour.   The most substantial and thorough research on women in 'pre-industrial' England to date deals with these later years.   Most important are Clark's *Working Life* and another early pioneering work by Ivy Pinchbeck: *Women Workers and the Industrial Revolution 1750-1850*.[21]   Both see similar changes taking place in women's work during the period c.1650–1850, but differ about their cause and timing.

The chief changes identified by both are the disappearance of many traditional female occupations, the growth of a class of idle women in more affluent social groups and the resort by their poorer sisters to waged labour outside the home.   Clark attributes these developments to the growth of capitalism (although she confounds capitalism with industrialization) and places their beginnings in the late seventeenth century. In agriculture capitalist development led to large scale farming which eventually dispossessed the descendants of many of the small independent farmers prized and encouraged by the Tudors and forced them, male and female alike, to turn to waged labour.   In industry capitalist development edged out small craftsmen and led to the concentration of increasing numbers of workers in workplaces away from home.   Taken together, these developments deprived women of their opportunities to share their husbands' work.   For wealthy women this led to the parasitism described by Olive Schreiner,[22] for the poor, increasing exploitation at the hands of wage-paying capitalists.   The increasing amounts of capital required in business combined with new skill specializations from which women were effectively excluded prevented the vast majority of women from carrying on their own business.   Pinchbeck attributes far more responsibility in this process to increasing industrial mechanization, although her analysis of the effect of large scale agricultural development is similar to that of Clark's.   The growth of factories in the late eighteenth and nineteenth centuries led to the destruction of handicraft industry and the separation of home and work. It also gradually removed many of the tasks of household production formerly undertaken by women to mass factory production.   Her view of these changes is less gloomy than Clark's since it maintains that female wage earners in factory industry were no more exploited than those previously working at home on out-work for capitalist employers and middlemen – an aspect of early capitalism of which Clark takes little account.[23]

These interpretations, most of them established early in this century, of the effects of industrial capitalism, have on the whole been accepted with little modification since and form the basis of much of the theoretical debate on the determinants of women's work in modern industrial society.[24] What historical modification there has been has usually been to the view of nineteenth century women's work – it has been pointed out, for example, that out-work, home-work and handicraft work, much of it involving women, survived into this century.[25] Even the concept of the idle middle class wife has been challenged.[26] But the picture of the antecedent conditions sketched above remains largely intact. Apart from its theoretical conveniences, one reason for the lack of modification to this view may well be the scarcity of sources available and the formidable methodological problems they present in use. Before examining the particular contribution of the papers in this collection to the field outlined above, a survey of the raw material available and its limitations will be useful.

One of the staple sources for the history of the earlier part of our period is court records (rolls). The most important here, in a collection of papers heavily biased towards urban life, are those of royal, ecclesiastical and borough courts. Surviving rolls are quite extensive and are made up of a mass of depositions, presentments, allegations, decisions and orders. They are perhaps the most systematically and regularly kept records, especially at the level of national judicial circuits. Year books, which were notes on the proceedings of cases, apparently by aspiring lawyers, can also be illuminating. Rarer, but also well kept, are taxation records. Again, these are best at a national level where, for example, the lay subsidies and poll taxes levied by the royal government in the fourteenth century provide a fairly comprehensive and hence valuable coverage.[27] Another important source is gild records and regulations – the nature and extent of these depends on the locality. In addition to these types of data, there is a variety of material to be found at local level. Household listings, baptismal registers, the 'Easter books' used by Sue Wright are examples of official records kept occasionally in individual towns.

Other important and widely used sources are personal records in the form of wills, testaments and inventories which can shed light on everyday life, inheritance customs, family relationships and so on. Personal papers become more extensive as our period progresses as diary-keeping became more common and correspondence more frequent due to higher standards of literacy and a more stable political environment.[28] Finally, there are literary sources, which also become more extensive in the later part of the period due to easier access to printing presses and, again, increasing literacy. Books and pamphlets of advice, warning and exhortation on a range of subjects appear in growing numbers as well as the more artistic works of fiction: plays, poetry, satires and, eventually, novels.

All these sources present fundamental problems in use, especially for historians studying women. Women, as is often pointed out, tend to be 'invisible' as far as many historical sources are concerned, rarely appearing, or doing so only fleetingly. This is due largely to their subordinate legal and political position which means that they were rarely householders, litigants or gild members. This is particularly so for married women whose rights and identity were largely subsumed under their husbands' and who present the added complication of a changing surname which makes them very difficult to trace, especially through remarriages. But the actual position of women who do appear in the records can be very difficult to ascertain. Take, for example, gild records, where women are occasionally recorded as members. It cannot be unquestioningly assumed that such women actually carried on a trade or enjoyed the same gild privileges as men. It seems clear that there were different types of membership.[29] To begin with, many gilds had social and religious functions which were as important as their role in regulating and protecting trade. Women might participate fully in the religious and social aspects of a gild while having only a limited role in its economic life. Moreover, within that economic life there could be different levels of participation: for example, someone might enjoy the privilege conferred by the gild to trade without having the right to participate in the governance of the gild. When this happened, women were probably usually in the former category. The sheer diversity of gild traditions add to the complications of determining the position of women within them.

Women, particularly widows, did, however, have one unique role within the gilds in that they could offer a way to membership for outsiders. Membership was often extended to the widows of craftsmen, but was transferred to their new husband if they married a man working the same trade. This raises the further important problem of how far female gild members actually carried on a trade themselves and how far it was in the hands of male relatives and employees – particularly if they were widows (a question explored here by Sue Wright). This in turn raises the question of the type and extent of the expertise acquired by the wives and daughters who frequently seemed to have assisted master craftsmen without official recognition. It also presents an interesting problem in those cases where husband and wife are found pursuing different gild crafts or trades or when gild privileges are granted to both husband and wife - examples of both have been uncovered by Diane Hutton and Kay Lacey.

Even such apparently straightforward aspects of gilds as their regulations cannot be taken at face value. For our purposes here, those regulating the employment practices of masters are most interesting. For example, from time to time there were prohibitions on the employment of women by masters except for their own wives and daughters. This throws interesting light on the employment of women in the trades concerned, and on the position of wives and daughters. But it also raises the problem of the reasons for the prohibition and its effect. It must have been enacted in response to what was perceived as an unacceptable level of female employment in the trade. But was this higher than formerly, or were economic conditions and male unemployment getting worse? Was it perhaps due to political pressure from male apprentices and journeymen prompted by their own precarious position? And why was female labour seen as unacceptable anyway? Frequently this must have been due to the threat of undercutting presented by female labour since women's rates of pay then as now tended to be lower than men's. This raises larger questions of the sexual division of labour and differential wage rates to which we shall return later.

Difficulties similarly arise with that even richer source - court records. Here the problem of typicality has been recognized for some time and not just in this period or in 'women's history'. It is obviously difficult to get a balanced view of a community and its life from court or police records. One of the many problems is judging the prevalence of a particular crime or misdemeanour at any one time: a flood of prosecutions for an offence could mean that its incidence had risen, or it could simply indicate more efficient policing or increased public concern about it for some reasons. Thus, for example, women prosecuted for illegal retailing could be part of a rising trend or could be the victims of a particularly vigilant town corporation. Moreover, it is difficult to assess how widespread the offence was: the authorities may have swooped successfully on all such lawbreakers or they may have been struggling in vain against a major problem, in which case even a large number of prosecutions may represent only the tip of the iceberg. Records of prosecutions and the like therefore have to be used very carefully and in close conjunction

with other data about the life of the community as a
whole.

However, court records are not confined to reports of
cases heard and decisions and penalties given. As David
Vaisey has pointed out, much useful incidental information
can often be gleaned from the statements of witnesses, the
comments of clerks and what were to contemporaries
unimportant incidental circumstances of a case: 'the most
valuable nuggets are to be found in the most unlikely-
sounding cases.'[30] Thus a source which has been well
worked over in conventional ways might, with a little
imagination and a lot of thorough tooth-combing, be made
to yield new insights.

The sources which are perhaps most obviously
fraught with problems of use and interpretation are
literary ones. Whether overtly polemical or not, they
obviously offer a highly subjective view of the world and
it is extremely difficult to determine how far and how
accurately the norms of contemporary society are reflected
therein. However, such sources still have valuable
potential, provided that their limitations are recognized.
Thus, they cannot be relied on to give concrete information on the nature and extent of women's employment
but may give some idea of the way in which it was
perceived, by women and others, of the status it enjoyed
and so on. In addition, the very appearance of such
tracts or other forms of literature, may have its own
sociological significance. Michael Roberts shows here how
literary sources, when carefully handled, can yield
images and ideals which themselves reflect important
facets of and changes in the society of a particular
period.

This, then, is the background of source material
and general methodological considerations against which
the papers collected here, with their specific foci and
varying approaches must be set.

We begin with a study by Kay Lacey of the legal
context of women's work in fourteenth and fifteenth
century London. This is a central issue as terms of
trading, ownership of land and goods, right to prosecute
for debt, in short, everything necessary for economic
activity was affected by law, whether it be parliamentary
statute, common law or borough regulation. Lacey threads
her way through the mass of complex and often conflicting
law governing women's work in London during this period
to determine what women's legal capacities may have been
in theory. She then compares their theoretical position
with what can be discovered about their actual work in
London at this time, and shows that the two frequently
did not coincide.

Diane Hutton puts women in roughly the same period

but a different town – Shrewsbury – under the microscope. She tries to ascertain the typicality of the few women appearing in the records and to reconstruct the working lives of women in general, examining the differences between the types and patterns of male and female work. She points out the need also to consider the work done by women without financial returns for the maintenance of individual households and families in assessing their overall contribution to the economy.

Sue Wright takes us on to the sixteenth and early seventeenth centuries with a detailed examination of women's work in Salisbury during this period. She discusses women's role both inside and outside the formal gild sector of the town's economy, trying to assess the extent of their participation in all areas, and the typicality and exact roles of the isolated examples which surface in gild and court records. She too discusses whether and how fluctuations in the town's economic fortunes affected the position of working women.

The last two papers move from the local study to the national overview. First, Michael Roberts gives us a different and little explored perspective on women's work in the seventeenth and eighteenth centuries. He presents five views of women's work, drawing largely, although not exclusively, on literary sources. Using these, he shows the ideological uncertainty and ambivalence surrounding women's work, and indeed work in general, during this period. He then relates these various and sometimes conflicting views to the economic reality of women's position and the changes probably taking place in it due to the development of capitalism and the first stages of industrialization.

A contrasting treatment of the effects of capitalism in its various stages of development follows in Chris Middleton's paper. He seeks firstly to evolve a clearer and more rigorous theoretical perspective on what pre-industrial capitalism comprised. He then argues that many of the characteristics of women's work which can be discerned under pre-industrial capitalism pre-date its development. In so doing he challenges many of the arguments frequently advanced about the reasons for sexual divisions of labour. He draws parallels over time, referring forward to the present as well as back to feudal society, to point up the similarities and continuity in women's work experience as well as the differences.

Women's work during this period, then, is viewed from a number of contrasting angles in this collection. There are, however, a few common themes and problems which occur throughout the papers and which may be drawn together briefly here and compared with other findings to date on the subject.

One of the most important of these is the association between home and work in this period. As seen above, this is often identified as a key difference, certainly for female labour, between pre- and post-industrial society. It would be impossible to deny that this theory has much in its favour. 'Pre-industrial' trade and manufacture was usually carried out in close proximity to domestic life, whether in the cottages of rural workers producing cloth or yarn under the putting out system, or in the shop or workshop of urban traders and craftworkers which was usually in the same building as a family's living quarters. It is also clear that members of the same family often pursued or assisted in the same economic activity. The example of this which arises most frequently in these urban-oriented papers is the one cited earlier of wives and daughters assisting in craftsmen's work. It was recognized that family and work relations were closely intertwined – hence the right of widows to inherit and continue their dead husbands' trade, or pass on his gild status to a new husband.

Furthermore, many household activities overlapped with commercial ones. For example, it is likely that many housewives still made bread, ale and homespun clothes for their households, but these were also produced for sale – Power's bye -industries. Often, as with bread and textile manufacture, these crafts had reached a fairly advanced degree of organization, and thus what counted as a standard female occupation within the household had become a trade in its own right outside it. But the lines were often blurred – ale was frequently made by house-wives, for example, hence the name 'alewife' and 'brewster'. How well defined this activity was for the woman concerned, that is, whether it constituted a distinct occupation rather than a sideline in surplus from ale made routinely for the household is difficult to say, not least because it doubtless varied with each case.

It is, however, possible to overdraw this identifica-tion of home and work, for both male and female labour. Many, possibly most, men worked away from their living quarters. Journeymen and apprentices, for example, worked on their masters' premises and were supposed to live as part of his household. But many journeymen were married, and for them there was a clear separation of home and work. It also, as Diane Hutton points out, ruled out family participation in their craft and put their wives in a quite different position to those of master craftsmen. For the far greater numbers working the land a similar case could probably be made. It has been pointed out elsewhere that the male population were frequently out of the household 'sowing, ploughing,

14

hedging, ditching, haymaking, harvesting.'[31]   To which may be added mining, foundry work, peddling and so on. The work of many women seems almost inevitably to have taken them 'abroad' out of the household.   For example, it is clear here, and has long been recognized, that poorer women were often 'regraters' or 'hucksters' — street traders who bought up produce and hawked it at undercutting prices.   But it is rarely acknowledged that this activity itself took them away from domestic confines. Women also, of course, worked on the land.   Only perhaps in the few rural households existing by cottage industry alone were members of the family in the house working together at their allotted occupations for much of the time.   In an urban context it was perhaps only in retailing businesses and the households of independent craftworkers that most of the family worked as a matter of course on related activities under the same roof.

Nevertheless, it must be admitted that for women the identification of home and work was stronger than for men.   To begin with, then as now, they bore the brunt of household management, unpaid domestic work, and child care.   For many 'huswyfry' was their work.   Also as noted above, it seems clear that many women developed a sometimes illegal byeline in selling goods which they produced for household use anyway.   But it is equally clear that women's activities were often not, apparently, linked to their housewifely roles.   Married women in the more substantial classes sometimes pursued occupations which were patently not extensions of their domestic activities — most spectacularly the female brokers and merchants cited by Kay Lacey.   Women who actually assisted in their husbands' or fathers' craft were by that very fact often straying beyond their household skills. This is not altered by the fact that, as Diane Hutton points out, they were often to be found running the retailing side of the business.   Skill in retailing does not seem to arise naturally from household tasks, except perhaps experience gained while marketing, yet it seems in general to have been an important female activity at all social levels.

This activity formed part of what here is often termed the 'informal economy' of the towns.   This can be broadly defined as economic activity which fell outside the formal systems of regulation and recognition imposed by the gilds.   It encompasses not only huckstering, regrating and the like, but also services such as nursing, searching the dead, laundering and servanthood itself.   The 'informal economy' included both men and women — by no means all trades were gild organized[32] and those that were represented, on the whole, elite groups. But while men were distributed, in unknown proportions, between 'formal' and 'informal' sectors, women's activities were concentrated almost exclusively in the latter, with the exception, of course, of those unusual and enigmatic females who appear in gild records. 'Informal' does not necessarily denote casual – many of the female activities falling under this heading were well defined occupations. The exclusively female craft of silk–making, for example, required a considerable amount of investment, equipment and work organization. Why such trades did not develop gild organization is an open historical question, as Kay Lacey points out. Women – only gilds were fairly common on the continent and it is difficult to see why they failed to develop in Britain. Power suggests that this was due to the tendency of women to pursue a variety of occupations in combination.[33] But, those female trades which seem the likeliest candidates for gild organization almost certainly demanded the full–time work and attention of the women who plied them. They also probably represented their most important means of livelihood, judging by the London silkwomen's petitions to the King about the threat of foreign competition in the fifteenth century. Michael Roberts explores the nature of occupational identity and discusses why it was strong for men while almost non–existent for women.

Another theme common to most of the papers here is the importance of the local social and economic environment in shaping the nature and extent of women's work. For example, a town's waning economic fortunes might account for repressive measures against women's employment in certain trades. The earlier the period the more pronounced local variations in economic organization and prosperity tend to be in general, yet their effect has often been overlooked. Clark shows little appreciation of the geographically uneven impact of capitalism on women's work and Power takes no account at all of such circumstances, although Pinchbeck undertakes, for the end of the period, a sophisticated analysis of the varying fortunes of women in different parts of the country.[34] More recent work on the early modern period has emphasized the importance of local conditions, demonstrating how different communities within a fairly small geographical compass could develop very diverse customs and work patterns.[35]

Economic conditions are perhaps the most obvious local factors affecting women's work, but there are others which are equally if not more important. One such is demographic circumstances. It seems increasingly clear that these have to be studied at a local level anyway, given the difficulty of obtaining reliable national data before the nineteenth century. Some of the more obviously influential demographic factors to be borne in mind when considering women's work are the incidence and average age of marriage, the incidence of remarriage and the number of children women could expect to bear or see survive. A more hidden phenomenon which is also important in this context is migration. Migration, especially between town and countryside, could affect both the pressure of the population and the balance of sexes in particular localities, which in turn affected women's position and work. The effect of migration depended rather on its causes and the districts concerned – to take a simple example, rural outsiders attracted to a town by its prosperity might be easily absorbed, those impelled there by disaster or decline in their home communities could pose a greater problem. Male and female migration often had different causes and hence different consequences for the communities concerned. Male migrants were more likely to be skilled workers looking for employment, females more likely to be driven by adverse personal circumstances. Michael Roberts and Sue Wright discuss some of the circumstances and results of female migration into towns. These factors have until recently been overlooked and it is noticeable that 'studies of demographic history often neglect the subject of women's work, while studies of women's work neglect the history of the family.'[36]

Finally, more intangible local influences may also be detected at work. Local customs, whose origins may not always be clear, could be important in determining the position of women, affecting as they did the status and treatment of widows and spinsters as well as, more obviously, the types of work women were expected or permitted to do. There was also the question of the individual's standing – recent work on the role of gossip and defamation suggests that a woman's status and livelihood could be affected in a number of ways by her reputation or connections or both. This, however, is a subject which is only now being tentatively explored.[37]

Perhaps one of the most striking facts to emerge from the studies gathered here is the similarity between certain aspects of women's work before and after industrialization. There were, for example, distinct sexual divisions of labour, in both the senses distinguished by Chris Middleton. Spinning, sewing, millinery, silk-working, laundering and nursing all seem to have been chiefly female preserves, while there were, of course, many activities which were mostly or exclusively male. Obviously, as seen above, this segregation was not total and there were a few areas where male and female participation was equally important, such as retailing and food production. In many ways, however, the association of women with particular occupations, and the nature of

17

those occupations foreshadow patterns of female labour in the last two centuries. Involvement in the provision of personal services, in certain aspects of textile manufacture and in retailing seems to be a continuing tradition of female employment. Nor, it seems, is there strong evidence to suppose that preceding capitalist organization in earlier centuries was responsible for these characteristics. The papers here reach back beyond what is often seen as the appearance of capitalist organization on a wide scale in sixteenth and seventeenth century England,[38] and similar characteristics can be discerned throughout.[39]

Capitalist industrialization may have made sexual divisions of labour more apparent, more widespread and more acute due to increasing specialization and job demarcation. But the question of how such divisions arose and why the sexes became associated with particular occupations remains. There is no simple or single answer. It is frequently argued (see above) that women's tasks are defined by their household 'duties', either in that their remunerative work was of a similar type, or that it could fit in with their domestic labours. So this explanation can easily be shown to be inadequate. As noted earlier, some female activities, such as regrating and huckstering, do not appear to have been closely related to household tasks. Others, such as the production of food, drink and clothing palpably were, but when carried on commercially were not female monopolies. Brewing appears to have been carried out largely by women before the eighteenth century, but baking was as much, if not more, a male occupation. Commercially, weaving was almost exclusively a male trade, while spinning was par excellence a woman's task. It is frequently argued that spinning was a woman's task because it was easily fitted around the needs of household and family. Clark claims that 'the convenience of spinning as an employment for odd minutes and the mechanical character of its movements which made no great tax on eye or brain, rendered it the most adaptable of all domestic arts to the necessities of the mother.' Yet she immediately goes on to comment that in the seventeenth century spinning 'became the chief resource for the married women who were losing their hold on other industries...'[40] Were these other industries equally flexible? More importantly, as Chris Middleton points out, the argument that certain types of work were undertaken by women because they could be fitted in with the care of household and children is based on a number of questionable assumptions.

Low pay also appears to be a perennial characteristic of women's work. In modern industrial society, this is often argued to be caused by the assumption that the great majority of female paid work supplements male income, which in itself is enough to support a family.[41] The notion of a family wage in itself appears to have developed during the nineteenth century partly due to trade union action to improve male pay and conditions, partly due to Victorian 'domestic ideology' which sought to confine women to hearth and home.[42] But the same argument has also been advanced about women's wages in earlier periods when contemporary suppositions were apparently quite different and women were expected to contribute substantially to a household's upkeep. Admittedly, this contribution was on the whole expected to be not in the form of money wages but of production for household or for sale. The same, however, was true of much male wage labour, also assumed to have usually been supplemental. A more complex web of power relationships lies behind this, especially given the distance between the idea of the female 'supplementary' and the male 'family' wage, and reality. The reality, as demonstrated for both the seventeenth and twentieth centuries is that many women supported, and support, dependants, while many single men did, and do not.[43]

The exploration of women's work in pre-industrial society, then, throws up a host of questions about its general nature and pattern and indicates how long-standing and obscure in origin many of its characteristics are. Any approach to solutions to such questions will only come from an increasing volume of careful research into the circumstances of female labour before modern industrial development. The papers gathered in this volume indicate some of the directions such research should take. It seems clear that much has already been done on the level of general theory and the need is now for more work on a local level which will test such generalizations. This is not simply because of local variation both in history and in the survival of evidence, but also because studies within narrow geographical boundaries allow more comprehensive analysis which can take in the interplay of several factors – demographic, economic, geographical and so on. The actual determinants of labour patterns, male and female, can be more effectively traced in such microcosms, where the effectiveness of individual sources of evidence can be increased by their combination. In addition, evidence needs to be pressed, pummelled and viewed from different angles to make it yield as much as possible. Finally the theoretical framework adopted consciously or unconsciously by the researchers concerned needs continual critical scrutiny to guard against the intrusion of present-day assumptions or inadequately formulated concepts. Only then will an accurate picture emerge of the patterns of women's work in pre-industrial society and of the factors which determined them.

Notes

1. I am indebted to Michael Roberts for his many helpful comments on the first draft of this introduction.
2. Wanda F. Neff, *Victorian Working Women*, London, Frank Cass and Co., 1966, p.11.
3. K. Casey, 'The Cheshire Cat: Reconstructing the Experience of Medieval Women' in B. Carroll (ed.) *Liberating Women's History*, Illinois, University of Illinois Press, 1976, p.224.
4. A. Clark, *Working Life of Women in the Seventeenth Century*, first published 1919, reissued with an introduction by Miranda Chaytor and Jane Lewis, London, Routledge and Kegan Paul, 1982. For a useful historiographical introduction to Clark's work see N.Z. Davis, '"Women's History" in transition: the European case' in *Feminist Studies*, vol. 3, no.3/4 (summer 1976) pp.83-103. On the subsequent neglect of the questions opened up by Clark see C. Hill's review of the new edition in *History Workshop*, Issue 15 (spring 1983), pp.173-6.
5. S.L. Thrupp 'Medieval Industry 1000-1500' in *Fontana Economic History of Europe* (ed. C.M. Cipolla), vol.1, p.221.
6. The following summary draws heavily on: E. Miller and J. Hatcher, *Medieval England - rural society and economic change 1086-1348*, Longman, 1978; S. Pollard and D.W. Crossley, *The Wealth of Britain 1085-1966*, Batsford, 1968; P. Gregg, *From Black Death to Industrial Revolution*, Harrap, 1976; M.M. Postan, *The Medieval Economy and Society*, Weidenfeld and Nicholson, 1972; J.L. Bolton, *The Medieval English Economy 1150-1500*, Dent, 1980; P. Deane, *The First Industrial Revolution*, C.U.P., 1965.
7. Gregg, p.82.
8. See A. MacFarlane, *The Origins of English Individualism*, Blackwell, 1978, for discussion of theories about the English peasantry.
9. Gregg, p.290.
10. See R.M. Hartwell, ed. *Causes of the Industrial Revolution*, Methuen, 1967, for a summary of the major explanations of industrialization and the objections to each.
11. Clark, p.12.

12. Lee Holcombe, *Victorian Ladies at Work*, David and Charles, 1973, p.4.
13. E.E. Power, *Medieval Women*, (compiled and edited after her death by M.M. Postan), C.U.P., 1975, p.53.
14. S. Alexander, *Women's Work in Nineteenth-Century London: a study of the years 1820-50*, London, Journeyman Press and London History Workshop Centre, 1983, p.27.
15. S. Rowbotham, *Hidden from History: 300 years of women's oppression and the fight against it*, Pluto Press, 1973, p.2.
16. R.T. Vann, 'Women in pre-industrial capitalism' in R. Bridenthal and C. Koonz, *Becoming Visible: Women in European History*, USA and London, Houghton Mifflin Co., 1979, p.195; D.M. Stenton, *English Women in History*, 1957, p.100.
17. Power, p.55.
18. A. Abram, *English Life and Manners in the later Middle Ages*, Routledge, 1913, p.33; F.W. Maitland and F. Pollock, *History of English law before Edward I* (2nd ed.), C.U.P., 1968, p.433.
19. A. Abram, *Social England in the Fifteenth Century*, Routledge, 1909, pp.131, 139; Clark, pp.65-6.
20. Those who have identified changes over time in particular aspects of female labour and reasons for them include: M. Roberts, 'Sickles and Scythes: Women's Work and Men's Work at Harvest Time' *History Workshop* 7, Spring 1979, pp.3-29; Abram, *Social England*, p.131; R.H. Hilton 'Women in the Village' in *The English Peasantry in the Later Middle Ages*, 1975.
21. I. Pinchbeck, *Women Workers and the Industrial Revolution 1750-1850*, first published 1930, reissued with introduction by Kerry Hamilton, Virago, 1981.
22. O. Schreiner, *Women and Labour*, London, 1911.
23. A view shared by what may be termed the 'optimist' school on the effects of the industrial revolution on women's work, which most notably comprises, along with Pinchbeck, M. Hewitt, *Wives and Mothers in Victorian Industry*, Rockcliff, 1958; Neff, *Victorian Working Women*.
24. For a succinct account and critique of Marxist-feminist debate around the effects of capitalism on women's labour see Michele Barrett, *Women's Oppression Today*, Verso, 1980, pp.176-186 and Roberta Hamilton, *The Liberation of Women*, George Allen and Unwin, 1978 passim.
25. R. Samuel, 'The Workshop of the World', *History Workshop* 3, 1977.
26. P. Branca, *Silent Sisterhood*, London, Croom Helm,

1975.

27. But not quite as valuable as they appear at first sight. See Postan pp.27–31 for discussion of their limitations.

28. R. Masek, 'Women in an Age of Transition 1485–1714' in B. Kanner (ed.) *The Women of England (From Anglo-Saxon Times to the Present)*, London, Mansell, 1980, p.142.

29. K. Casey, 'Women in Norman and Plantagenet England' in Kanner, p.89.

30. D. Vaisey, 'Court records and the social history of seventeenth century England' *History Workshop*, 1 (spring 1976), p.185.

31. M. Chaytor, 'Household and Kinship: Ryton in the late sixteenth century and early seventeenth century' in *History Workshop*, 10 (autumn 1980), p.30.

32. K. Thomas, 'Work and Leisure in pre-industrial society' *Past and Present*, 29, 1964.

33. Power, p.62.

34. Pinchbeck, *Women Workers*.

35. M. Spufford, *Contrasting Communities: English Villages in the sixteenth and seventeenth centuries*, C.U.P., 1974; J. Goody, J. Thirsk and E.P. Thompson, *Family and Inheritance: rural society in western Europe 1200–1800*.

36. L.A. Tilly and J.W. Scott, *Women, Work and Family*, London, Holt, Rinehart and Winston, 1978, p.7. For demographic work on England relevant to the questions raised here see: E.A. Wrigley and R.S. Schofield, *The Population History of England 1541–1871*, Edward Arnold, 1981; J.C. Russell, 'Population in Europe 500–1500', *Fontana Economic History* (ed. C.M. Cipolla), vol.I, pp.25–70; D. Herlihy, 'Life Expectancies for Women in Medieval Society' in *The Role of Woman in the Middle Ages* (ed. R.T. Morewedge), Hodder and Stoughton, 1975, pp.1–22.

37. J. Sharpe, *Defamation and Sexual Slander in Early Modern England*, Borthwick Papers, no.58 1981 .

38. But see MacFarlane, p.195 for a summary of the difficulties involved in defining and dating the rise of capitalism.

39. On sexual divisions of labour in English society see also Roberts, 'Sickles and Scythes' and C. Middleton 'The sexual division of labour in feudal England' *New Left Review*, 1979.

40. Clark, p.9.

41. H. Land, 'The Family Wage', *Feminist Review*, 6, 1980, pp.55–78.

42. C. Hall, 'The Early Formation of Victorian Domestic Ideology' in S. Burman (ed.) *Fit Work for Women*,

London, Croom Helm, 1979, pp.15–32.
43. E. Rathbone, *The Disinherited Family*, Edward
Arnold, 1924; Clark, pp.65–6.

1 WOMEN AND WORK IN FOURTEENTH AND FIFTEENTH CENTURY LONDON

Kay E. Lacey

> A woman . . . though a citizen . . . cannot bear civilia, or publica onera of tne city; she cannot doe any thing for the benefit of the city; she cannot perform watch, and ward; she can bear no office in the city; neither can she be of any of the Companies; she cannot be Attorney; she may be a Free-Woman, but this is only to have her will (as many so have) but to no other purpose.[1]

Introduction

The important economic role played by women in medieval society frequently goes unacknowledged in studies of urban life of the fourteenth and fifteenth centuries. But contemporary legal documents abound in references to merchant women and female apprentices and from these sources, it appears that very few occupations were actually denied to women. Furthermore, the freedom of women within the 'home' and the fact that they were expected as wives or daughters, to participate in their husbands' or fathers' business activities, and sometimes even act as their agents, suggests that medieval women were accepted as sharing fully in all areas of family life.[2] A haberdasher, Thomas Canons, sent his wife 'to the Citee of London to doo dyvers thyngys at his Commaundement', and another wife Margery Smith, even though sick, 'cam to London and agreed with other of her creditors' because her husband Robert could not be found.[3] As these examples show women were expected to be competent in matters concerning their husbands' business activities. Competence would include reading and writing abilities and some schools which took women did exist in some medieval towns.[4] They were, however, generally excluded from performing public rights and duties. They could not be members of universities, or be clerics, judges, members of Parliament etc., or hold public office.[5] There were exceptions. Some noble, gentlewomen, and merchants' wives are recorded as being constables of castles and guardians of prisoners or collecting loans for the King.[6] Women, unless they worked on their own account as sole merchants, traders, apprentices or as servants in the towns, were also still largely dependent on fathers or husbands.

London women's participation in the economy appears to have increased after 1350, which may have been related to the Black Death and the resultant male labour shortage, but may equally well have been related to the general increase in legal documentation. A clear decline in women's participation can be observed in the same documentary sources from about 1480, which may be related to growing attempts by gilds and livery companies to exclude single women (or *femme sole* traders) from various occupations. The evidence shows fewer women merchants active on a large scale in the sixteenth century.

As late as 1722 the borough laws of London allow for women to trade and work on their own account in the City. However, by this time they are no longer found in the wide range of occupations they pursued in the Middle Ages, and are concentrated in the traditionally female trades in which they had always had a monopoly (spinning, laundering, nursing etc.).[7]

The main concern of this article is a survey of the occupations practised by women in the period. Before considering these, however, it is necessary to look at women in the context of law and custom in the City of London. Every woman who lived in the City of London and who worked there as a citizen or freewoman was bound to obey the customs of London and could enjoy the privileges resulting from London's special borough status and law. The same women were also bound to obey canon law when it touched upon such matters as testaments, marriage, adultery, defamation, broken contracts or promises etc. They were also governed by the common law when involved in some types of criminal proceedings, land litigation or contract law, which were not covered by borough customs and the customs of London. Many different types of law regulated women's lives, often when common law or borough customs was unable to minister justice in a certain matter, women would apply to chancery, to obtain a decision through equity. Medieval women would have been conversant with the different types of law which governed their lives, and would have been aware of the different courts to which they have had to apply to receive 'justice'. For this reason, it is necessary to be aware of how important different laws were in women's lives, as they could govern and regulate women's status in society, or their ability to work in certain occupations, or affect their capacity to own land or chattels, or to make contracts.

In general it may be said that the images of medieval women seen through courtly love and the Church, bear little resemblance to the activities of women in the world. Ideological influences of the Church and of literary conventions, were however assimilated into legal thinking, which was as inconsistent and conflicting as literary and religious opinion. Canon, civil, common law and borough custom often contradict each other on the legal status and abilities of women. Law itself may not reflect the real activities of women in society. Canon law was the basis of the judicial proceedings of the Church, which was recognised as binding by the community. Civil law, was based on Roman law, and should be distinguished from both canon and common law. It played little part in affecting the lives of English subjects. Common law was the general law of the community, separate from local and borough customs. It was administered by the King's Courts and was believed to have been derived from ancient and universal usage. It relates to the law of the King's ordinary judges, and does not include special courts and equity (chancery). Borough custom varied from town to town, though many boroughs followed similar laws to those of London on which they were based.

Common Law

The common law was almost entirely directed towards married women and widows. Single women are rarely mentioned, perhaps because they were regarded as having rights equal to those of men. It was concerned primarily with women in relation to marriage and towards rights and duties within marriage. Its form was dictated by the two-fold desire to preserve the husband's superiority and to protect the rights of the wife and children.

On marriage, a husband acquired control of his wife's freehold interests for the duration of the marriage, because, by the law and custom of England, the husband was entitled to have the inheritance of his wife, and was seized of it for his lifetime. Husbands thus gained guardianship of land and possessions and any actions concerning these had to be brought either by, or against, both husband and wife. If the husband had a child by the wife then he was entitled to hold the land acquired by marriage by the 'courtesye of Englande',[8] which meant that he held it in trust for the child. An important part of the common law which affected women was concerned with land or possessions, acquired by husbands on marriage, or which passed to women on their husbands' death. Dowry was the money or property which the wife brought to the husband on marriage. Dower was the portion of a deceased husband's estate which the law allowed to his widow for her life. The maritagium was that part of the marriage portion or dowry given to the husband, which returned to his wife after his death. The morning gift was the gift made by the husband to the wife on the morning after consummation of the marriage. Dower and dowry feature considerably in the common law relating to women.

Dower and dowry were also important in canon law where private marriages (i.e. not taking place in church) were concerned as the gifts confirmed that the marriage had taken place and so secured ecclesiastical recognition for it. [9]

Some of the earliest laws applicable to the fourteenth century including ones on dower and dowry, were compiled around 1100, and they became known as the *Leges Henrici Primi* (the Laws of Henry I). They were a collection of laws of various kinds, including Anglo-Saxon, and the surviving manuscripts were transcribed in about 1201–1350. One of these laws stated that:

> If a wife survives her husband she shall have in permanent ownership her dowry and her maritagium which had been settled on her by written documents or in the presence of witnesses and her morning-gift and a third part of all their jointly acquired property in addition to her clothing and her bed. [10]

The *Leges Henrici Primi* was written at a time when there were three great laws, those of Wessex, Mercia and the Danelaw, and many local customs. By the time of Glanvill, the next great legal author of the twelfth century, whose treatise was written in about 1187–9, there still remained local and feudal diversity but there was also a permanent court of justices, under the Crown, and it marks the beginning of the common law. Glanvill gave a definition of dower, and of the property which can form part of the dower, and the wife's rights in relation to it. He also discussed what happens when a husband dies: the dower may be vacant, in which case the widow can take it; or it may be all occupied, or part vacant, part occupied. He then gave remedies: when the land is all occupied the writ of *unde nihil habet* had to be used in the King's court to secure the widow's possession of the land, and when part vacant, part occupied, the same writ had to be used in a feudal court. Glanvill stated that a woman could not claim more than her third at the time of marriage and she could not alienate any of her dower during the life of her husband.[11] He then explained that this is because the husband had complete control of his wife's property and actions during his lifetime:

> For since legally a woman is completely in the power of her husband, it is not surprising that her dower and all other property are clearly deemed to be at his disposal. Therefore any married man may give or sell or alienate in whatever way he pleases his wife's dower during her life, and his wife is bound to consent to this as to all other acts of his . . . a woman is bound to obey her husband that if he wishes to sell her dower and she opposes him, and afterwards the dower is in fact sold and purchased, she cannot when her husband is dead claim the dower from the purchaser if she confesses, or it is proved against her in court that it was sold by her husband against her will.[12]

Women, as wives or widows were not completely without rights or protection from the law. The argument used by Glanvill to explain why women did not have control of their own property was also used to explain women's position in relation to contract law, which I shall discuss later, as it is important in understanding women's position in trade.

Widow's rights to dower were protected by the common law. They could recover dower by a writ of *pone*.[13] If a husband sold his wife's dower after he endowed her with it, he was required either to regain it, or to give her reasonable lands in exchange.[14] If none of the dower land was vacant she had the right to cause a writ of *unde nihil habet,* to be brought.[15] A husband could only alienate his wife's inheritance with the consent of their heirs and then only for the term of their lives.[16] A woman's rights were to be protected because whilst she was in the power of her husband 'She could not contradict him in any matter nor act against his will, and thus could not, if her husband were unwilling, take care for her own right.'[17] Widows were thus entitled to a third of their husbands' property as dower, and could bring a writ of *cui in vite* to regain any of the freehold property which they brought with them. But a widow's rights in the latter could not supersede those of the heir, 'because the general rule is that a woman never shares in an inheritance with a man, unless there is a special rule in a particular city by ancient custom of that city.'[18]Another commentator elaborates further on this subject, saying that even though the widow recovered her dower, she could lose it in several ways, 'as where her warrant loses the two other parts by judgement without any collusion', or she may be deprived of it by the custom of the county particularly in Kent, 'and sometime there was such a usage in London and many other places, that as soon as a widow is married to another husband, or becomes with child by any other man than her first husband, she may be immediately ejected from her dower.'[19] This particular custom is not mentioned by Bracton, a royal clerk, who wrote a law book on the laws and customs of England before 1256. The book was in circulation by 1277. Neither does the writer of the *Fleta seu Commentarus Iuris Anglicani,* written about 1290 mention it. [20] It did not play a large part in the development of the law, and the writing of Glanvill and Bracton, were more popular, and are referred to frequently in the Year Books (records of judicial proceedings) and in commentaries on the law until the seventeenth century. Bracton, although he wrote after Glanvill, does not appear to have superseded the latter, and both carried equal weight when discussing precedent. A sixteenth century commentator on the law said that there was a custom whereby the wife could have the third part of her inheritance of which her husband was 'seasyd in dede or in law after the spousellis' whether there were children or not, to hold as dower for her lifetime. But she must be over twelve when her husband died or she could not have her 'dowrye'.[21]

A discussion of law both canon and common relating specifically to wills and to contract, may highlight some of the more noticeable legal disadvantages which affected women, and married women in particular.

Canon law and testaments

Medieval law, canon, civil and common, relating to women was 'coloured by the canonist's conception of marriage as a sacrament which makes the husband and wife one flesh, and gives the husband dominion over the wife.'[22]

Canon lawyers basing their beliefs on Scripture, generally held that matrimony could only be dissolved by death. The Church allowed that divorce might be possible under certain circumstances (non-consummation, consanguinity and impotence) but was reluctant to grant it. Divorce was available under the common law on the same grounds but was more easily obtainable. Canon lawyers also held that 'the wife as long as she liveth is subject to the law of her husband by Saint Paul.'[23] This view is reflected in the *Lawes Resolutions of Womens Rights,* a sixteenth century statement of common law, which said that the status of women had been determined in Genesis, chapter three:

> Eve because shee had helped to seduce her husband hath inflicted on her, an especiall bane. In sorrow shalt thou bring forth thy children, thy desires shall be subject to thy husband, and he shall rule over thee.
> See here the reason . . . that women have no voyse in Parliament, they make no lawes, they abrogate none. All of them are understood either married or to bee married and their desires are subject to their husband, I know no remedy though some women can shift it well enough. The common law here shaketh hand with divinitie.[24]

However, canon law did accord women some legal rights which were denied to them by the common law, as for example the right to make a testament. The legal status of women in common and canon law can be considered in three aspects: first, their rights with respect to property, secondly, their right to make a will and/or testament, and thirdly, in the extent of their criminal and civil responsibility.

Common law dealing with property and land reflected women's position under the canon law in relation to wills and testaments. It is important to understand the distinction between a will and a testament, as the terms were frequently, and wrongly, used interchangeably. A testament was a bequest of moveable goods and chattels, a last will expressed the desire or wish of executors or people to dispose of real estate in the way indicated. There were also differences in these instruments in the language used. The testament was supposed to be written in Latin, the *ultima voluntas* in French or English. Until the reign of Henry VIII wills could be written or nuncupative (an oral wish proved by witnesses or an unsealed document): thereafter they were required to be in writing. Women could make testaments but not wills. This stemmed from the fact that, while they could own chattels and dispose of them in accordance with their own wishes, they had no such rights over land.

It is worth illustrating some of the confusion surrounding the use of these terms. The distinction between them is rarely found in the thirteenth century when they were often made together, and in the later fourteenth and the fifteenth centuries the last will became more common than the testament. A testament for fourteenth and fifteenth century canonists was an instrument written with due legal form and appointing one or two executors. A will, or *ultima voluntas,* was also frequently referred to as a codicil, *(codicillus)* which was, strictly speaking, an addition to a will. The lawyers of Archbishop Chichele used three expressions to describe a will: *testamentum, ultima voluntas* and *codicillus.* In the late sixteenth century another slightly different view emerges with a writer who said that a codicil might be an addition to a testament or be made by a man dying intestate. The testament, which was defined by the appointment of an executor, could contain the last will, but every last will was not a testament, the difference lying in the appointment of the executor. Further, no testator could die with two testaments, but he could leave many codicils.[25]

Canon law claimed that bishops had jurisdiction over wills bequeathing property in *pios usos.* By the thirteenth century the ecclesiastical courts exercised extensive jurisdiction over wills bequeathing personal estate and in theory could claim a tithe from the deceased's chattels. Since Papal codes made little provision for extensive testamentary business church lawyers built up a testamentary law on the basis of Roman civil law.[26] Canon law had a monopoly on proving testaments which evoked the jealousy of common lawyers whose own monopoly over cases concerning wills and real estate was far less lucrative.[27]

The occasions when a wife did make a testament were possibly inspired by canon lawyers who maintained that a wife could make a testament in the normal way.[28] An early canon law statute of 1261 attempted to establish a testamentary capacity for married women. It stated that those people who impeded the 'just customary and free' making of wills by married women were to be excommunicated.[29] This structure was again repeated in a provincial council of Archbishop Stratford in 1342. The statute gave women, married or unmarried, the power to make testaments, and those who impeded them were to be excommunicated.[30] In 1344 the Commons in Parliament complained that this action by prelates was against reason, 'et q [ue] neifs et femmes poent faire testament, q'est conte reson.' The King's ambiguous response was that law and reason would be done.[31] After this the lay courts maintained the widower against the wife's executor unless the widower had consented to probate of the will. The spiritual tribunals then admitted that the wife only had such testamentary power as her husband allowed her, and his consent could be revoked at any time before the will was proved.[32] A fifteenth century writer said that, 'it would be extraordinary that because of marriage wives could obstruct us in our lifetimes in the respect of making wills.'[33]

But some clergy still supported women's ability to

make testaments freely and they allowed their execution:

> and the last wills of ascripts and of other persons
> of servile condition, of women also both married and
> unmarried and of their own wives and of other
> men's wives, which things they do against the
> Customs of the Church hitherto approved, unto
> the . . . injury of the Church's rights . . . [and]
> any who offend in these be excommunicated. [34]

The writer contends that because of this constitution
married women can make a will, especially 'where such
women hath brought a large fortune to her husband, who
perhaps had nothing of his own before.' [35]

In contrast to canon law, the common law of
England did not permit married women to make wills or
testaments, although single women were free to do so. A
reason for this is given in the discussion of a common
law case:

> no other person can make a testament save he who
> can claim property [in the chattels] ; but a wife
> cannot claim property, and consequently she cannot
> make a testament. Besides if a wife died intestate,
> the ordinary will not intermeddle in the matter;
> because she has no chattel that is her own in her
> husband's lifetime. [36]

Only married women who had the permission of their
husbands or who were executors of others could make
testaments. The common law stated that married women
were unable to make a testament or will. Glanvill said
that:

> A woman of full capacity may make a testament; but
> if she is in the power of her husband she may not,
> without her husband's authority, dispose of chattels
> which are her husband's, even in her last will. Yet
> it would be truly kind and creditable to a husband
> were he to allow his wife a reasonable division,
> namely up to that third part of his chattels which,
> she would have obtained had she survived her
> husband; many husbands in fact do this, which is
> much to their credit. [37]

Married women could not bequeath lands and other
property, or devise them to their husbands, because it
was thought that there would be a danger of the heirs
being disinherited, due to the constraint and influence of
the husband. [38]

In Henry VIII's reign a statute enacted that wills

or testaments made of any manors, lands, tenements or other hereditaments, by covert (married) women, were not to be good or effectual in the law.[39] The same applied to those under 21 years old and idiots.

If a woman made a will and testament concerning lands and chattels before marriage but died intestable because her husband was alive, it was void because:

> It is necessary to the validity of a testament, that the testator have ability to make it, not only at the time of the making thereof, when the testament receiveth his essence or being; but also at the time of the testator's death, when the testament receiveth his strength and confirmation.[40]

If the wife outlived the husband, a testament made during marriage was invalid, unless she approved and confirmed it after the death of her husband. A wife could not make a testament of goods or chattels without the licence or consent of her husband:[41]

> because by the laws and customs of this Realm, so soon as a Man and a Woman are married, all the goods and chattels personal that the Wife had at the Time of the Celebration of the Marriage, or after, and also the Chattels real, if he over-live his Wife, belong to the Husband, by Reason of the said marriage.[42] And therefore with good Reason she cannot give that away which was hers, without the Sufferance or Grant of the owner.[43]

But with his licence and consent a wife could make a testament even of her husband's goods.[44] If a husband did consent to his wife making a testament of his goods, he could revoke it at any time before it was proved.[45] A *femme covert* (married woman) who was an executrix to another person, could make a testament of those goods and chattels, without the licence of her husband, because they were for the use of another, and were not her husband's.[46] If she was a legatee as well as executrix she could not make a testament because as a *femme covert* the goods belonged to her husband, and therefore she would need his consent.[47] Also the profits accruing to her as executrix would become the property of her husband.[48] In 1497 Fineux C.j. summed up women's executory position in common law:

> Then as to the question whether a femme covert can make an executor or not, she can do so well enough without the consent of her husband, in the case where she is another's executor, or of such things

> or duties of which [the husband] never had
> possession ... And by the spiritual law she can
> make her executor of some things of which the
> property and the possession are in her husband,
> that is, of her personal apparel; and so she can by
> the common law by the consent of her husband; but
> without the consent of her husband she cannot, the
> possession and the property being wholly in the
> husband.[49]

Apart from the exception of the *femme covert* executrix the
opinion of the common law generally held that married
women were unable to make wills and testaments, because
they did not own any property. But even common law
lawyers did not always agree on this point.[50]

The canon law provided general rules for the
protection of a widow as a *miserabilis persona*, and
defended her free choice of state, either in widowhood or
remarriage.[51] Christian teaching also emphasised the
importance of donation in alms, and the pious gift became
associated with the testament, becoming known as
eleemosyna. Bishops acquired the right to supervise these
legacies in alms, and also claimed the supervision of the
wife's dowry which was part of the *legitim*.[52] In conclusion, under the canon law, there was a tendency to limit
the proprietary abilities of the married woman. The lands
of her dowry were controlled by the husband, and the
profits accruing from it were administered by him. But
the wife was believed to retain ownership, and thus it
was believed she could recover her dowry on termination
of the marriage.[53] But all chattels that she brought with
her, or that she acquired after marriage belonged to her
husband. Only the dower could not be owned outright by
the husband. The disposition of moveable property
originally allowed only the freedom to bequeath chattels
within a 'quota system', allotting a portion to the wife
and children.[54]

Common law and testaments

Canon law, then, attempted to allow the wife a testamentary bequest, and limited the testamentary freedom of the
husband, allocating a portion of moveable property to his
widow. In contrast, the common law was generally un-
favourable to the wife's position in relation to chattels.[55]

The common law is contradictory on what was the
standard custom of the realm relating to the disposition
of a testator's goods. In 1366 the Lords in Parliament
said that an action for *legitim* (or thirds) could not be
maintained by any common custom or law; and such

actions continued to be dealt with by ecclesiastical courts.[56]
A sixteenth century lawyer citing the reign of Edward I
said that *legitim* was part of the common law of the
realm.[57] But medieval lawyers were not so certain.

The common law lawyer Glanvill stated that
excepting certain local usages, it was general custom that
freemen with dependents, having paid their debts, were
allowed to distribute a third of their chattels as they
chose.[58] The remaining thirds, the *legitim* were reserved
for the wife and the heir. If the heir only survived then
one half of the chattels became *legitim*, and the remainder
could be disposed of by the testator at will. The free
portion would be distributed as the testator desired and
did not have to be allocated for pious uses.[59] Bracton and
the Fleta agree with Glanvill on customary usage, adding
that the testator without dependents was free to dispose of
all his moveable property.[60] But the common law courts of
the fourteenth century refused to acknowledge that the
tripartite division was the custom of England.[61] Yet Magna
Carta (1215) recognised that the wife and children could
claim reasonable shares in the dead man's goods[62] Bracton
stated that if the testator did not leave a wife, then half
was to be used for pious purposes, and half reserved for
the heirs. If there were no heirs then the distribution
would be half for the wife, and half for the dead. If
there were no wife or children, the whole was to be used
for the dead.[63] He said that these were the general rules
unless contradicted by the particular custom of a city or
borough.[64] He cites a custom of London which was that if
a specified dower was settled on the wife, whether in
money or other chattels, she could rightfully claim
nothing more, except by her husband's grace and favour,
that is, if he left her something in addition to her
dower.[65] The reason given was that before debts were paid
she would have the whole of her dower, and except as a
matter of grace, children had no more rightful claim than
wives 'for a citizen could scarcely be found who would
undertake a great enterprise in his lifetime if at his
death, he was compelled against his will to leave his
estate to ignorant and extravagant children and undeser-
ving wives.'[66]

Thus the husband can encourage good conduct and
virtue and compel wives and children to good behaviour.
Bracton's statement of the custom is confirmed in a
document of 1246 concerning a widow's claim to more than
her dower which was disallowed.[67] A London will of 1290
reads like Glanvill, the debts of the testator were to be
paid, and the remainder was to be divided into thirds, to
the wife, children, and for funeral and other bequests.[68]
Whether this distribution was custom or choice is not
known. What is probably the earliest reference to the tri-

partite division as part of London 'city' law occurs in a
document of around 930–40 which lists the canon laws of
the City of London. This mentions that excepting the first
in rank, the remainder of a man's possessions, were to be
divided into three parts to the wife if she were of the
world and was not a party to the deed, to the King, and
to 'Societas'.[69]

Borough custom and testaments

London borough custom relating to wills differed from the
common law in the procedure of proving and in freedom of
disposition, as did other English boroughs.[70]
    When a citizen of London died, after the payment of
his debts, if he had a wife and child, his goods were
divided into three parts, for the wife, children, and
pious uses. The wife and children could claim their share
against the executors, before the Mayor and Aldermen of
London.[71] The writ, *De rationabili parte bonorum*, was
used both at common law, and in the Mayor of London
court, against the administrator of an intestate freeman,
to compel the distribution of a widow's or children's
shares from his estate. If either did not exist the property was divided into two parts and distributed.[72] This
division of property was, as we have seen, generally the
custom of England whether a will existed or not.[73] But the
custom eventually only remained in force in Wales, York
and London, and did not survive as the common law of
the realm.[74] As I have shown these restrictions on the
disposal of chattels was not a peculiar custom of London,
and was part of the common law in the reign of Henry II,
and it is probably much older, being based on Anglo–
Saxon law.[75] It continued in use in London until William
and Mary's reign, when it was abolished by Parliament.[76]
By the seventeenth century the general rule throughout the
province of Canterbury denied to the wife and children
any 'legitimate part' or *legitim*, and allowed the testator
to dispose of all his fortune. But the tripartite division
was followed in London and 'the north of Britain, after it
had ceased to be part of the common law.[77] The law of
legitim prevailed in both London custom and the common
law in the thirteenth century. A few cases in the Year
Books concerned actions in the fourteenth and fifteenth
centuries brought by widows and children to claim
legitim. But the origin of their right was disputed. Some
cited the authority of Magna Carta, or the common custom
of the realm. But both reasons could be denied as valid [78]
because claims for *legitim* in theory should have been
taken before an ecclesiastical court. However, why Westminster judges sanctioned the procedure at one time, and

at another would refuse to allow it as it was contrary to law, is unknown.[79]

When the custom of London is cited concerning women, it probably refers to the tripartite division and may imply that freebench is also to be given (see below). There are many cases of men in other parts of the country leaving their wives one third of their goods after 'the custome of the citie of London.'[80]

To judge by a case decided in 1368 or 1369, another custom of London gave a widow half of her husband's goods. The wife of Henry Bredforde brought a case against his executors claiming one half of all his goods and chattels, as her reasonable part according to the custom of the city of London. But the executors said that Henry had two sons by a former wife and therefore she should only have a third part. The Mayor and Aldermen stated that the custom of London was that, even though the citizen had issue surviving, a second wife should have half his goods and chattels, and so she obtained her claim.[81] But, as this is the only example of a claim for a half, perhaps the Aldermen made a mistake, or the two sons had received settlements before their father's death.

London custom differed from common law in that it gave to widows freebench. Freebench was an estate in copyhold lands or tenements which a wife had at the death of her husband, and she held it for the term of her life, for her children.[82] For her freebench, or frank bank, she was to have the rents in the City of which her husband was seised in fee when he died. In the tenement where she and her husband dwelt at the time of his death, she was to have the hall, the principal chamber and the cellar, and use of the oven, stable, privy and the yard. When she remarried she lost her freebench and her dower of the same tenement, except dower of other tenements according to the law.[83] Alice de Harwe, wife of John de Harwe obtained her freebench from the Sheriffs of London in 1314, in a tenement of her late husband, viz. the hall, principal chamber and the cellar beneath, and a common easement in the kitchen, stable, common privy and courtyard. The rest of the tenement she shared with two female cousins of her husband.[84] Another woman, Cristina, wife of Thomas Clenche, was given her freebench in 1384, viz., the principal tenement of which her husband was seised at his death, according to ancient custom of the City. She was also given a third of the other tenements in the city of which the husband died seised, to hold the same by way of dower.[85]

At common law a widow only had a right to residence in the principal tenement for forty days, but in London she had a right for life, so long as she remained unmarried.[86] It is probable that in London when a widow resigned her freebench, she could then take her dower, but was unlikely to enjoy both together. If a widow remarried she then gained her dower in place of free-bench. Perhaps Bracton was confused when he said that London widows lost dower on remarriage, and meant free-bench.[87]

A sixteenth century writer said that London's wealth and prosperity had flourished because merchants who acquired riches spent them in the City. Also after a merchant died:

> Yet his goods may remaine as among his wife and children in use and propertie, so to the generall strength of this city in account and reckoning. For we often see ye one rich mans wealth passeth to the increase of the good estate of another citizen, either by marriage of the widow, or of the orphan: so that the citie though deprived of a member or inhabitant, yet is not destitute of such as may discharge his employment and place.

He added also that if the custom of London regarding a widow's and children's inheritance was abolished, such wealth would be dissipated 'by deedes of giftes and cautelous conveyance to strangers, not only the wife and children may be distrested, but also the state of the city much weakened, and in danger of a great disreputation and decay.'[88] The custom of tripartite division was especially important in London in that merchants tended to have goods only in moveables or in trade, and because of this wives were uncertain as to whether they would be able to claim their dowry 'commonly called thirds, as they might if their husbands were seased of lands in fee simple.' Children also could only depend on their fathers 'travaile'.[89]

Another practice in London was the entailing of property. This became more frequent after the 1285 statute *De Donis*, which gave the donee a life estate, and as a result the custom of London ensured that a widow could be given no more than a life estate in her husband's property.[90] London citizens in their testaments frequently left property to their wives with remainder to their children in successive tails.[91] This practice was well established by the reign of Edward II. In London a husband could not devise tenements (buildings) to his wife for any higher estate than the term of her life, neither could the wife claim any higher estate on pain of losing the whole, nor could the husband devise tenements in the right of his wife, or devise tenements which were jointly purchased by husband and wife. If they had tenements held for the heirs of the husband, then the husband could devise the reversion, and the testaments devising tenements were to be enrolled in Husting (the borough law court), and there proved by two men before the Mayor and Aldermen in full court.[92] Men who held tenements jointly with others could devise them, but infants, and married women could not, even with the permission of their husbands.[93] Freemen of the City could also devise tenements in *mortmain* which was a privilege denied at common law, without licence.[94]

In 1399 the Mayor, Aldermen and Sheriffs of London stated that no testament of lands and tenements could be admitted to probate or enrolment unless the seal of the testator were affixed to it, and two witnesses at least were to testify concerning the seal of the testator.[95] The custom of London also required that cognizances and confessions (relating to business transactions and legal cases) of women should be recorded before the Mayor and one alderman, or before the recorder and one alderman, or before two aldermen, and such deeds of indentures etc. were to be entered and enrolled in Hustings, as were to be testaments, and other writings.[96] In London although a woman had no power of devise of landed property, she was allowed to make a testament bequeathing her chattels.[97] In 1256 William de Munchanesey appeared in the Court of Hustings desiring probate of the testament of his wife Paulina, which devised all her tenements in London, but as she was *sub potestate viri* this caused some debate. The Mayor and citizens after much altercation, said that no married woman could or ought to devise any tenements, and if she did so, it would be void. Sales, gifts, demises, and alienations which she made of land, tenements or rents were to be held good only if she herself came into Husting with her husband and made affidavit as to the same.[98] Thus a wife's testament could only receive probate if she had previously come into Hustings and declared her intention.[99] But this sometimes did not happen in practice.

The will of Henry de Greenford was enrolled in June 1307. He left nothing to his wife Emma and she quickly remarried (for the third time) a tiler, Walter Cope, and together they disclaimed their single and joint interest in her former husband's principal property. She died soon after and all attempts by her executors (who were also Henry's) to enrol her will with Henry's in June 1307, failed because she was *femme covert*, both when she made it (as Emma Wylekin, under her first husband), and when she died.[100] The majority of women who made wills were presumably single or widows. In the period 1393–1403 in Hustings there were 101 men and only 13 women leaving testaments.[101] In the Archdeaconry court for the same period only 62 out of 439 wills or testaments were made by women, or 14.3%. Of this number 14 made no reference to husbands or children, but they may not have been single women.[102] Only 5 women making independent testament were survived by their husbands, or 1% of the total.[103]

One 'will' was made by a married woman, Isabelle Dove, wife of Thomas, citizen of London, directing her executors 'to pay her dettis, her bequestis; and the remenant for to Kepe to the vse of the husbondes of the seyde Isabell, unto his comying home fro beyonde the see.'[104] Such a 'will' (as she called it) is unusual. In conclusion married women under the common law were generally unable to make wills because they could not own property or chattels. It was not unusual for a husband to bequeath his wife her own clothes. In the 1417 will of Walter Rede, he left his wife Emma £100 sterling as dower, utensils, and her clothes and ornaments.[105] A London mercer, john Coventry, left his wife Alice 1,000 marks sterling, all her clothes and ornaments, and other necessaries for her body. If she thought that this was insufficient she was to have nothing 'except what the law allows her without other advantage.'[106] According to the legal historian Holdsworth, the common law 'tended to magnify the control of the husband to such a degree that it literally gave him the chattels of the wife, and denied the wife any capacity to own them.'[107]

Common law and contract

Under common law, the rule that married women could not own chattels, had been established before the end of the thirteenth century.[108] A woman who was hanged at the beginning of the fourteenth century was said to own no chattels because she had a husband.[109] In 1428 it was stated that a husband and wife could not hold their chattels in common.[110] This rule was effective as early as 1306, and in a debt case it was stated that the demand for a chattel 'supposes that the property in a chattel may be in the wife during the life of her husband, which the law does not allow.'[111] The standard historical theory of the community of goods between husband and wife is tenuous; rather a married woman gave her possessions and her self to her husband, who then becomes the 'one person' of which the law speaks. For in law husband and wife are one person: 'this conglutination of persons in Baron and Feme, forbiddeth all manner of feoffing and giving by the one unto the other, for a man cannot give any thing unto himself.'[112]

Because a married woman could not own chattels she was in theory unable to make contracts. Under the common law the status of a married woman in the fifteenth century was that of a minor, for she was unable to take full responsibility for her actions. But a woman in a town could become a *femme sole,* and her husband would then be her guardian, and she would be able to trade as if she were single, and be allowed to make contracts. *Femmes soles* were usually responsible for their own debts. Wives could act as their husbands' agents,[113] and in this case, the husband would accept responsibility for her contracts and debts, if they had been previously authorised or subsequently ratified by him because they were his contracts.[114]

Generally the common law principle was that *femme coverts* were unable to make contracts, or even buy goods without their husbands' prior assent. Neither does the question of agency seem to have been discussed in relation to married women, although it was relevant to servants, who often had a similar legal status to wives. In 1506 Fineux C. J. said that:

A married woman cannot make a contract to her husband's loss or prejudice but can if it is to his profit. Thus I can give a married woman a gift and the husband agree to it, but if a married woman make a contract to buy something in the market this is not valid since the cost may be a burden to her husband. But my wife can buy something for her own use. and I can ratify the purchase. If I order my wife to buy necessities and she buys them, I shall be held responsible because of the general authorisation given her. But if my wife buys things for my household like bread etc., without my knowledge I shall not be held responsible for it even if it was consumed in my household.[115]

In a law case of 1313–14 a debt was demanded from a husband under contract made by the wife. It was stated that: 'The deed of the wife is . . . the deed of the husband, for they are but one person, and consequently the husband is answerable for his wife's contract.'[116] But it was argued by another lawyer 'that no contract made by the defendant's wife during coverture ought to or could charge her husband'. To this Tilton J. replied that if a husband profited from the contract, then he should be made liable. In conclusion, a husband was liable to his wife's contracts if it gave him profit or advantage, but he was not liable if the wife made the contract without his consent and will and it was not to his benefit.[117] Thus in the case of a woman who was dependent on her husband, he was only held responsible if debts were contracted with his notification. As women could not theoretically in law own chattels, they could also not be guilty of the tort of appropriating them.[118]

In cases relating to the occupations of married women who did not trade as *femme sole,* it must be assumed that in London, they were bound to follow the common law concerning such matters, and the women would be regarded as being under coverture. As the husband had responsibility for his wife's chattels he also had the liability for debts incurred before marriage and torts committed during the same period. In 1447 Thomas Charles in a law case in the city of London had to pay the debt of £29 4s. 8d. contracted before his marriage, by his wife Elizabeth when she was *sole.*[119]

A woman who was *covert baron,* then, was over - shadowed by her husband's protection and supremacy. [120] But in many towns a married woman could register as a trader with the town authorities, and be treated as a *femme sole* in relation to her occupation. Women traders who were known as *sole* usually had responsibility for their own debts.

Some towns by proviso or by local custom made allowances for increasing the legal capacity of married women (i.e. allowing them *femme sole* status). If borough customs had not included provisions for married women traders who were technically *femme covert* it would have been impossible for a wife to have lawfully made a contract, or be liable for any debt, because married women could own nothing.

Borough custom and contract

In London so long as women registered in the correct manner there were unlikely to be disputes concerning their occupation. Presumably married women registered in Guild-hall before the Mayor and Aldermen, but no lists of admissions survive. Recognisances concerning the business of married women were taken before the Mayor at the Guildhall.

A London contract case in Chancery concerning debt illustrates the problems that might sometimes be encoun-tered by people trading with married women. In the 1490s, Johanne Horne, a widow, late the wife of William Horne, salter and Alderman of London was involved in a case of debt over silk which she purchased from John Ffynkell, Knight and draper.[121] She sealed the obligation with her seal, and in the life of her husband had 'shewynd' and affirmed to Ffynkell that she was a sole merchant:

> and that she after the custome of London myght in
> her own name bye and selle and that all contracts

and bonds by her and in her sole name made shuld not withstanding her cou(ver)ture be god and effectual in the law to all her customers.

But he could not find record in the city that 'she was admytted to be sole m(er)chaunte and so is like to lese his ocid dutie ayeste all right and conscience.'[122] When a woman was not registered as *'sole'* then the common law would be followed in such cases, hence Ffynkell's concern that he might have no redress.

Another London chancery case illustrates that wives who traded in the city were a normal occurrence, in the words of one husband,

> that where the comune yise within the said citee is, and of longe tyme hath been that wyfes of men of worship and thrifte unfraunchised in the same citee have by the sufferance of their husbondes in the absence of them used to by and selle all manere of merchandise towards thencrease and lyving of them and ther household the dutees of all which bargaines comyng or grohying hath alwey ben contente by suche wifes or for nowne paiement of them by ther husbondes . . .[123]

A London act of the early fourteenth century states:

> where a woman couverte de baron follows any craft within the city by herself apart, with which the husband in no way intermeddles, such a woman should be bound as a single woman as to all that concerns her said craft. And if the husband and wife are impleaded, in such case the wife shall plead as a single woman in a Court of Record, and shall have her law and other advantages by way of plea just as a single woman. And if she is con- demned, she shall be committed to prison until she shall have made satisfaction; and neither the husband nor his goods shall in such case be charged or interfered with.[124]

The custom also states that

> If a wife, as though a single woman, rents any house or shop within the said city, she shall be bound to pay the rent of the said house or shop, and shall be impleaded and sued as a single woman, by way of debt if necessary, notwithstanding that she was coverte de baron at the time of such letting, supposing that the lessor did not know thereof.[125]

Another custom concerning married women was recorded:

> where plaint of debt is made against the husband,
> and the plaintiff declares that the husband made the
> Contract with the plaintiff by the hand of the wife
> of such dependant, in such case, the said defendant
> shall have the aid of his wife, and shall have a
> day until the next court, for taking counsel with
> his wife. [126]

A married woman was usually considered as *covert
de baron* in pleas of debt but it was common, in the
words of one who was imprisoned: 'contrarie to the law of
this land, to make a woman that hath a husband to
answere as a woman sole.'[127]Only married women who were
registered as traders, should have been made to answer
for themselves in debt cases. Thus in London female
traders who chose to be known as *sole* women, and who
had registered as such, were not dependent on their
husbands to answer for them. Margaret, widow of John
Salisbury was presented by the fishmongers in 1440,
before the Mayor and Aldermen, and affirmed that she
might in future enjoy the benefits of the custom of London
touching such traders.[128] With the exception of the woman
trading as *sole* the law allowed little individuality or
independence to a wife.

It appears that women could become free of the city
by one of the usual qualifications with the exception that
during coverture their freedom was suspended.[129] In many
towns there was a custom which explains why more women
were not admitted to the franchise. For example, the
practice of allowing people who were not citizens to pay
fines for living and trading in the borough created a
class of tradeswomen and tradesmen with inferior
rights. [130] Obviously many women would have had this
status in the towns.

The definition of the *sole* woman raises the
question of her legal status in trade. An act of 1363
restricted men to one trade each, but left female
'Brewers, Bakers, [Carders, Spinners and Workers as well
as of wool, as of linen cloth, and of silk, Brawdesters
and breakers of wool,] and all others that do use and
work all Handy Works' free to work as they had done
formerly, [131] in several trades. By the fifteenth century
the status of the married *femme sole* was more clearly
defined although she still needed to declare publicly her
intention to be *sole*. In Lincoln the ordinances seem to
have been based on those of London,[132] as they stated
that if a married woman followed any craft without her
husband she was to be charged as

44

a sole woman as touchyng suche thynges as longeth to hyr crafte. And yf a pleynt be takyn ageyn syche a woman, sche schall answer and plede as a sole woman, and make hyr law, and take other avauntege in courte by plee or other wyse for hyr dyscharge. And if sche be condempned sche schall be commyt to preyson tyll sche be agrede with the Pleyntyf. And no godes nor catell that longeth to hyr husbonde schall be attached for hyr nor chargyd. [133]

A similar custom was also followed in York. [134] In London an action of account or debt was maintainable by custom against a single woman and against children under age (15 for girls, 14 for boys), if they were traders or kept open shops for craft or trade, and actions of debt could be taken in the same way for anything that concerned their craft or trade. [135] In London if a woman was bound with her husband, or if she made the contract by her hand she could be made answerable. [136] Women were also made sureties for others, thus indicating that they were considered to have a responsible part in financial dealings. [137] In conclusion women who were known as sole traders could take responsibility for their actions, and where they were impleaded in cases of debt, they could wage their law with men and women, when the action concerned their trade or craft. [138]

In London the widows of freemen were allowed to become freewomen of the city, and were thus able to continue in their husbands' trade as members of the craft guild, or as if they were members. Evidence for this comes from the regulation that married women practising crafts by themselves could take apprentices. There were considerable numbers of freewomen in London. In 1464 it was recorded as ancient custom in the city that every woman married to a freeman was, after his death, a freewoman of the city so long as she remained single. [139] Widows were also allowed to continue working in their husbands' craft by some guilds provided that they did not marry men who followed other crafts. [140] An example of this can be seen in the recognisance of a vintner's widow who was admitted to the freedom to follow her husband's craft on being publicly presented to the warden and brothers. [141]

Women and work in London

Women could be members of guilds, although they probably had fewer rights than male members. They engaged in trade in the same way as men. In towns other than London women and men sometimes had to pay a feudal tax

conferring the right to trade, but in this men and women were treated equally. [142]
    Women could gain guild membership through inheritance, as daughters or widows of members. But wives usually had to wait until their husbands died to obtain membership because it was unusual for women to become free through patrimony, redemption, or apprenticeship. [143] Women were called 'sisters' in merchant guilds, but they never had the same positions in guilds as men, as they were not allowed to participate fully in council or social events. One woman, a member of the York Merchant Adventurers, was on the council of the guild in 1474-5, but this is a rare example.[144] In England, in contrast to France and Italy, there were no all women craft guilds, [145] and perhaps because of their absence, there was less segregation of occupations. Mixed guilds probably also ensured that women could participate in many varied trades as they were not often deliberately excluded from professional trade within a guild, although their admittance was regulated. Marriages arranged within guilds ensured that the secrets of the mystery were protected, and that the interests of guild members were guarded from unfair competition by other traders.[146] The only guild composed solely of women was a religious organisation dedicated to St. John the Baptist in Boston, Lincolnshire, founded in 1366. On the Baptist's day they had to dance together and pay a fine. [147]
    Although women were denied higher education they could enter craft guilds and receive a formal training, but it is probable that many women learnt their crafts and trades informally. In London women or girls could be apprenticed to a trade by the same method and under the same conditions as a man. Women who had girl apprentices were required to be *sole*. Wives who took a separate craft and were declared *sole* could have female apprentices. A statute of 1405-6 decreed that no man or woman worth under 20 shillings a year could apprentice his son or daughter to any craft within any city or borough. [148] Some towns appealed against this law, including the citizens of London who said that it interfered with their ancient custom and they believed that every freeman might apprentice his son or daughter to any other freeman. Their request was granted.[149] The appeal of Oxford on the same grounds was rejected.[150] Norwich was successful.[151]
    In London general regulations on apprenticeship were applicable equally to male and female. The 1413 ordinances drawn up for the support of rebuilding work at the Guildhall, stipulated that the increase in payments at the beginning and end of apprenticeship were to be paid by male and female alike.[152] Women were specifically included in guild regulations which suggests that they

arose from actual practice. London apprentices were to enrol within their first year; and a proclamation of 1415-16 was addressed to 'every man and woman having apprentices'.[153] There are frequent references to girls who were bound as apprentices to both husband and wife to learn the wife's craft. [154] When wives worked with their husbands, apprentices were frequently bound to both, and it is probable that in these cases when the husband died the wife had to retain and teach them. One case that occurred in 1429 shows what was expected of merchants' widows. John Haccher who had been apprenticed to Richard Gosselyn Ironmonger, and had served for nine years, asked to be admitted to the Freedom of London on the grounds that Beatrice the widow, 'who by the law and custom of the City and the will of the deceased ought to have kept up his household and instructed his apprentices, had dismissed and allowed him to depart and refused to maintain and teach him.' As she had sold everything belonging to the business he was admitted.[155] Obviously it was expected that widows would continue in their husband's businesses and they were legally required to find alternative position and employment for apprentices if they decided not to work in their husband's occupation. [156]

As far as women's own apprentices were concerned, a London ordinance of the early fifteenth century states that:

> Those married women who are accustomed to practice certain crafts in the city by themselves without their husbands, are to take girls as their apprentices, to serve them and to learn their crafts, and these apprentices are to be bound in service by indentures of apprenticeship to both the husband and the wife in order to follow the mistery of the wife.[157]

The practice of women working apart from their husbands can be seen among the parish clerks of London, whose guild regulations allowed them to take apprentices only 'to all such maner craftes, as their wifis usen and occupien.'[158] Many girls were bound to female pursers, [159] throwsters, [160] and broiderers.[161] Many girls seem to have been bound under age. Petronilla, daughter of John Oxwyk, was apprenticed at 7 or 8, in 1393-4.[162] An orphan girl was apprenticed at 11.[163] Another orphan girl who had been apprenticed by the Mayor and Aldermen to a mercer's widow ran away and married Richard Bun, a draper's apprentice. [164] A carpenter had enrolled Katherine Lightfoot against her will, her father's and her friends', and as she was under the age of 14 she was exonerated. [165] A woman of the same name supplied 2,000 tiles to the

King for Shene Palace.[166]   Another girl was exonerated because her masters Thomas and Alice Glanton were not free of the city, 'neither was the said Alice practiced or skilled whatsoever in the said mistery of a brouderer,' wherein she had pretended to be trained.[167] Complaints of non-enrolment were also common,[168] and could result in exoneration from service.

Both apprentices and masters could appeal to the guild officials or to the Mayor and Aldermen for redress. One mistress Alice Virly, in 1414 left the city and did not make provision for her apprentice, Agnes Wawton, though she should have assigned her to another of the same mistery, or provided for her to be taught.[169] Apprentices were not always well treated, as is shown by the case of Agnes, wife of John Cottiller, who was in the habit of beating her girl apprentice with a stick.[170] But apprentices could also be punished for bad behaviour. John Shadwell, apprentice of Margaret Shadwell, was sent to prison, and in 1445 an apprentice was flogged in the Goldsmith's Hall for trying to strangle his mistress.[171]

Apprentices were usually bound for 7 to 10 years and girls were required to be over 14. Agnes Snell of Hoo, Kent, apprentice of Agnes Haunsarde had been bound for 10 years.[172]   Alice Harflete had been apprenticed for 11 years to a poulterer and a Shepster to learn the latter's trade.[173]

Men could also have female apprentices.[174]   Two out of seven apprentices in the will of Richard Somery, mercer, were women.[175]   One man apprenticed his two daughters to a public notary, one died young and the other married, so they may never have practised.[176]

It is apparent, then, that the female worker was recognised in industry and trade independently of her role as wife, widow, or daughter. Another example is provided by the wife of a 'boteman' of London who bought linen cloth from a mercer as one 'who was a sole merchant in the art of Shepster.'[177] The range of occupations open to women were very varied. Several women occur as barber surgeons.[178] But the physicians were to send a petition to Parliament bewailing the 'worthless and presumptuous women who usurp the profession' and asked for the imposition of fines and prison sentences for those who attempted to 'use the practice of fisk (physic)'.[179] Perhaps these informally trained women were encroaching on what was considered a male profession.

One woman practising as a healer, was Alice Shevyngton, a servant of William Gregory of London. Alice had served William for three years at a yearly wage of 16 shillings, but in her fourth year she often absented herself from his service to cure persons of sore eyes, and when he suggested she should make amends she took out an action of debt against him.[180] A number of women occur as apothecaries,[181] but most women involved in caring for the sick were midwives[182] or nurses. The profession of midwife was barred to men, as men were not allowed to be present when a child was born. Women who worked as nurses in a professional capacity were common: the two London infirmaries of St. Mary without Bishopsgate, and St. Bartholomew's, employed women to care for those in childbirth, and for children orphaned when born there. [183] One of the earliest permanent homes for women was St. Katherine's-by-the-Tower.[184] The hospital office of nurse was only honorary but they were supplied with food and clothing. Some women acted as nurses privately. Robert de Eye, a pelleter, recovered a bed in 1365 as payment for his wife who had cared for William de Langford for four years.[185]

The following examples of the occupations in which women participated may give a fuller idea of the kinds of work open to them in London.

An occupation which was probably more profitable for the owners of brothels than for those who practised it, was that of prostitution. Attitudes towards prostitution and prostitutes were often contradictory. Many men had mistresses, and if not condoned, this practice was at least largely disregarded by the church.[186] But women who were prostitutes seem to have been morally condemned by Society. In early fourteenth century Bristol prostitutes were ordered to proclaim their profession openly by wearing a striped hood.[187] In 1344 prostitutes, like lepers, were forbidden to live within the walls of Bristol.[188] The London regulations of the early fourteenth century stipulated that brothels were not to be set up within the walls of the city, neither were courtesans nor brothel keepers to work there under pain of imprisonment.[189] The punishment recorded in 1285 for women found to be of ill-fame was imprisonment for forty days. A warden was appointed to specify the areas to which they were assigned and they were not allowed to wear minever (on dress or hood). [190] The earliest reference to the legal regulation of the stews in Southwark is of 1611-2.[191] In the early fourteenth century boatmen were not allowed to carry people across the Thames to the stews except in daytime. [192]

By 1393 it was believed that affrays and dissensions arose in the city because of men consorting with 'harlots' at taverns, or at the brewhouses of hucksters, in the city and suburbs. Flemish women were especially blamed, and such women were only allowed to live in the stews in Southwark or Cokkeslane. The punishment for wandering in other areas was the loss of her upper garment with her hood.[193] In 1417 Robert Chichele, Alderman, attempted to abolish stews within the city itself, and the punishment for every offence was a fine of £5.[194]

The Bristol regulations were probably based on these of London. Like London they allowed for the doors and windows of prostitutes houses to be removed to force them to conformity, or to move. In 1366 in London the watchmen of Broad Street ward took away the doors and windows of a chamber where Jean Upholderster dwelt, because she was a woman of bad character.[195] From the number of indictments in the wards it would appear that there was a conscious policy to control prostitution. The Postern in Langhornesaley, Cornhill, in 1421, was indicted because 'strumpets' entered there by night,[196] and in the following year it was said that behind the Pye at Quenhithe was a privy place, where strumpets and pimps had their covert, so the place was closed at night time.[197] In London many women were indicted as being 'strumpets' and bawds. Alice, wife of John Cheyney, and Isabel Cobham in 1422 were said to have committed fornication with two priests and other unknown men.[198] In 1367 Joan, wife of William at Grene, was sworn not to keep her house as a brothel.[199] In 1422 Gerard Clayson and his wife, occupiers of the 'estewsheus' (stewhouse) in Grub Street, Cripplegate without, were indicted as receivers and maintainers of harlotry.[200] Zenobius Martyn of Langbourne ward was indicted as a bawd and associate of prostitutes. He kept a lodging house in 1373 for aliens, and was also a broker even though he was not free of the city, and he had housed prostitutes.[201] One unfortunate man, Thomas Bunny, in 1362 had bound himself to Thomas Rose, Shedder, for four years. But his master sold his estate to Joan Hunt who kept stews on the far side (south) of London Bridge. He was forced to do grievous work, carrying water in 'tynes' and he fell and injured himself. She then incited Bernard her lover to beat him and when he fell sick he was thrown out. When he recovered she wanted him to return.[202]

In conclusion, prostitution was blamed for riots and arguments that arose in the city. The City authorities tried to control prostitutes by allocating two areas where they might live: along the Thames in Southwark outside City control, and in Cock Lane. Certain areas in the city were blamed for immorality and these were subject to closure. Flemish women were not free of the city and were probably forced by poverty into this profession, and the numerous pimps who lived in the city exploited this circumstance. Even honest girls could be lured into a life of immorality. In 1385 Elizabeth, the wife of Henry Moring, under cover of the craft of broidery took in female apprentices, and then incited them to prostitution, in her own house in the Parish of All Hallows near the wall, and elsewhere, keeping the earnings so gained.

Because of this offence, and to deter other women from such scandals, she was punished by the pillory. It was said that later offences would be punished by prison.[203]
Women of better reputation kept hostels and lodging houses.[204] Numerous women were ale-wives.[205] The ale-wife of the 'Bosommes Inn' took an action of trespass against a former customer, who now lodged at 'Ye Falcon' saying that he had encouraged her ostler to leave her service.[206] In 1418, out of 234 paid up members of the brewers company, 39 were women.[207] In 1420, out of 300 brewers, less than twenty were women. In 1356 when thirty brewers were appointed to serve the king only one was a woman.[208] In 1414 Jone Harold was admitted to the Brewers' Company, paying 12 pence quarterage, entitling her to wear the livery.[209] She occurs in a debt case, as the wife of John Harold, tailor, selling bread and ale to the wife of Henry Barton with whom she made a tally for 36 score of bread. The normal price was a penny a score but Jone was asking 12 pence a score, a debt of 47 shillings![210] Many women occur as brewers, and some clearly have possession of breweries.[211] One father left his daughter the lease of a brewhouse for eight years, at the end of which she was to keep five quarters of malt to set herself up in business to support herself.[212]
Many women were indicted for not selling ale according to the Assize of Ale, many were called hucksters. A great number like the wife of Ballad Emmot at the Red Latys by St. Magnus, were accused of selling ale in hanaps[213] (probably tankards).
Women occur frequently as hucksters, one Alice Norwell, was a *sole* merchant *in arte huxsters*.[214] Hucksters were retailers of small goods, in shops or stalls. The term is frequently associated with female brewers and bakers. By 1421 it had acquired pejorative connotations.[215] Regratresses are often associated with hucksters. Regraters bought up market commodities, especially victuals, to re-sell at a profit in the same place, or at another market. Forestallers bought goods before they arrived at market or before the hour appointed for their sale and profited by their resale. Forestalling and regrating were often accused of causing rises in prices and shortages. One woman who forestalled was Juliana Tanner. She forfeited 424 eggs to the Chamberlain worth 2s. 6d. for this offence in 1372.[216] Poulterers were frequently called forestallers and regraters.[217]
Female bakers were common in the city and some had their own bakehouses.[218] Women, though not so common in some victualling trades as others, do appear. In 1383 out of 128 members of the livery of grocers (merchants rather than artisans) only one was a woman.[219]
Women were also active in more traditional trades, such as laundering.[220] One occupation open to women that was not self-employed, was that of servant.[221] Edith

Hyman was paid only £4. 16s. for 9 years service to Walter Rawlys.[222] Servants, if fortunate, were left property or goods by their masters.[223] One woman received a hall and two shops, another land and houses, and a third 20 marks and a home in the testators almshouse.[224] One servant was given 9 pence a week to support herself.[225] In the lower classes the practice of sending daughters into service as an alternative to marriage was equivalent to the practice in other classes of sending children away to other people's houses as preparation for marriage. It must be born in mind, however, that some types of service were prestigious, e.g. in the Royal household.

Women were not only active in the less prestigious occupations. They could act as brokers. Sanche Snoth undertook to sell for a skinner of London '3 furres of blak shankes and 6 furres of blak lambe' at a price set by him. It was agreed that if she was unable to sell at this price she was to pay him or return the furs.[226] Another woman is found in 1365 as a pawnbroker. Mariotta Convers accepted a gold nouce set with stones worth 50 marks from John Count de Harecourt. She pledged it to John Lapy of Florence for 20 marks and he sold it to Bartholomew Fotenaunt and it afterwards came into the hands of Gillemyn de Nerny, a Lombard. As a pawnbroker had no right to assign pawn to another Mariotta had to make restitution.[227] Women also lent money, sometimes on a large scale. Alice de Perrers lent 200 marks to Richard de Kent in 1365 and had to sue for its return.[228]

Other occupations held by women were sometimes unusual. One woman in 1453 was an armourer[229] and Alice, wife of Thomas de Cantebrugge, had armour and other goods worth £200 stolen from her house.[230] In 1408 the Keeper of the King's Wardrobe owed money to Alice Drax who was a 'boke bynder'.[231] At the end of the fifteenth century Joyce Pylegrome of London, 'a straunger', was stated to be a 'bokeseller'.[232] Women were also artists. One in her will left her apprentice the third best part of copies and instruments appertaining to the making of pictures and one of her best chests to hold them in.[233] Another received payment of £26, from the Churchwardens of St. Mary at Hill for doing 'gilte' and painting the tabernacle of our lady.[234]

The wife of john Hert, haberdasher, at the beginning of the fifteenth century is frequently referred to as a 'jeweller'.[235] There are several other references to women jewellers,[236] one of whom tried to recover some debts.[237] There were also female wiredrawers of gold and silver.[238]

Joan Hille, widow of Richard Hille, who died in 1440 carried on his business as a founder. In his will he mentioned a shop, 4 male apprentices, and two female servants. [239] Unfortunately Joan did not work long as her will was proved in the following year. [240]

Sometimes only single instances of women holding certain occupations occur, there was a waterbearer,[241] a spurrier,[242] a herb wife,[243] a flax wife,[244] and others sold hooks,[245] iron goods,[246] hammers,[247] lime,[248] hurdles,[249] poles,[250] ropes,[251] tents,[252] and old clothes.[253] Some even owned ships.[254] A husband and wife who were foreigners sold oxen.[255] Other foreign women frequently seem to have kept shops or bought and sold as freewomen.[256] Deonys Browne, widow, was indicted because of the tubs and boards of fishmongers in front of her shops in Bridge Ward.[257] There were sellers of fish in shops and burlesters who sold fish in the street.[258] Many women were fishwives.[259] Only in one instance do women appear to have held an office technically forbidden them. In 1422 John of Ely was indicted because he had let the office of assayer of oysters at Queenhithe, London, to farm to women, who it was said did not know how to perform it. It was also said to be not 'worship to this city that women should have such things in governance.'[260] Other women connected with the sale of food were floaners,[261] butchers,[262] and maxsters.[263] One woman Margaret Bate had a 'warehouse and shoppe' from which her servant sold and lent divers merchandise.[264] She also sold russet cloth, ludlows and medleys to foreign merchants.[265] Women were often described only as merchants.[266]

Women appear to have been concerned with almost every process in the manufacture and finishing of all kinds of cloth, with the exception of dying and weaving.[267] Female weavers of wool occur in other towns, but I have found no evidence of them in London during this period.[268] Spinsters[269] and shepsters[270] are the trades which seem to have been most commonly followed in connection with the manufacture of cloth. Alice Swaby supplied the Royal household and her work was divided amongst several women who made many things from a 'Shavying cloth' to towels, altar cloths and surplices, shirts and sheets.[271] Agnes Shepster and another woman made 159 sheets of holland cloth for the Royal household over a period of one and a half years.[272] Margaret Swan supplied sheets and pillow covers.[273] Other women dealt in linen cloth.[274] Needlewomen and sempstresses were also employed by the household.[275] There were thredwomen,[276] pouchmakers,[277] purse makers,[278] cappers,[279] hurers,[280] tailors,[281] drapers,[282] and mercers.[283]

Women were also active in importing cloth[284] as well as exporting.[285] Christiania Combemaker exported thrums and imported 'Combehedes'[286] as well as making instruments for the preparation of wool, as a separate business.[287] Some women were even merchants of the staple. In a list of merchants pardoned for offences against the statutes regulating trade, of 350, 19 were women.[288] Margaret Parker was one such merchant of the staple, supplying a John Heron with wool.[289] Another was Margaret, daughter of William Gregory, Alderman and Mayor, who married John Croke, Alderman, in 1470. Although John Croke and William Gregory were skinners, Margaret herself made extensive shipments of wool, some of which she exported from Sandwich in 1478.[290] In her husband's will she was left a third of his goods as dower and 'all her clothes and jewellery and all good monies and debts which I and Margaret have acquired through merchandise and dealings in wool.'[291] Margaret was a wealthy woman in her own right and lent money to Sir William Stokker, her son in law, an Alderman and Draper, when he was unable to pay the customs or subsidies or contribute to a loan to the King. When he died he owed her £133 11s. Numerous debts owing to Margaret are listed in her will in detail.[292] She was a capable business woman and looked after her husband's interests after his death. Thomas Betson, her granddaughter Katherine's husband, has left us an account of a meeting with Margaret in 1478.

> And God wote she made me right sullen chere with hir countenaunce whyles I was with her; me thought it longe till I was departid. She brake to me off the tayll I told her betene the Vicar that was and hir: she said the Vicar never ffared well seth, he took it so much to hart . . . I had no joye to tary with her, she is a ffyn mery woman, but ye shall not know it nor yit ffynd it, nor none of youres by that see in her.[293]

John and Margaret had seven sons and five daughters. [294] Through marriage they were related to the London families of Stonor, Walden, Marowe, Ryche, Stokker, Hille, Tate and Wood. Their extensive connections help to explain their trade relationships and alliances with these families. They owned considerable property in and around London, living in the city in comfort, with plate and jewellery. At least seven servants were mentioned in Margaret's will, proved in 1491. John had died 10 years before.[295]

Elizabeth Kirkeby in the late fifteenth century was also engaged in trade on a large scale. George Bulstrode, Draper of London, acted in Seville for her for a year and he sent £4,000 of merchandise to her from there, and had intended to marry her. John Heron was her executor.[296]

One craft which deserves special attention is that of silkwork, because it appears to have been solely in the hands of women until the end of the fifteenth century.

Unlike other major European towns engaged in the manufacture of silk and silk goods, they did not have guild
status, but the women within the industry appear to have
worked closely together to protect their interests. Many
silkwomen also appear to have been wives or daughters of
Aldermen, and it was probably an occupation which was
socially acceptable for the wealthier merchant families.

Women composed virtually all the labour-force in the
silk industry; they made laces, ribbons, girdles and
small articles. They collectively tried to safeguard their
interests, and in particular, they feared foreign competition. It is clear that the industry suffered particularly
throughout the second half of the fifteenth century. The
term silkwoman, seems to have been applied to any woman
concerned with the production or sale of silk. Silkwomen
were distinct from mercers' wives, and they followed a
defined occupation, separate from the trade of their
husbands' or fathers' crafts. Silkwomen followed the same
rules and worked under the same conditions as workers in
other crafts. A prospective apprentice was bound by an
indenture made by parent or guardian and her future
mistress. Whilst learning the craft girls would be sent on
various errands and perhaps entrusted with some money
transactions.

The silkwomen were concentrated in London, perhaps
because silk was an expensive luxury, and so it was not
profitable to work elsewhere. Their trade often involved
large sums of money and dealing with foreign merchants.
Because of the financial risks of their trade, many silkwomen operated as *femmes soles*.

It is possible that the petitions presented by silkwomen,
which led to five acts between 1455 and 1504, forbidding
the importation of certain silk goods, may have been
inspired by xenophobia as much as an actual threat to
their craft.[297]   An earlier petition of 1368 expressed anti-
alien feelings and a fear of monopoly. Some silkwomen
delivered a bill to the Mayor and Aldermen of London
complaining that a Lombard, Nicholas Sarduche, had been
purchasing all the silk and then raising its price. The
women also petitioned the king, and a writ was issued
ordering the civil authorities to give them justice; an
enquiry was held and Sarduche found guilty of the
accusations.[298]

In 1455 it was again necessary for the silkwomen to
seek protection from foreign competition, and they petitioned parliament:

> the silke-wymmen and throwestres of the craftes and
> occupation of Silkework within the Citee of London,
> which be and have been craftes of wymmen within
> the same city of tyme that noo mynde renneth unto

the contrarie. That where it is pleasying to God that all his creatures be set in vertueux occupation and labour according to their degrees, and convenient for thoo places where their abode is, to the norishing of vertue, and eschewying of vices and ydelness. And where upon the same craftes, before this tyme, many a wurshipfull woman within the said citee have lyved full honourably, and therewith many good Housholds kept, and many Gentilwymmen and other in grete noumbre like as there now be moo than a M, have been drawen under theym in lernyng the same Craftes and occupation ful vertueusly . . .

But Lombards and other alien foreigners, who wanted to destroy these crafts, 'and all such vertueux occupations for wymmen within yis lande', so that they could become rich and could transfer the occupations to other countries, brought 'daily' into England 'silk throwen Rybens, and laces falsly and decyrably wrought, corses of silke', and other goods which concerned the silkwomen's craft. The silkwomen complained that they could not make the products themselves because no unwrought or raw silk was being brought into England, except for that of poor quality. They claimed that the sufferance of this grievance, 'hath caused and is like to cause, grete ydleness amongs yonge Gentilwymmen and other apprentices . . . and also laying down of many good and notable Housholdes . . .' They (successfully) asked Parliament to ask the King to ban all finished silk from coming into England.[299]
 In 1463 a petition was granted to protect wrought silk and other goods from foreign competition.[300] In 1482 the London silkwomen were again struggling to survive as silks of 'Jewish and Saracen' origin were being sold in England. Importation of foreign silks was then forbidden for four years.[301] Although there were, clearly, considerable numbers of silkwomen in London their monopoly could not have lasted throughout the period, for in a petition of 1482 occurs the phrase 'as well men as women, and yonge damsels, beyng servauntes and apprentices to the said craft of silke work.' Men came to dominate and professionalise the trade, and this culminated in the large silk industries of the seventeenth and eighteenth centuries.
 Some women supported their husbands. William Balaile, home from Normandy, was admitted to the freedom of London so that his wife could keep an open shop to support him in her way of business as he was incapable of work.[302] Cristian Baxter, a single woman brought a charge of debt against John Davell, citizen and draper,

who was imprisoned in Ludgate. She then charged his wife Ann, who petitioned the Chancellor saying her husband for his meat and drink had only her 'daily labor and hande crafte' and she had two children upon her 'daily burden and charge'.[303]

Conclusion

Women, then, were involved in considerable economic activity despite the constraints which were in theory placed on them by the various overlapping bodies of law. Nor were they ever full members of craft guilds: they could not hold guild office or have any voice in the guild's regulation. In addition, women were admitted to some of the more specialised crafts only if they were wives or daughters of masters of the craft – for example, the girdlers', braelers' and pynners' guilds passed restrictive legislation against women and prohibited their employment, except for the wives and daughters of members.[304]   But only five out of 500 guilds in England excluded women altogether, and even where the affairs were managed by a company of priests, women were admitted as lay members and had duties and claims on the guild like men.[305] Women were also often present at guild feasts, in their own right or as companions of men,[306] and their participation in guild activities as members of a master's family indicates a recognition of the close ties of the family even within economic life.

In conclusion, it is evident that women played an important part in the economy in the production of consumer and producer goods and in the provision of services. More research is needed before statements can be made about the wages paid to women, but it is unlikely that they had equal earning power with men. Although Sir John Fortescue held that women did not have the powers of concentration required in business,[307]   yet as we have seen there were many capable business women in his day. Although excluded from civic office (being unable to be members of Wardmote) the trading and manufacturing activities of women suggest that they were accepted as citizens in their economic capacity provided that they declared themselves *sole*. Finally, townswomen appear to have enjoyed more freedom and respect in practice than they were ascribed in theory or in law.

The writer of the *Lawes Resolutions of Womens Rights*, said that once a woman was under couverture, that mastership was called by citizens, after *Esops Fables*, 'Leonina Societate',[308]   but as the wife of Bath said:

who peyntede the leoun, tel me who?
By God, if Wommen hadde writen stories,
As Clerkes han with-inne hir oratories,
They wolde han writen of men more wikkednesse
Than all the mark of Adam may redresse.[309]

NOTES

I should like to thank Dr. Caroline Barron for reading
and commenting on this article, Dr. Christopher Harrison,
and my parents, Mr. and Mrs. K. Lacey, for making
this research possible.

1. J. Brydall, *Camera Regis, or, A Short View of
    London* (London 1616).
2. For accounts of women participating in family
    affairs see, A. Hanham ed., *The Cely Letters 1412-
    1483* (London, 1975, Early English Text Society –
    hereafter referred to as E.E.T.S.). N. Davis, ed.,
    Paston Letters and Papers of the Fifteenth Century,
    2 vols. (Oxford 1971). The joint share of a husband
    and wife in business matters is publicly acknowledged
    when husband and wife brought actions of debt
    against a third party. For example, see A.H.
    Thomas ed., *Calendar of Plea and Memoranda Rolls
    preserved among the archives of the Corporation of
    the City of London at the Guildhall ad.1413-1437*
    (Cambridge 1942), p.45, (1416). Hereafter cited as
    C.P.M.R. P.E. Jones ed., *C.P.M.R. ad. 1437-1457*
    (Cambridge 1954), p.31, (1440).
3. Public Record Office, London C1/48/37 and C1/33/261.
    Hereafter cited as *P.R.O.*
4. *Thrupp*, op. cit. pp.155-161. A.F. Leach, *The
    Schools of Medieval England* (London, 1915), p.89.
    A.F. Leach, *Educational Charters and Documents,
    598 to 1909* (Cambridge 1911), pp.xvii, xlviii.
    F.J. Furnival, ed., *Early English Meals and
    Manners:...* (London, 1868), pp.xiv-xvi.
    R. Dybaski, *Songs, Carols and other Miscellaneous
    poems* (London 1907), pp.xiii-xxxiii. M. Aston,
    'Lollardy and Literacy' *History*, 62 (1977), p.349.
    M.S. Serjeantson, ed., *Legendys of Hooly wummen.*
    (E.E.T.S. London 1938). F.J. Furnivall and
    C. Horstmann eds., *Life of St. Catherine of
    Alexandria* by John Capgrave (E.E.T.S. London 1893).
    A. Goodman, 'The Piety of John Brunham's daughter,
    of Lynn.' in D. Baker, ed., *Medieval Women*
    (Oxford 1978). S.B. Meech ed., *The Book of
    Margery Kempe* (E.E.T.S. London, 1940), pp.3,21,29.
    H.G. Richardson, "Business training in Medieval

Oxford" *The American Historical Review*, vol.XLVI,
Jan. 1941, no.2.
I intend to deal with this subject in a future
article.

5. For example, Margaret 'Countess of Northfolk, to
    whom no place in parlement myght apperteyne by
    cause she was a woman.'
    J. Strachey, J. Pridden, and E. Upham, eds.
    *Rotuli Parliamentorum ut in petitiones et Placita in
    Parliamento* (London 1767-1777), vol.iv, p.270,
    (1425). Hereafter cited as *Rot. Parl.*

6. The Duchess of Suffolk, Constable of the Castle of
    Wallingford. Sir H. Nicholas ed., *Proceedings and
    ordinances of the Privy Council of England* (London
    1837), vol.VI, pp.255-6, (1455). Hereafter cited as
    Proc. Priv. Council. Dame Agnes Fo[r]ster,
    custodian of Lord Gravyle and Sir Cardot Malort.
    She was the widow of a London Alderman. *P.R.O.*
    C1/31/44 (between 1458-84). The Countess of
    Hereford, *Proc. Priv. Council.* (London 1834),
    vol.1, p.343 (1410). M. Harris ed., *Coventry Leet
    Book 1420-1555* (London E.E.T.S. 1907-13), vol.1,
    p.123. A. Abram, *Social England in the Fifteenth
    Century* (London 1909), p.143.

7. J. Green, *The Priviledges of the Lord Mayor and
    Aldermen of the City* (London, 1722). I. Pinchbeck,
    *Women Workers and the Industrial Revolution,
    1750-1850* (London 1981). See chs. viii, xii, in
    particular p.303.

8. T.F.T. Plucknett and J.L. Barton eds., *St. German's
    Doctor and Student* (London 1974), dia.1, ch.VII,
    pp.52-3. Hereafter cited as *D.&S.* (1523):
    > by the law and custom of England the husband
    > shall have all the inherytaunce of his wife
    > durying wherof he was seased [in dede] in
    > the ryght of his wyfe durying the spouselleys
    > in fee or in fee tayle [generall] for the term
    > of his lyfe/yf he have any chyld by her to
    > hold as tenaunt by the courtesye of Englande/
    > *but otherwise he shall have nothing in her
    > inheritance.*

9. M.M. Sheehan, 'Canon Law and Married Women's
    Property', p.114. In *Medieval Studies*, Vol.XXV,
    Toronto, 1963. Hereafter cited as *Canon Law.*

10. L.J. Downer ed., *Leges Henrici Primi* (Oxford, 1972),
    p.225, no.70,22.

11. G.D.G. Hall ed. *The Treatise on the laws and
    customs of the realm of England commonly called
    Glanvill* (London 1965), book VI, no.1, p.58
    (c. 1187-1189). Hereafter cited as *Glanvill.*

12. *ibid.*, book VI, no.3, p.60.

13.   *ibid.*, book VI, no.5, p.60.
14.   *ibid.*, book VI, no.13, p.65.
15.   *ibid.*
16.   *ibid.*, book VII, no.3, p.76.
17.   *ibid.*, book XI, no.3, p.135.
18.   *ibid.*, book VII, no.3, p.77.
19.   F.M. Nichols, ed. *Britton*, vol. II (Oxford, 1865), liv. V, ch. XX, p.291 (13th century).
20.   H.G. Richardson and G.O. Sayles eds., *Fleta Sue commentarius iuris Anglicani* c.1290, vol.II (London, 1955). Hereafter referred to as *Fleta*.
21.   *D & S*, dia.I, ch.VII, p.53.
      For further information on the medieval law relating to women I refer the reader to T.E. (possibly Thomas Edgar), *The Lawes Resolutions of women's rights or the Lawes provision for women* (London 1632), B.L. 1481, b.46. A late sixteenth century compilation of the law relating to women. Hereafter cited as *Lawes Res.* See also A.W.B. Simpson, *An Introduction to the History of Land Law*, (Oxford, 1961), pp.60–66, 77–87.
22.   W.S. Holdsworth, *A History of English Law*, vol.III (London 1923), p.521. Hereafter cited as *Holdsworth*, see also p.521, n.3 where he cites Hawkins, P.C. i. 93:
               A husband and wife are considered but one person in law, and the husband by endowing his wife in marriage with all his worldly goods, gives her a kind of interest in them.
      See also, *Canon Law*, pp.109–124.
23.   *Lawes Res*, book 2, section XXVII, p.67.
24.   *ibid.*, book I, section III, p.6.
25.   I owe much of this information to Nigel Ramsey who kindly lent me his unpublished paper 'Lawyers as Feofees to uses and as Executors'. See p.6. Hereafter cited as *Ramsey*. *Holdsworth*, p.521.
      F. Pollock and F. Maitland, eds., *The History of English Law*. (London 1911), 2nd edn., vol.II. hereafter cited as *P & M*. On testaments see: R.J.R. Goffin, *The Testamentary Executor in England and Elsewhere* (London, 1901), pp.35–78; E.J. Jacob ed., *The Register of Henry Chichele Archbishop of Canterbury 1414–43*, vol.II, (Canterbury and York Society, vol.42, Oxford 1937), pp.xxi, xix, xx. Hereafter cited as *Reg. H. Chichele;* M.M. Sheehan, *The Will in Medieval England* (Toronto, 1963), pp.178, 192; H. Swinburne, *A treatise of testaments and last wills*. 5th edn., pp.2,6 (statutes 32 H.8 and 34 H.8), 15. Hereafter cited as *Swinburne*.
26.   Sir H.B. Vaisey, *The Canon Law of the Church of England*. (S.P.C.K. London, 1947).

27. *Reg. H. Chichele*, p.xxi.
28. J. Marshall, 'The Position of women in the Middle Ranks of Society in 15th Century England.' Unpub. dissertation, St. Andrews MA, 1968.
29. D. Wilkins ed., *Concilia Magnae Brittoniae et Hiber nae a Synodo Verolamiensi 446 ad. Londiniensem, 1717...* (London, 1737), Concilium Lambethense. Statutes of Archbishop Boniface XVIII of Canterbury, 1261:

> Statuimus, ne quis alicuijus solutae mulieris, sive conjugate, alienae vel propriae, impediat vel peturbet, seu impediri aut peturbari faciat, seu procuret justam et consuetam testamenti liberam factionem: quod si fecerit. Sciat se excommunicationis innodatum sententia ipso facto.

30. *ibid.* vol. II, p.705 *P. & M.* vol.III, p.429.
31. *Rot. Parl.* vol.II, p.149, no.9 and p.150, no.9. 'that villeins and women can make testaments, is against reason.'
32. *P. & M.* vol.II, p.429.
33. *ibid.* p.430. Citing *Lyndwood's Provinciale*, p.173.

> "Mirum est quod nostris diebus mariti nituntur uxores suas a testimenti factione impedire."

34. J.V. Bulland and H. Chalmers Bell. eds., *Lyndwood's Provinciale.* (London, 1929), p.66.
35. R. Burn, *Ecclesiastical Law*, (London 1797), 6th edn., vol.IV, p.50. Citing *Lyndwood* p.173. Hereafter cited as *Burn*.
36. G.J. Turner ed. *Year Books of Edward II*, vol.X (Selden Society, vol.63, London 1947), p.241 (1311). Case of Thyke v Fraunceys, concerning the wife of a plaintiff who with his assent made a testament. Roubery, J. argued that Magna Carta allowed a woman to have a rightful share of her husband's goods and therefore she could claim property. But Herle said that a villain could claim property against everyone except his own lord; but a woman could claim against nobody in the lifetime of her husband.

> qe autre persone puisse fere testament qe cely qe proprete porra clamer; mes femme ne peut proprete clamer, nec per consequens testa- mentum facere. E d'autrepart si femme devie intestat l'ordinarie s'entre mettera point; e la reson pur ce q'ele n'a'd nule chatell qe seon seyt vivant son baroun.

37. *Glanvill* book VII, s.5, p.80.
Full capacity – unmarried.
Potestate – married ('in the power of').
38. *Swinburne*, pp.79–80.

39.   T.E. Tomlins and W.E. Taunton, eds. *The Statutes of the Realm* (London 1817), vol.III (34 and 35 H. VIII), ch.5 p.903 (1542), n. (32 H. VIII) ch.1 p.745 (1540).   Hereafter cited as *Stat. Realm*.

40.   *Swinburne*, p.80.

41.   *ibid*. p.80.   Sir R. Brooke, *La Grande Abridgement* (London 1586), fol.256, n.21.   Hereafter cited as *Brooke*.

42.   *D. & S*. dialogue I, ch.VII, p.51.
      the husbonde shall have all the chatellys
      parsonellys that his wyfe had at the tyme of
      the spousellys or after for his own right:
      (and also chatellys reall yf he over lyve his
      wife/but yf he sell or gyve away the chatellys
      reallys and dye by yt sale or gyfte the
      intereste of the wife is determyned/ and els
      they shall remayne to the wyfe yf she over
      lyve her husbonde). (1523).

43.   *Swinburne*, p.80 and see *Lyndwood*, book 3, ch.V, p.66.

44.   *Swinburne*, p.80.

45.   *Burn*, p.52.   *Swinburne*, p.81.   *Brooke*, Devise, fol.230. n.34 (24 H. VIII).

46.   *Swinburne*,   p.8.

47.   *ibid*. p.82.

48.   *ibid*. and see also *Burn*, pp.55-6.

49.   C.J. is conventional legal terminology for Chief Justice, J. for Justice. *Holdsworth*, op. cit. vol. III, p.544 and see R. Tottil ed., *Year Books E.V. - H.VIII*. (London 1567). 12. H. VII Fo. 24.d.
      il ne poit allez bien sa[n]s assent son baron
      en case ou est exec[utor] a un auter home
      avant, ou de tiels chos ou duties dont il ne
      unques avec possession come en les cases avant
      dit. Et par espiritual ley il poit faire
      exec[utor] des ascuns chosez do[n]t le
      propertie, et le possession en le baron. S. de
      son aparade de son corps is sint par le comen
      ley, et par assent de son baron, mes sauns
      assent de son baron le possession, et le
      p[ro]perte est tout en le baron, mes icy le
      baron ad prove le testament son feme le quel
      est prove son assent.

50.   For example Bracton says that,
      A woman who is sui juris can make a will,
      just as any other person may, and dispose of
      her property and the extant fruits of her
      dower, whether they have been separated from
      the soil or not, a thing she formerly could not
      do but now may as a matter of favour.   But
      if she is under her husband's authority she

will not be able to make a will without his consent. Nevertheless, because it is only proper, she is sometimes permitted to dispose by will of that reasonable part she would have had if she had survived her husband, especially things given and granted her for personal adornment, as robes and jewels, which may be said to be her own.

S.E. Thorne, *Bracton on the Laws and Customs of England* (Selden Society, Massachusetts, 1968), pp.178–179. *Glanvill,* book VII, S.5, p.80.

51. *Canon Law,* p.111.
52. *ibid.,* p.112.
53. *ibid.,* p.113.
54. *ibid.,* p.114.
55. *P. & M.* II. pp.432–33. *Holdsworth,* III. pp.525–8.
56. *P. & M.* vol.2, p.351, citing *Year Book 40. E. III.* f.38. (Mich. pl.12). See Mowbray's comments on the Lords.
57. He only refers to writs of particular counties. Fitzherbert, *La Graunde Abridgement* (Richard Tottel, London, 1577), detinue pl.60, 34 E.I. not [E.II]: 'Usage del pais'.
58. G.E. Woodbine, ed. *Glanvill De Legibus et consuetudinibus Regni Angliae,* (London, 1932), book VII, C.5. pp.104–5.
59. *ibid.,* and see *Sheehan,* p.294.
60. *Bracton,* vol.II, p.178.
    Fleta, vol.II, p.193.
61. *Sheehan,* pp.294 and 288 n
    P. & M. vol.II, pp.351–2.
62. *P. & M.* vol.II, p.350 (Magna- Carta 1215, c.26), citing cases relating to the use of Magna Carta, *Year Book 13, 7 E.II,* f.215 and *Year Book 17 E.II,* f.53.b.
63. *P.& M.* vol.II, p.350. *Bracton,* vol.II, p.178.
64. *Bracton,* vol.II, p.178.
65. *Bracton,* vol.II, p.180.
66. *ibid.,* p.181:
    > vix enim inveniretur aliquis civis qui in vita magnum quaestam faceret, si in morte sua cogeretur invitus bona sua relinquere pueris indoctis et luxuriosis male meritis.

    On the custom of London see also p.267, and vol.3, pp.389–400.
67. *Bateson,* vol.II, p.121 (Liber de Antiquis Legibus) and see *Sheehan,* p.294.
68. *Sheehan,* p.294.
69. F. Liebermann ed., *Die Gesetze der Angelsachsen.* (Halle. 1903), vol.I, p.173:
    > Decretum episcoporum et aliorum Sapientum

London." (VI. Aethelstan).

Et excipiatur inprimis captale repententis de pecunia ipsa, et dividatur postea superplus in tres partes: unam patem habeat uxor eius, si in eo munda sit et ipsius facinoris conscia non fuerit; reliquum dividatur in duas partes: dimidium habeat rex, dimidium societas.

70. *Sheehan*, pp.294-5. Limitation on the testator: a Cambridge custom of 1299 mentions the reservation of one half of the chattels to the wife - M. Bateson, Ed., *Borough Customs*. (Selden Society, London 1904), vol.II, p.xcviii. Hereafter cited as *Bateson*. For other variants of local custom see *Bateson*, vol.II, pp.xcvi-xcix and pp.119-20 (Bristol). R.R. Sharpe ed., *Calendar of Wills proved and enrolled in the Court of Husting, London 1258-1688*. (London 1889). Part I. pp.xxxiii-xxxiv. Hereafter cited as *Husting Wills*. *Chichele*, vcl.2, pp.xxxvi, xliii, and p.393. The Earl of Salisbury, after debts and legacies paid, left half his moveable and immoveable goods to his wife.

71. Sir H. Calthrop, *Reports of Special Cases touching several Customs and Liberties of the City of London* (London 1670), pp.109-10. Hereafter cited as *Calthrop*.

72. A. Pulling, *A practical treatise on the laws, customs, and regulations of the City and port of London* (London 1862), p.180. Hereafter cited as *Pulling*.

73. *ibid.* p.181 and see *Glanvill* book 12, c. 20. pp.145-6.

74. For the laws of Wales see D. Jenkins and M. Owen eds., *The Welsh law of Women* (Cardiff 1980). For York, see *P. & M.* vol.II, p.348. The tri-partite division in York lasted until 1692. *Pulling*, p.181, *P. & M.* pp.314-56, *Sheehan*, p.186. The custom of thirds to the wife and children remained in use until the eighteenth century, in London and York:
Bracton, vol.III, p.388.

in accordance with the custom of our city of London (or 'York').... render to B, who was the wife of C her reasonable dower.... From the free tenement which belonged to.... her late husband, in London (or in another city, such a one, or in a suburb of London),.... let the plea proceed in the court of the citizens according to their custom ... and the custom in those parts is that wives of deceased husbands have their free bench in the lands of sokemen and hold for life in the

name of dower, but if they remarry after the
death of their husbands, the custom in that
county is that they lose the dowers they have
in the name of the first husband.

See *Hustings Wills*, vol.1, p.xxxix.   The 1391 revised
version of the Statute of Wales states that if Welsh
women and men hold land by English tenure, then
dower was to follow English law.   Welsh widows were
also entitled to a third of the goods and chattels of
their husbands, and his moveable goods if there
was a child.   If there was no child the widow was
to receive half the moveable goods, so long as she
had not cohabited with another man during her
husband's lifetime.   The last clause is similar to
chapter 34, Statute of Westminster 11 (1285).   The
clause relating to half the goods is similar to the
Welsh law concerning separation by death, where the
goods of husband and wife ought to be equally
shared.

R.R. Davies, 'The status of women and the Practice
of marriage in late medieval Wales'. in D. Jenkins
and M. Owen eds., op. cit. p.102 citing B.L. Add.
Ms. 10,013, f.5v. *ibid.*, p.102, n. citing *P. & M.*
11, p.405.   Bleg. 61. 5–6. Lat. A. 51/4; Cvfn 73/9a.

75.   *Hustings' Wills*, vol.1, p.xxxiii.
76.   *ibid.* p.xxxix.   Britton intimates that by his time
widows ceased to lose their dower obtained from
their first husband, when they remarried.   But
Bracton said that such a custom was in force in his
day; and according to Sharpe this is corroborated
by the evidence of wills.   See *Hustings' Wills*,
vol.1, p.xxxiii.
77.   *P. & M.* vol.11, p.349.
78.   *ibid.*, vol.11, p.351, citing Reg. Brev. orig. 1426,
Year Book 40 E.111 f.38. (Mich. pl.12) and see
Fitzherbert, Detinue. pl. 60 & *Year Book 7 E.11*
f. 215; *Year Book 17 E.11* f.536.
79.   *P. & M.*, p.352.   For a legal debate on the custom
of boroughs touching 'the reasonable part' of a
husband's goods, see *Lawes Res.*, book IV, p.238.
80.   *Wills and inventories... and the northern Counties
of England from the eleventh century onwards*
(Surtees Society, London 1908), part 3, p.62.
81.   H.T. Riley ed., *Liber Albus: The White Book of the
city of London* (London, 1861), pp.338–9.   For the
case see R.R. Sharpe ed., *Calendar of Letter Books
.... of the city of London. G.* (London 1905), p.250,
(12 March 43 E.111. 1368–9), and p.250, n. where
a later copy is said to state that this custom holds
goods only when the children have already received
settlement from the father.   Hereafter cited as

    Liber Albus.
82. *Hustings' Wills*, p.xxxix.
83. *Calthrop*, p.113. The estate in copyhold lands which the wife had for dower on the death of her husband was also according to manorial custom. see R.R. Sharpe ed., *Calendar of Letter Books ... of the city of London, E* (London 1903), p.33. See also on Freebench. *Hustings' Wills*, vol.1, p.xxxix.
84. *Letter Books. E.* pp.33-4, and *Liber Albus*, p. 339.
85. R.R. Sharpe, ed., *Calendar of Letter Books .... of the city of London, H* (London, 1907), p.253.
86. *ibid.*, p.253 and *Letter Book E*, p.33. *Liber Albus*, pp.392-3, 338-9. *Hustings' Wills*, p.xxxix. *ibid.*, vol. 1, p.448. *Letter Book. G.* p.448. *C.P.M.R.* 1881-1412. p.177 (1391). *Calthrop*, p.165. In older boroughs the widow could be endowed of lands, but she was not dowered of a third, but of the moiety and ceased to have rights in the chief messuage. If there were no lands other than the chief messuage she received at the church door a dower of specified chattels or a money dower. *Bateson*, vol.2, p.cx.
87. *Bateson*, vol.2, pp.cx, 126, 121.
88. Anon, *A Briefe Discourse, declaring and approving the necessarie and inviotable maintenance of the laudable Customs of London: Namely, of that one whereby a reasonable partition of the goods of husbands among their wives and children is provided.* (Henry Midleton, London, 1584), S.T.C. No.16747, pp.44-5.
89. *ibid.*, pp.25 and 23.
90. *Ramsey*, p.5. *Sheehan*, p.276. *Bateson*, vol.2, pp.119-20 on Torksey Customs, circa. 1345. *Hustings' Wills*, vol.1, pp.102 and 125.
91. *Hustings' Wills*, vol.1, pp.96 (1291), 105, 106 (1292), 108 (1293) etc., and p.445.
92. *Calthrop*, p.105. Term of Life altered by Statute of 32 H.8. C.1 (wills) and see, L.O. Pike ed., *Year Books of the Reign of King Edward the third Years XVII and XVIII* (London 1903), XVIII Ed.III, Hil. Pl. (25) p.554 (1443-4).
93. *Calthrop*, p.104.
94. Devise in mortmain without licence applied only to freemen. Privilege confirmed by Charter 1 Ed.111 (6 March 1326-7). See *Liber Albus*. By 13.H. VI (1434) an ordinance of the common council would not allow any devise or testament in mortmain, unless examination proved that no deceit or fraud was intended, for the purpose of devising land under colour of Freedom. See *Hustings' Wills* vol.1, p.XXXVII.
95. A.H. Thomas ed., *C.P.M.R. 1381-1412.* (Cambridge

1932), p.262.

96. *Liber Albus*, p.161.

97. *Chichele*, p.XXXVII, citing no.27 of the articles of agreement between the Bishop and the Mayor of Salisbury in I.S. Davies ed., *Tropenell Cartulary 1*, 197 on the custom.

98. *Hustings' Wills*, 1. p.xlii.

99. *Bateson*, vol.2, p.109 and *Sheehan*, p.276.

100. Pricilla Metcalf, 'Seven Centuries in White Hart Court', in *Guildhall Studies in London History*, vol.IV, no.1 (October 1979), p.5. *Hustings' Wills*, vol.1, p.188.

101. *Hustings' Wills*, married women stated that they had made wills with the consent of their husbands. *ibid.*, pp.501 and 599 (Margaret Holyn) and Y.13. 12.H.VII. Trin. pl.2, p.24.

102. I owe this information to Robert Wood. Taken from the Archdeaconry Court, London: Register of copy wills and administrations, Guildhall Library, M & S. 905111.

103. *ibid.*, Agnes Twykford (1393), 1393.F.16; Joan Seles (1396) 1396 F.14; Alice Okle (1395) 1396 FF. 15v.16; Isobel Coleman (1403). 1403 F.7; Alice Benyngton (1395) 1403 F.8v made by licence of her husband William.

104. F.J. Furnival ed., *The Fifty Earliest English wills in the Court of Probate, London. 1387-1439*. (London E.E.T.S. 1882), p.103. (More. Commisary Court of London. f. 1434-5). 379 bk.

105. *Hustings' Wills*, i. p.413.

106. *Chichele*, pp.XXXVII and 405:
    'Ex lege habere potuit sine avantagio sive incremento aliquali.'

107. *Holdsworth*, vol. III, p.524.

108. A.J. Horwood ed., *Year Books of the Reign of King Edward the First*, 30 and 31, (London 1863), pp.522-3:
    Although a woman be condemned for man-slaughter, the Justice will not enquire concerning her chattels, if she be under coverture, because all the chattels belong to the husband.
    Tot seit ceo issi qu une feme seit dampne pur mort de home, Justice ne enquerre nent de ses chateaus si ele seit covert de baron, pur ceo qe touz les chateauz sunt au baron.

109. R.B. Pugh ed., *Calendar of London Trailbaston trials under Commissions of 1305 and 1306*, (London 1975), p.72, no.107. In London a woman convicted of theft was hanged and it was stated that she had no chattels as she had a husband.

110. *Year Book. 7.H.VI.* Mich. pl.6 'Le baron et sa feme no poit aver bien en common.'

111. A.J. Horwood ed., *Year Books of the Reign of King Edward the First* Years XXXVIII–XXXV (London 1879), 34. E.1, p.312 (1305–6).

112. *Lawes Res.* book 111, s.111, p.120 citing 27.H.VIII, fol.27.

113. For an example of a husband appointing his wife to be his attorney, see, W. Baildon ed., *Select Civil pleas: 1200–1203*, vol.1 (London 1890), pl.155. The Statute of Westminster 11. 1285, chapter 3, allowed a wife whose husband made default to raise her voice in court and plead in defence of her title. For an analysis of the statute see *Lawes Res.*

114. *Holdsworth*, vol.III, p.529. (*Year Book 27 H. VIII.* Mich. pl.3 1535–6):

> Un femme coverte nad ascun volunte, mes la volunte del baron est sa volunte; et donques quand le baron agre a un acte fait per sa femme, cest agreement fait cest l'acte le baron.

115. R. Tottel ed. (London 1567). 21. H.VII. pl.64. Fo. Xl.b.

> Car [fe] m e covert ne puit faire chose que tourne son baron en preiudice ou charge y sa contracte, mes il est able de faire chose, par quel son baron ava avantage, car si ieo done bienz al feme covert, ces est bon, et le bar [on] puit agre a ceo, mes si fe [m] e covert fait contract, ou achate chose en martat, ceo e [st] void, pur ceo q [e] puit este que ceo serra charge al bar [on] , mes sa feme puit achat chose a ma use, et ieo puis agree a ceo, et issint si ieo co [m] ma [n] de ma fe [m] e de achater chose necessarie et c. si et achat ceuz, ieo serra lie y ceo, par cest comman dem [n] t general, et si ma feme achat chose a gard mon householde, co [m] e pain et C. et ieo nay conusans de ceo, com [n] t q [e] il soit expende de en mon houshold, ieo ne serra charge pour ceux.

116. F.W. Maitland & W.V. Harcourt & W.C. Balland, eds., *Year Books of Edward II*, vol.VII: The Eyre of Kent, 6–7 E.11. 1313–14 (London 1912), vol.11, and other judgements, p.46.

117. *ibid.* p.4. (Anon v Musket) and case of Anon v. Anon. p.48. (See also *Year Book 2 H.VIII.* Mich. Pl.3.)

> Et ne [st] se [m]ble al cas lou home fist contract oue un moign car la e [st] un disabilitie en le moign issint q [ue] l'agrem[en]t le soveraigne ne poit faire c [eo] bon, mes

issint nest un feme covert, donqz si cest
assumption soit bone tanque le baron disagree,
et il appiert icy que le bar[on]   ad agree,p[ur]
q[ue]   ce[t]   agrement fait lassumption bon.
and   *ibid.*, per Brook, J. (1535).

118. *Holdsworth*, vol.III, p.532.
119. P.C. Jones ed., *C.P.M.R. 1437-57*, p.97 (1447) and
pp.101-1 (1447).
120. *Lawes Res.*, book III. s. 1. pp.117-8.
121. *P.R.O.* Prerogative court of Canterbury wills: Horne
1. (d. 1497) and Horne 36. (d. 1499).
122. *P.R.O.* C1/201/32:
And that she could because of the custom of
London make contracts and be bound in her own
name even though she was married, and such
agreements would be good in the eyes of the
law .... But there was no record of her
admission to be a "sole" merchant and so he
was likely to lose his true duties and rights,
against all moral rights.
123. *P.R.O.* C1/43/293:
Because of the commune of the city, it was
ancient practice that the wives of worshipful
and thrifty men that were not free of the city,
by the allowance of their husbands and without
their help, used to buy and sell all types of
merchandise, which helped towards increasing
their wealth and standard of living. The duty
of the same bargains coming or going were
always satisfied by the wives, without husbands
paying the debts.
See also *P.R.O.* C1/43/160, 43/291-1, 43/294, 31/476,
43/158-9, concerning a silk purchase in September
3. E.IV. (1463).
124. *Liber Albus*, book III, part 1, p.181.
125. *ibid.*, pp.181-2.
126. *ibid.*, p.182. For dating of the Liber Albus, a
compilation of 1419 on the customs of London, see
W. Kellaway,'John Carpenter's Liber Albus.' in
Guildhall Studies in London History, vol.III,
no.2, April 1979, p.77.
127. *P.R.O.* C1/32/344.
128. *C.P.M.R. 1437-57*, pp.35-36 (14 Dec. 1440). For her
avowal see *Corporation of London Record Office*
(London), Journal III, p.73, hereafter cited as
C.L.R.O.
129. M.K. Dale, 'Women in the Textile Industries and
trade of Fifteenth Century England.' Univ. of
London M.A. Thesis, 1928, p.35. Hereafter cited as
Dale.
130. F. Aidan Hibbert, 'Tensers: An Historical investig-

ation into the Status and Privileges of Non-gildated Tradesmen in English Towns.' in *Transactions of the Shropshire Archaeological and Natural History Society,* 2nd Series, vol.III (Shrewsbury 1891), pp.253-264. See also, J. Meadows Cowper. *Intrantes: A list of persons admitted to live and trade within the City of Canterbury, on payment of an annual fine. From 1392 to 1592* (Canterbury, 1904), pp.2-238. For example see p.66 (Margaret Halke, Chandler, 1429-30).

131. A. Luders, T.E. Tomlins, J. France, W.E. Taunton, and J. Raithby, eds., *The Statutes of the Realm, from original records and authentic manuscripts* (London 1810) vol.1, p.380 (37 E.11. ch.6-10) and see p.380 n. '[Websters, Filersters and Spynsters as wel of lynnen as of Wullen Webbe, and of them Carders and Kembers of wul].' Hereafter cited as *Stat. R.*

132. *Liber Albus,* p.181. *Bateson,* vol.1, p.227 (Lincoln Cap.32. 1480-81).

134. M. Sellers, ed. *York Memorandum Book* Part II 1388-1493 (Surtees Society) vol.II, p.144, (London 1914) hereafter cited as *York M. Bk.*

135. *Liber Albus,* p.193.

136. *ibid.,* p.182.

137. For example see *P.R.O.* C1/37/8.

138. *Bateson,* pp.185-6:

> Et lou femmes en liex cases sount empledez et gagent lour ley, elles purront faire lour ley ovesques hommes ou femmes a loure voluntee.

In Worcester any man's wife who became a debtor, or surety, or bought or sold anything, or hired a house was to answer as a 'woman soole Merchant', without the naming of her husband. See *Bateson* ·p.227 (1467) and *York M. Bk.* vol.II, p.145. The laws of Winchelsea, Rye and Hastings enacted that

> si femme covert de baron soit emplede de plee de dette, covienant enfrint, ou chastell deternu, et ele soit tenuz par marchaunt soule, en respondr sanz presence de son baron.

> if a married woman is empleaded in a plea of debt infringing their coverture, or their chattels detained and she was bound as a sole merchant she is to reply without the presence of her husband.

in *Bateson,* vol.I, p.227 (Winchelsea 15th century). See also *York M. Bk.* vol.II, p.145. See also London examples of waging law, A.H. Thomas ed., *C.P.M.R. 1381-1412* (Cambridge 1932), p.51: case of Matilda, widow of Hugh Holbech (23 May 1384). *C.P.M.R. 1437-1457,* p.149: Margery widow of William Crowche, claiming her 'right as a free woman of the

City to wage her law.' (4 July 1454).

139. *C.L.R.O.* Journal, VII, f.89:

quod quelibet femina que in virum suum
aliquem liberum hominem civitatem ceperit et
eidum viri suo libero hominem eiusdem civitem,
existentem tempre mortem eiusdem viri matrimon-
ialum copulat fuerit post mortem viri sui
[   ] et fuit . . . ubera femina
eiusdem civitati diu et tam diu femina illa
sola ac vidua permanserit et infra eandem
civitatem residens fuerit alteri viro non
copulata.

it was recorded as ancient custom that every
woman married to a freeman of the city, is
after the death of her husband, a freewoman
as long as she continues his widow and resides
within the city and also fertile women, unmarried and widows of the same city, who have
and who are residing and remaining there for
a long time, are not whilst living in the city
to join together with other men. (11 Jan. 1465).

140. A. Abram, 'Women Traders in Medieval London' in
The Economic Journal, vol. XXVI (London 1892),
p.283. Hereafter cited as *Abram*.

141. *Guildhall Record Office*, Recognisance Roll, 21 m.4.
and see *Dale*, p.22.

142. *Bateson*, vol.I, p.309; vol.II, pp.172-183. M. Bateson,
ed., *Records of the Borough of Leicester. Being a
series of Extracts from the Archives of the Corporation of Leicester, 1327-1509.* vol.II (London 1901),
pp.382-3.

143. J.M. Imray '"Les Bones Gentes de la Mercerye de
Londres", a study of the Membership of the medieval
Mercers' Company,' in A.E.J. Hollaender and
W. Kellaway eds., *Studies in London History
presented to P.E. Jones* (London 1969), p.163. In
1427-8 Alice Bridenell was admitted to the freedom
because her great-grandfather had been a mercer.

144. M. Sellers, ed., *The York Mercers and Merchant
Adventurers 1356-1917* (Surtees Society London 1917)
vol.129, p.64, Mariona Kent. For other women see
pp.52 (1440), 60 (1467). Hereafter cited as *Sellers*.

145. On France see E. Dixon 'Craftswomen in the Livre
des Metiers.' *The Economic Journal*, vol.V, (London
1895), pp.209-228.

146. *York M. Bk.* no.120, pp.ix, lxi, 77, 209, 243:
no.124, pp.112-4, 160. *Sellers*, no.129, pp.39, 40, 56.
M. Harris ed., *The Coventry Leet Book or Mayor's
Register* (London 1907-13), vol.I, p.xxx.

147. *P.R.O.* C.47/76. Guild certificate of 1389, and see
H.F. Westlake, *The Parish Guilds of Medieval*

England (London 1919), pp.19, 36–48.

148. *Stat. R.* 7. H.IV.C.XVII (1405-6) vol.II, pp.157-8.
149. *ibid.*, 8. H.VI.C.XI.
150. *Rot. Parl.* vol.V, p.205.
151. *Stat. R.* II. H.VII.
152. H.T. Riley ed., *Memorials of London and London Life in the XIIth, XIVth, and XVth Centuries . . . AD 1276-1419* (London 1868), p.590. Hereafter cited as *Memorials*. R.R. Sharpe ed., *Calendar of Letter - Books preserved among the Archives of the corporation of the city of London at the Guildhall* (London 1909), Letter Book I, pp.111-2 (14 March 14 H. IV. 1412-3). Hereafter cited as *C.L. Bk.*
153. *C.L. Bk.* 1, p.134 (3.H.V. 1415-6).
154. *P.R.O.* C1/72/73. *C.L.R.O.* Mayors Court Files, 3/171. *C.L.R.O.* Journals II, f.20, III, ff.43, 886.
155. *C.P.M.R. 1413-37*, pp.230-1. For another case see Philippa Fawconer, *ibid.*, p.280 (1434).
156. *ibid.*, pp.280, 208. *P.R.O.* Ancient Deeds, A. 8643, C.3879.
157. *Bateson*, vol.I, pp.229-30 (1419). Recorded in Ricart's Kalender (Bristol), p.103. On female apprenticeship see R.R. Sharpe, ed., *C.L.BK.E. 1314-37* (London 1903), p.200:
> Les femmes couverts qu usent certyns craftis deinz la citee par aux mesmes saunz loure barouns, poent prendre femmenis a loure apprentice pur eux servier et apprendre loure .. endenturez d'apprenticialitee all baroun et su femme pur apprendre in mistere la femme.
158. *C.L.Bk.K.* (London 1911), p.291 (1443).
159. *C.P.M.R.* 1413-1437, pp.42-3 (1516). C.L.R.O. Journal III, f.73b. *P.R.O.* Ancient Deeds. A.8267.
160. *C.P.M.R.* 1413-37, pp.166-7 (1423), *C.P.M.R.* 1437-57, p.88 (1445).
161. *C.P.M.R.* 1413-37, pp.146-7 (1422).
162. *C.L.BK.H.* 1375-99 (London 1907), pp.405-6 (1393-4).
163. C.L.BK. G. . . . *1352-74* (London 1905), p.105 (1358-9).
164. *C.L.BK.K.* 1413-37, p.229 (1429).
165. *C.P.M.R.* 1413-37, p.229 (1429).
166. In 1383 a Katherine Lightfoot supplied painted tiles and was paid 15s. for these for the King's bath. M. Wood, *The English Medieval House* (London 1965) p.373 and *P.R.O.*, Exchequer Kings Rembrancer Accounts 473. A Katherine Lightfoot married Henry Yevele the Architect and master builder.
167. *C.P.M.R.* 1413-37, p.146-7 (1422).
168. *ibid.*, pp.71 (1419), 166-7 (1423). *C.P.M.R.* 1437-57, p.65 (1445).
169. *C.P.M.R.* 1413-37, p.12 (1414).

170. A.H. Thomas, ed., *C.P.M.R.* . . . *1323-1364* (Cambridge 1926), p.277 (1364). A.H. Thomas, ed., *C.P.M.R.* . . . *1364-1381* (Cambridge 1929), p.54 (1366).
171. W. Prideux, *Memorials of the Goldsmiths' Company* (London 1576-7), 2 vols.
172. *ibid.*, p.166 (1423).
173. *ibid.*, p.208 (1427).
174. *C.L.R.O.*, Journal III, ff.16, 18.
175. *Guildhall Library*, Commissary Court of London wills, 250, v.3. (1430).
176. *C.L.BK.L. (EIV-HVII)* (London 1912), pp.141-238.
177. *C.L.R.O.*, Mayors Court files, 3/66: 'Que sole merchandisat in arte de Shipster.' Shepster was a cutter of material.
178. *C.L.BK.s.* E, p.205, H; p.352, C; p.125, S. Young, *The Annals of the Barber-Surgeons of London* (London 1890), pp.260, 38.
179. B. Ehrenreich and D. English, *Witches, Midwives and Nurses* (London 1976), p.35. G.N. Clark, *A History of the Royal College of Physicians* (Oxford 1764), pp.54-5. C. Rawcliffe, 'Medicine and Medical Practice in Later Medieval London' in *Guildhall Studies in London History*, vol.v, no.1, October 1981, p.16.
180. *P.R.O.* C.1./66/264 (1415-80 or 1483-5).
181. *Hustings' wills*, vol.I, p.569; vol.II, pp.40, 248.
182. *ibid.*, vol.II, p.218. W.H. Hale, *Precedents and proceedings of the ecclesiastical Court of London. A Series of Precedents and proceedings in criminal causes* (London, 1973, reprint), p.34. Hereafter cited as *Hale*. R.M. Wunderli, *London Church Courts and Society on the Eve of the Reformation* (Speculum, Cambridge Massachusetts 1981), p.17. *Calendar of the Close Rolls preserved in the Public Record Office.* Edward III, vol.VII, AD 1343-46 (London 1904), p.430 (1344).
183. R.M. Clay, *The Medieval Hospitals of England* (Oxford 1966), p.26.
184. *ibid.*
185. *C.P.M.R.* 1364-1381, p.25 (1365) pelleter = fellmonger.
186. For late 15th century ecclesiastical court cases of the Commissary court of London, concerning prostitution see *Hale*.
187. F.B. Bickley, ed., *The Little Red Book of Bristol* (Bristol 1900), vol.II, pp.229-30, no.30.
188. *ibid.*, vol.I, p.33, no.11 and 12.
189. *Liber Albus*, pp.239, 246-7, 509-10.
190. *ibid.*, p.246.
191. A. Pulling, *A Practical treatise on the laws, customs and regulations of the city and Port of London* (London 1842), p.151 8H.II. 1161-2 act. [assize?].

192. *Liber Albus*, p.242.
193. *Memorials*, p.535 (II.R.II 1378-9) and *C.L.BK*.H. p.402 (1393).
194. *Memorials*, p.647 (5.H.V.).
195. *C.P.M.R. 1364-81*, p.57 (1366).
196. *C.P.M.R. 1413-37*, p.132 (1421).
197. *ibid.*, p.138 (1422).
198. *ibid.*, p.122 (1422).
199. *C.P.M.R. 1364-1381*, p.7 (1367) and p.58 (1366).
200. *C.P.M.R. 1413-37*, p.154 (1422).
201. *C.P.M.R. 1364-1381*, p.151 (1373).
202. *ibid.*, p.54 (1366).
203. *Memorials*, pp.484-5 (1385) and *C.L.BK*.II. p.271 (1385).
204. *C.P.M.R. 1413-1437*, p.128 (1421) and p.132 (1421).
205. *P.R.O.* C.1./11/222, 61/379, 67/146 and see 'Accounts of St. Margaret Southwark.' *The British Magazine* XXXii, pp.496, 489, 488.
206. *ibid.*
207. S. Thrupp, *The Merchant Class of Medieval London* (Chicago 1962), p.42. Hereafter cited as *Thrupp. C.L.BK*.I, pp.233-4 (1420).
208. *C.L.BK*.I, *Abram*, p.284.
209. W. Herbert, *The History of the Twelve Great Livery Companies of London*, 2 vols., London 1886-7, vol.I, p.63. Hereafter cited as *W. Herbert*.
210. *P.R.O.* C.1/76/59.
211. *C.L.BK*.C. c.1291-1309 (London 1901), p.47 (1299). *C.L.BK*.D. c.1309-1314 (London 1902), p.201 (15th century). *C.L.BK*.E. p.71 (1316). *C.L.BK*.H. p.215 (1383) p.293 (1386). *C.L.BK*.F.c.1337-1352 (London 1904), pp.114 (1344), p.78 (1347-8).
212. *Hustings' Wills*, vol.1, pp.145-6.
213. *C.P.M.R. 1413-37*, p.140 (1422).
214. *C.L.R.O.* Mayor's Court files bk.3, no.6.
215. *C.P.M.R. 1413-37*, p.158 (1421) concerning criticism of all bakers, brewers, taverners, hostillers and hucksters as greatly defective in Crepulgate ward (within).
216. *C.P.M.R. 1364-1381*, p.139 (1372).
217. *ibid.* p.21 (1365). *C.L.BK*.H. pp.1-134.
218. *P.R.O.* C.1/64/105, 64/75. *C.P.M.R. 1364-81*, p.187 (1375). *C.L.BK*.D. p.242 (1310). *C.L.BK*.K. p.358 (1326-7).
219. *Abram*, p.284.
220. *P.R.O.* King's Remembrancer wardrobe Accounts, 4047/23 f.4, 4041/2 f. 40.6. 16. H. Littlehales, ed., *The Medieval Records of a London City Church 1420-1559* (St. Mary at Hill). (E.E.T.S. London 1905), p.78. Hereafter cited as *Littlehales. C.L.BK*.E. p.270. W.H. Overall, ed., *The Accounts of the Churchwardens*

of the Parish of St. Michael Cornhill, 1456-1608
(London 1871) pp.40,60. Hereafter cited as *Overall*.

221. *P.R.O.* Cl/124/32, 1 20/22, 17/44, 66/201, 407/390.
Calendar of the Patent Rolls. H.IV. 1401-5 (London
1905), p.163 (22 Oct. 1402). Hereafter cited as
C.P.R.

222. *P.R.O.* C.1/151/116.

223. *Hustings' Wills*, vol.1, 363.

224. *ibid.* vol.I, p.292; vol.II, p.548.

225. *ibid.* vol.I, p.345.

226. *P.R.O.* C.1/113/76.

227. *C.P.M.R. 1364-81*, pp.30, 35 (1365).

228. *ibid.*

229. *C.P.R. H.VI. 1452-61* (London 1910), p.105 (May 8
1453 Armourers).

230. *Liber Albus*, p.437.

231. *P.R.O.* King's Remembrancer Wardrobe Accounts, 405/14.

232. *P.R.O.* C.1/218/2.

233. *Hustings' Wills*, vol.I, p.576.

234. *Littlehales*, p.142.

235. *P.R.O.* C.1/7/92. *C.L.R.O.* Journals 1, f.566, ii;
f.100.b. *C.P.R.* H.V. 1416-22 (London 1911) p.291
(Joan Hert 'Citesein and Jeweler' Nov. 30 1420).
C.P.R. H.IV. 1408-13 (London 1909) p.33. (Joan Cok
'Jeweler' Nov. 24 (1427).

236. *C.P.R.* H.IV. 1408-13 (London 1909), p.19 (July 13
1409), p.326 (Oct. 24 1411 Joan Cok 'Jeweler').

237. *P.R.O.* C.1/16/45.

238. Wiredrawers - people who made wire. *C.L.BK.*L.
p.320 (1496-7). P.E. Jones ed., *C.P.M.R. 1458-1482*
(Cambridge 1961, p.112 (1476).

239. *Guildhall Library*, Commissary Court of London wills,
1. (1440). 4. 44v. (St. Bot. Aldersgate).
J.C.L. Stahlschmidt. *Surrey Bells and London Bell
Founders*, (London 1884), p.51. *Victoria County
Histories*, Hampshire, vol.III (London 1908), p.165.

240. *Guildhall Library*, Commissary Court of London wills,
1. (1441). 4. 62.

241. H.C. Coote, 'The Ordinances of some secular Guilds
of London, 1354 to 1496' in *Transactions of the
London and Middlesex Archaeological Society*, vol.IV,
January 1871, part 1, pp.56-8, 7. (1495).

242. Spurrier - a spur maker. *C.L.R.O.* R.R. Sharpe.
Calendar of Letters, manuscript 100.

243. *C.L.BK.*K. p.293 (1444).

244. *C.L.BK.* C. pp.244 (1305), 117 (1302-3).

245. *P.R.O.* King's Remembrancer Wardrobe Accounts,
405/14.

246. *ibid.* 406/9.

247. *ibid.* 409/12.

248. F. Devon, ed., *Issues of the Exchequer, Henry III*

to *Henry VI* (London 1837), p.48.
249. *ibid*. p.49.
250. *ibid*. p.52.
251. *P.R.O.* Ministers Accounts, general series, 963/10.
252. W. Campbell, *Materials for a History of the Reign of Henry VII* (London 1773) 2 vols. vol.1, p.561. Hereafter cited as *Campbell*.
253. *C.L.BK.* E. pp.151, 158, 161 (1321-1322).
254. *C.P.M.R. 1364-81*, p.114 (1370).
255. *C.P.M.R. 1413-37*, p.153 (1422).
256. *ibid*. and pp.136 (1422), 151 (1423).
257. *ibid*. p.139 (1422).
258. *Hustings' Wills*, vol.I, pp.150-1, 317, 11, 93.
Calendar of the Close Rolls, 1364-1368 (London 1910), pp.745 (July 12 1364). *C.L.BK*.G. p.169.
259. *Memorials*, p.456.
C.P.M.R. 1413-37, p.138 (1421).
260. *ibid*. pp.138-9 (1421).
261. Flaoner - a maker of pancakes/crepes. *Husting's Wills*, vol.1, p.105.
262. *C.L.R.O.* Mayor's court files, 4/3.
263. Maxsters - makers of Malt. *P.R.O.* C.1/17/343.
264. *C.P.M.R. 1458-1428*, p.43 (1467).
265. *P.R.O.* King's Remembrancer Accounts, various: E.101/128/30, 31.
266. *P.R.O.* C.1/137/33, 127/65. *C.P.M.R. 1323-64*, p.212 (1344). *Memorials*, p.75.
267. Women could dye leather, see *Memorials*, p.365.
268. M. Curtis, 'The London Lay Subsidy of 1332' in G. Unwin, ed., *Finance and Trade Under Edward III* (Manchester 1918), pp.35-92 and see p.59.
269. Spinsters - women who span wool. *P.R.O.* C.1/246/66. 66/252.
270. Shepster - a female cutter of material. *P.R.O.* King's Remembrancer Wardrobe Accounts (Henry V to 28 Henry VI). *P.R.O.* C.1/253/6.
271. *P.R.O.* King's Remembrancer Wardrobe Accounts, 410/7. 10. 18-19. *P.R.O.* King's Remembrancer Enrolled Accounts, 361/6, m.53.d. 55.d.
272. *P.R.O.* King's Remembrancer Wardrobe Accounts. 413/1.
273. *ibid*. 416/3, f.27.
274. *ibid*. 415/10, f.6 and see *P.R.O.* C.1/30/47, 93/6 and *C.L.R.O.* Mayor's court files. 4/263.
275. *Campbell*, vol.II, p.218. Sir N.H. Nicholas, *Privy Purse expenses of Elizabeth of York... Wardrobe Accounts of Edward IV* (London 1830) p.118. *Overall*, p.13.
276. Threadwomen - women who made thread. *C.L.BK*.H., p.186 (1387). *ibid*. B, p.182.
Husting's Wills, vol.I, p.67.
277. Pouchmakers - makers of Pouches/bags. *Guildhall*

Library, Commissary Court of London wills, reg. 3.
f.250. *Guildhall Library,* Archdeaconry Court of
London wills, reg.1. f.329.
278. *C.P.R. 1441-6* (London 1908) p.265.
279. Cappers – makers of knitted caps/hats. *C.L.BK.*H.
pp.413-18, 431.
280. Hurers – makers of or dealer in hats and caps.
*C.L.BK.*I. p.258 (1420).
281. *C.L.BK.* H. p.341. *W.* Herbert, vol.2, p.413.
282. *C.L.R.O.,* Journal xi, f.209.b. *P.R.O.* C.1/67/307-8.
283. *Husting's Wills,* vol.I, pp.628, 489, 462. W.D. Selby,
*The Charters, Ordinances and Byelaws of the Mercers'
Company* (London 1881), pp.72-3.
284. *P.R.O.,* Customs Accounts 194/18 m.69, 73/25 f.2.
203/4 ff.3.b. 8.b. 106, 146, 176, 20.b. 38.b.
285. *ibid.,* 128/8, f.14.b. (Margaret Barre Sandwich
1463) 128/15 and 194/19 (1438).
286. Combehedes – teasels nailed in wood boards, used
for raising the knap of cloth. *ibid.* 72/17 (London).
287. N.S.B. Gras. *The Early English Customs System: a
documentary study . . . thirteenth to sixteenth
centuries* (Cambridge Mass. 1918) pp.47, 488, 494,
500.
288. *C.P.R. 1494-1509* (London 1916) pp.447-9.
289. *ibid.* pp.447-9, 130.
290. *Dale,* p.139. C.L. Scofield, *The Life and Reign of
Edward the Fourth, King of England and of France
and Lord of Ireland.* 2 vols. (London 1923), vol.2,
p.420.
291. *P.R.O.,* Prerogative court of Canterbury wills, 33,
Wattys:
> Tam omni vestimenta et ornamenta corpori suo
> spectantia quemeciam omnia bona denarios et
> debita que ipsa Margareta ex Lana mea habuit
> et inquisiuit racione proprie mercandiscionis
> sue.

> All her clothes and jewellery of her body and
> all good monies and debts which Margaret and
> I have through our dealings in wool.
292. E. Veale, 'The London fur Trade in the Late Middle
Ages, with particular reference to the Skinners
Company.' Unpublished London Ph.D. 1953 pp.439-40
and see *P.R.O.,* Prerogative court of Canterbury
wills, 6, Dogett.
293. C.L. Kingsford, ed., *The Stonor letters and Papers,
1290-1483.* 2 vols (Camden Soc. London 1919). Vol.2,
no.224, p.64:
> And God know she made me depressed with her
> countenance whilst I was with her; I thought
> it a long time until I left. She told me the
> story that I told her about the late vicar and

her: she said the vicar had not fared well since because he took it so much to heart . . . I had no pleasure staying with her, although she is a fine merry woman, but

294. Brass of John and Margaret Croke. Church of All Hallows Barking, London.
295. *P.R.O.* Prerogative Court of Canterbury wills, 6. Dogett. 4. Logge.
296. *P.R.O.* C.1/116/34-7.
297. *Stat. R.* vol.II (R.II – H.VII). 33 H. VI. Ch. V. (1455) pp.374-5.
298. For silkwomen see P.R.O. C.1/43/291, 416/3 and C.244/125 (55.a.).
299. *Rot.Parl.* vol.V. (18.H.VI – 11.E.IV). 34 H.VI (1455) p.323.
300. *Stat. R.* vol.II. 3. E.IV. ch.3. (1463) pp.395-6.
301. *ibid.,* vol.II. 22 E.IV. ch.3 (1482-3), p.472.
302. *C.L.R.O.* Journal V. f.210.6.
303. *P.R.O.* C.1/80/12. 18/189.
304. *Abram*, p.138-9.
305. T. Smith and L.T. Smith. *English gilds: the original ordinances of more than one hundred English gilds, together with the old usages of the City of Winchester, etc.* (E.E.T.S. London 1870) p.xxx.
306. For example see Masons. *C.L.BK.*L. p.184. The Lorimers (1488), Saddlers (1490), Weavers (1492), all mention sisters of the crafts. *C.L.BK.*L. pp.265, 274, 291.
307. *Thrupp*, p.173.
308. *Lawes Res.*, p.125.
309. W.W. Skeat, *Chaucer: Complete Works*, (London, 1969) pp.573-4, lines 691-6.

Glossary

'Courteseye of Englande'

A tenancy of land devolving on a man from his wife on her death, providing she was seised of her land and had a child of the marriage, who was born alive and capable of inheriting the wife's lands. Husband held estate of wife's land for his life. If there was no child by the marriage wife's real estate devolved to her heirs.

Seised

Possession of land by one who occupied and used it, common law – freehold estates. The person seised of the land could exercise all the rights of an owner, a person not seised could not exercise these rights until he/she recovered seisin by action, two persons could not simultaneously possess the same land, but several persons could be seised of different estates in the land.

Fleta seu commentarius Iuris Anglicani

Commentary on English law. Title from legend that unknown author wrote the work in the fleet prison.

Unde Nihil habet

A writ of dower, where a widow claims dower of lands, which she does not have.

Cui in vita

('whom in his lifetime'). A writ where a man died seized of lands in fee simple, fee tail or for life, in the right of his wife, and alienated the same before his death. After his death the wife had this right to recover the land. She had to show her title to land, by purchase or inheritance.

Pone

A writ removing a county court case to the court of common pleas.

Devise

A disposition or gift of property made by will. Applicable to real property. 'Bequeath' refers to personal property.

Codicil

A supplement to a will.

Ultima voluntas

The last wish of a testator gives effect according to his true intentions.

Testamentum

A will. A declaration of intention in expectation of death.

Solemnitas

Seriousness. Solemn procedure.

Laicum feodum

'lay person's fee'.

Miserabilis persona

Miserable character. Anyone capable of having and being subject to rights.

Elemosyna

'alms', for pious and charitable uses.

de rationabili parte bonorum

In reasonable good parts.

Copyhold

Under feudal landholding the lord of manor allocated lands

to free and unfree tenants, which were held according
to the customs of that manor and manorial court. Copyhold
could pass from tenant to tenant.

Redemption

Rights conveyed by a proprietor to another, rights of
security. They might be redeemed on payment of money
etc.

Apprenticeship

Binding of a person to another by contract to serve with
a master for a term of years to learn a trade or skill.
Apprenticeship usually lasted 7 years. Boys being bound
at 14, and girls at 12 years old or over.

Miniver

A type of fur.

Legitim

The right of children, spouse and church to have one third
each of a deceased person's estate, if all are living. If
one party is satisfied before death, or is dead the
remainder obtain half.

Consumatio

Completion of requirements.

Perfectio

To complete or finish.

Dower

The right of a wife on her husband's death to a third of
the land of which he was seised for life. She could not
be deprived of it by an alienation except in limited ways.

Dowry

Property given to a woman on marriage by her family
which accrued to her husband.

Tail

A freehold estate of inheritance in land which descends
to specified descendants of the body of the devisee,
rather than to heirs general. It was created by the
Statute de Donis. 1258.

Mortmain

(dead hand). Under the feudal system incidents of
wardship, marriage, relief etc. became chargeable on the
death of a vassal, but did not if they were vested in a
corporation or the church which never married or died.
Statutes or crown licence were required before land could
be passed to the Church etc. See Magna Carta 1215,
The Provisions of Westminster 1252, Statute de viris
religiosis 1279, Statute of Westminster II 1285, Statute
1392. Penalty was forfeiture to the crown.

Husting

A Law Court in the city of London.

Cognisances

Knowledge of matters entitling the Mayor to demand that
the plea be heard before him, concerning obligations.

Recognizances

Obligations or bonds acknowledged before a court of
record etc. and later enrolled in a court of record. The
person bound is obliged to cause the performance of an
act, e.g. paying a debt.

Probate

Proof that a deceased person's will has been proved and
registered in the court and a right of administration of
the effects has been given to an executor.

Feoffing

(to give in fee). Transferal or creating of a freehold
interest in land of free tenure. It included the livery
of seisin (holding of land by occupier). Usually
accompanied by charter or conveyance as a record.

Patrimony

Rights applicable to person's patrimony or estate,
including rights to property and of obligation distinct
from personal rights, concerning inheritance.

2 WOMEN IN FOURTEENTH CENTURY SHREWSBURY

Diane Hutton

The role of women in the medieval economy has attracted considerable attention in recent years.[1] Sadly, though historians interested in the subject of women and work in medieval England have to content themselves with evidence which is far from satisfactory.

On the face of it Eileen Power would appear to have produced a fairly comprehensive account of the position of women in late medieval society.[2] Much of her research for her chapter on working women in the town and country, however, was based on regulations and literary accounts. It would be a great mistake to consider such images as typical representations of female activity.

Gild and civic regulations were not necessarily strictly obeyed. Indeed the frequency with which such regulations were reissued would seem to indicate that the authorities found enforcement difficult. A ban on women working in a particular craft does not mean that they did not continue to do so illegally. Clearly the existence of such a ban is a good indication that women were already working in that particular industry. The ban may well have been introduced as a solution to unemployment amongst male craftsmen created by competition from cheaper female labour. Possibly the profits to be made from employing this cheap female labour may have been sufficient to induce an employer to risk the punishment of a fine and defy the ban.

Conversely, regulations authorising women to work in a particular craft are no sure indication that large numbers did so, nor that they participated on an equal basis to men with equal wages, the opportunities of apprenticeship and entry to the mastery. Such an authorisation may well have been introduced in times of labour shortage.

Ideally the historian needs to investigate the exact circumstances under which each individual regulation was introduced; but this is not always possible. Not even complete silence on the subject of women can be taken as an indication that women did not participate. The most one can say about such regulations is that they represent a situation which the civic and craft elite would have liked to bring into existence.

The use of medieval literature is fraught with similar problems of interpretation. In any case, social and economic historians should not rely solely on literary references. Research into the role of women in the medieval economy must be based on more concrete data. Very often, however, 'concrete data' simply does not exist. Indeed at times it is difficult to see to what extent it is possible to investigate the economic role of women in late medieval society, given the male bias of the surviving documentation.

In most documents the household is represented by its head, the eldest male. Women are seldom mentioned. For example, the most common form of taxation in the late thirteenth and early fourteenth centuries was the lay subsidy. This was a tax levied on the moveable goods belonging to each household, but only the head of the household would be named in the assessments. The only women mentioned in taxation documents of this kind were widows who had not remarried after the death of their husbands and who remained in their own independent households without any male heirs living on the premises, seemingly a rare occurrence in the late medieval town.

Similarly many wives were not named in documents which enumerated population by household. C.V. Phythian-Adams, in his book *Desolation of a City*, found that the Coventry census of 1523 does not record the name of any wife when her spouse was present.[3] Instead the words *et uxor* are appended to the husband's name in each case. The same is true for some earlier census data, such as the poll taxes of 1379 and 1380/1 which could be used to provide information about the structure of the medieval household.

In the case of the urban household it was the husband, as head of the family business, who enrolled in the merchant gild or represented the artisan workshop at meetings of the craft gild. So the absence of female names from lists of gild membership does not necessarily indicate that women did not participate in the productive activity of the household.

Despite these apparent limitations, however, it is still possible to attempt an investigation into the role of women in the medieval urban economy using the occasional glimpses which the sources provide.

The sources for fourteenth century Shrewsbury are by no means unique in their survival. Nevertheless Shrewsbury has been particularly fortunate in that many detailed copies of the lay subsidy returns from 1297 to 1336 have survived.[4] These have been especially useful in the study of the artisan workshop, since those rolls compiled between 1297 and 1322 contain not only the names of taxpayers and amounts of tax paid but also exact details of their moveable possessions. Many of these goods were tools, raw materials and finished products of trade and industry. For example, Richard de Upton, a smith, was assessed in 1309 for iron worth four shillings, charcoal worth five shillings and a forge worth four shillings as well as other household goods such as cloth, wheat, meat and utensils. In all the total value of his moveable goods amounted to twenty-five shillings.[5]

Occasionally women were taxed and most would appear to have been widows since their husbands can be traced as paying tax in earlier years. In addition many wives could well have carried on their own separate trades, but their raw materials and finished goods were included under their husbands' entries in the taxation documents. Much of the cloth or malt listed among Richard de Upton's goods, for example, might have been for use by his wife in her own textile or brewing trade. In the case of some taxpayers this can often be confirmed by reference to later subsidies when, after her husband's death, the widow is herself named in the taxation returns and possessed large amounts of malt or cloth. She may well have had to turn to brewing or textile manufacture to support herself after the loss of her husband's income.

Unfortunately such taxation documents give no indication of the actual labour employed in an industrial or trading enterprise. So there is no way of telling to what extent wives and daughters helped out in the workshop itself rather than earning a separate income from their own bye-industry.

Perhaps the main limitation of such evidence is that it only shows us the upper strata of urban society. Generally those with less than ten shillings worth of moveable goods were not taxed. So such documents cannot be used to study the economic activity of women from the lower ranks of urban society. In all somewhere between fifty and seventy-five per cent of the population was excluded from such documents. Furthermore many widows would have fallen below this ten shilling level after the death of their husbands. Most widows only appeared in one or two subsidies and then either remarried, died or became too poor to be liable for taxation.

Another very important source, this time dealing equally with people from all levels of urban society, is court records. Amongst the Shrewsbury documents there is a good series of court rolls from 1308 onwards, including the fortnightly pleas of debt, trespass, detention of chattels and breach of contract as well as the twice yearly view of frankpledge concerning breaches of the peace and sales of bread, ale and other victuals without licence.[6]

Amongst the pleas of debt and trespass, it is possible to find the occasional case which is concerned with a trade or industrial dispute. Some of these name both husband and wife as plaintiffs or defendants. This provides some evidence that the wife was at least given some say in the running of the business and could be held responsible in a legal capacity for any infringements committed.

Indeed such cases might even relate to the wife's own independent business dealings. Rarely did a married woman appear in court without her husband and this could be an indication that in Shrewsbury the status of 'femme sole' did not exist. In many towns, such as Lincoln or London, the husband of any woman who had the status of *femme sole* could not be held liable for debts incurred or offences committed during the course of her separate business activities.[7]

Thus the nature of the Shrewsbury court records makes it very difficult to distinguish a wife's own business dealings from those of her husband, although obviously the economic activities of single women would appear quite clearly in the records, even though in practice most of them acted through an attorney. In fact, in the majority of cases concerning industrial and other disputes only the husband was named. So there is no way of knowing for certain whether his wife participated in the running of the family workshop or helped out in a practical way. Also, although these court records do not display any particular craft or occupational bias, obviously only the wealthier members of society could afford recourse to law. Some servants and poorer traders, however, appear in court as defendants in pleas.

On the other hand, the lower orders and especially the petty traders are frequently mentioned in the view of frankpledge records. There are countless prosecutions for trading without licence, forestalling and regrating. Many women are named for brewing offences, selling bread and ale without licence, forestalling and regrating victuals in addition to various offences of assault, disturbing the peace and being common scolds. The danger here is that this clear evidence for the participation of women in economic activity over-emphasises their role as hucksters, brewstresses, tapsters and the like.

Also filed amongst these court records are two early lists of tensers for 1351 and 1361.[8] Tensers were usually petty traders who were not members of the Merchant Gild but had purchased the right to buy and sell in the town

on an annual or periodic basis. Although excluded from
the ranks of the Merchant gild, women apparently had the
right to become tensers and there are a few female names
in these two lists, mainly as cooks and brewers, with one
skinner and a glover. Perhaps the absence of females
from the other crafts listed, including fishers, butchers,
mercers, tailors, bakers, shoemakers and drapers, is a
significant indication of their non-participation in such
occupations.

Certain other Shrewsbury documents also mention
females and occasionally give occupations, such as the
detailed fragment of a local copy of the 1380 poll tax.[9]
Whereas wives were just entered alongside their husbands
as *cum uxore*, widows and single women householders
were named and occasionally their occupations were
stated. Maid-servants were also named, so the Poll Tax
can be used to calculate the ratio of male and female
servants living in as well as the number of children over
the age of fifteen years still living with their parents.
The majority of families listed in this fragment of a poll
tax return consisted of only husband and wife, possibly
with children under taxable age. Only three couples had
offspring over the age of fifteen years still living with
them and none of the offspring were married. Women were
much more likely to remain single than men : thirteen out
of eighteen single householders were female and a further
four out of six single persons with servants living in
were women.

Finally, no civic or gild regulations exist for
Shrewsbury in the fourteenth century and there are only
one or two isolated sets of regulations surviving from the
mid-fifteenth century. So it is possible to conduct a
detailed study of women in a medieval urban economy
without the temptation to place overdue reliance on these
formal and legalistic sources.

In the early fourteenth century Shrewsbury was one
of the most important boroughs in the country. According
to the 1334 lay subsidy the town ranked seventh in a list
of provincial towns after Bristol, York, Newcastle, Great
Yarmouth, Lincoln and Norwich – paying a tax of £94.[10] It
was by far the wealthiest borough in the entire area of
the northern Welsh Marches and the north-west Midlands,
serving a hinterland covering Shropshire, north Hereford-
shire, west Staffordshire and south Cheshire.

The growth of the town can be attributed to its
strategic siting and prosperous hinterland. The early
settlement was situated on top of a hill, surrounded on
three sides by a broad meander loop of the river Severn,
which made it an excellent defensive site and a key
fortress in the Welsh Borderland. It is situated in the
centre of the lowland plain of north Shropshire, an area

of heavy settlement particularly in the Severn Valley; and lay on the crossing of two important routeways from Chester to Gloucester and Bristol via the river Severn; and from London and the lowlands of South-East England and the Midlands to North Wales and Ireland.

The town may have suffered badly during the mid-fourteenth century population crisis, since according to the first poll tax of 1377 Shrewsbury only ranked seventeenth in the list of provincial towns with a total tax-paying population of 2083, an estimated population of 4000.[11] It was just a little larger than its nearest rival, Hereford, which ranked nineteenth in 1377 with a tax-paying population of 1903 – an estimated population of 3800. Nevertheless Shrewsbury was still the most important town in the county, marketing produce from and producing goods for sale in the small market towns and villages of the surrounding countryside.

If economic importance can be measured by occupational diversity, it is probably significant that at any one time in the early fourteenth century documents there were at least fifty different occupations mentioned. By the 1370s and 1380s this had risen to between sixty and seventy occupations.

A large proportion of the discernible working population was employed in manufacturing, closely followed by the production and sale of food and drink. Only a tiny fraction appear to have been engaged in building, services, transport and the mercantile sectors of the economy. Of the manufacturing occupations, leather working was by far the greatest employer of skilled full-time labour in the town. This is understandable since Shrewsbury is close to the cattle rearing region of the Welsh Marches and was a major cattle market for the area. At least a third of these leather workers were shoemakers and the others included tanners, saddlers, glovers and skinners in more or less equal proportions.

It would appear that, in the first half of the fourteenth century at least, the Shrewsbury cloth industry was mainly concerned with finishing raw cloth produced in the surrounding countryside, especially dyeing and making it up into garments. A change took place, however, in the middle of the century. From about the 1350s and 1360s onwards, there was a rapid growth in the number of weavers and other cloth producers in the town, along with such allied trades as cardmakers and wiredrawers.

Of the other manufacturing industries in the town there was the usual range of metal workers, woodworkers, as well as such crafts as bottle makers, rope makers and horners. So all in all, Shrewsbury was a fairly typical English medieval borough and it is safe to assume that the situation of women therein was fairly representative of that of countless women in other towns throughout the country.

The sources for fourteenth century Shrewsbury have been used here to investigate two aspects of the subject of women and work in the medieval English town. Any references to women participating in trade and industry, either on their own or helping their husbands have been noted in an attempt to ascertain to which crafts and trades women had access in reality. Whilst doing this it is also important to discover how commonplace it was for women to work in such occupations, distinguishing the isolated case from a general trend. Perhaps the most important feature of the Shrewsbury sources if that they are relatively free from craft bias. If medieval women did work in certain crafts, such as metal-working or building, they would be just as likely to appear in the court and taxation records as women engaged in cloth production. For example, court cases are just as likely to refer to debts incurred over metal goods as for cloth; and if widows did take over from their deceased husbands as metal workers their supplies of iron and charcoal would appear clearly in the subsidy assessments.

Mere evidence of female participation in a particular trade or industry, however, does not investigate the issue of the sexual division of labour within the medieval urban economy fully. It is also crucial to ascertain to what extent this participation was on a basis of rough and ready equality with men. Women may have been denied apprenticeships and excluded from the mastery but their contribution within the workshop itself and the urban economy as a whole may have been more than just that of a cheap source of labour. Only a full investigation of the evidence will answer this question.

As argued above, it may be significant that no references have been discovered at all to women participating in woodworking, building or the metal industry. Even Isabella widow of Roger the Locksmith only had malt, cloth, a calf and four pigs amongst her moveable goods in 1313.[12] So it would appear that she turned to the more traditional female occupations of brewing and cloth working to support herself after the death of her husband. This, of course, does not mean to say that wives of smiths or carpenters, for example, did not assist in the running of the family business, although complete silence on the part of the court rolls in this matter would seem to be significant. Certainly, though, it would appear that the widows of such craftsmen were not able to put their experience, if any, to productive use after their husbands' death and indeed may have been prevented from doing so.

As far as the cloth industry was concerned, one

would expect to find evidence of female participation. Traditionally medieval women were employed in the preliminary processes and especially in spinning, rather than in weaving or the finishing crafts. Much of this work would have been taken in by housewives of the town and countryside alike as a supplement to the family income and is therefore very difficult to trace in the sources.

In Shrewsbury there are no clear references to women engaged in spinning, apart from five women who between 1377 and 1383 all owed money for wool which they had 'bought' from William de Preseley, an important wool merchant and clothier.[13] This wool would have been spun into yarn at home, possibly for their own domestic use. Although, it is far more likely in view of the large amounts of wool involved, up to thirty nine shillings worth in some cases, that the yarn was destined for use by the weavers of the town.

The term 'bought', however, need not necessarily indicate a straightforward sale. From a very early date the English cloth industry had been organised on a 'putting out' basis. That is, the merchant-entrepreneur put out wool for spinning to women of the town and villages. He paid them a certain amount for their labour after they had returned the finished yarn to him. In the same way he then put the yarn out to weavers to be made into cloth and put the cloth out to fullers, dyers, shearers and possibly even tailors to be processed.

As the research of Georges Espinas on the Flemish cloth industry has shown, at each stage of production the merchant conducted a series of transactions, or 'sales', with the producer whereby he 'sold' the raw wool or cloth to the producer and agreed to buy back the finished product at its new value, the difference between the two prices being the wage paid to the producer for his labour.[14] So William de Preseley could have been putting out wool for spinning to these five women and when they failed to deliver the yarn on time he took them to court for the value of the wool.

In all five cases their husbands cannot be traced and their names would indicate that they were single women or possibly widows. One woman, Felicia le Bribster, may also as her name implies, have engaged in brewing.

One other interesting point about the sexual division of labour in the preliminary stages of cloth production has emerged from this research. Whilst half of those with the occupational surname 'le Kembster' (a comber) were female, most of whom would appear to have been single, all five of the carders ('carpator lane') in the late thirteenth century evidence were male.

Weaving on a craft basis is always thought to have been a predominantly male activity and in fourteenth century Shrewsbury only two women were definitely engaged in weaving. A further five had 'le webbe' as their surname and not all were just married to weavers. One of these two female weavers provides an interesting illustration of how women frequently became involved in more than one occupation, often simultaneously. In the court rolls of the 1370s and 1380s Alice de Lye was frequently described as a weaver (webbe) and in 1383 she owed William de Preseley large amounts of money for wool 'sold' to her on at least three separate occasions – the amounts being thirty shillings, thirty shillings and twenty shillings. But in the view of frankpledge of the same year she was fined for being a common bribster and breaking the assize of ale. [15]

There are also two examples of male weavers with female servants. One in particular of these servants was clearly connected with the occupation of weaving since she is described as Amicia servant of John Condeover weaver when in 1384 she was taken to court for breach of contract by her former employer Nicholas the weaver of Doglane. [16] This could well be an example of what was quite a commonplace occurrence in the post–Black Death labour shortage – the enticing away of skilled servants.

These examples of women helping out in weaving are not very numerous, particularly in view of the fact that weaving was an essential skill for any self–respecting medieval housewife. Many weavers' wives may, in fact, have helped their husbands produce the cloth. Indeed ordinances elsewhere allow wives and daughters to help in the domestic workshop of weavers; but these women need not have been exclusively engaged in such work. [17] There are several examples in Shrewsbury of weavers' wives brewing and selling ale or retailing other victuals, particularly in the late fourteenth century. [18]

Of course cloth produced for sale was of much higher quality than the coarse cloth made by wives for household use, but the techniques involved were the same. So it seems unlikely that a master weaver did not call upon the skill of his wife and daughters to help out in commercial production whilst producing for the household at one and the same time. As is often the case with the study of medieval artisan production, it is impossible to distinguish between the paid work done by the craftsman and the unpaid labour of his family.

Fulling is not normally considered to have been a female activity since it often involved heavy labour, namely beating cloth with hammers. But there are two interesting examples of women involved in this particular aspect of cloth production, at least on the organisational side.

Margery the Walker appears to have been in partnership with Alan the Walker, although the exact relationship between them is unknown.[19] Together they took John Lok to court in 1382 for a debt of two shillings and four pence owed to them for fulling cloth. Margery also appeared in court several times between 1394 and 1399 for brewing offences and as a hostler selling horse bread, hay and oats.[20] If this was the same Margery the Walker, there must have been some change in her occupational circumstances in the intervening twelve years.

A more interesting example is Alice wife of Yockes Carnifex.[21] Yockes himself was a butcher. In 1384 he took action against Hugh Walker for detaining twelve cloths of crude wool price thirty six shillings and eight pence which Hugh received in Yockes' house from Alice. She could have been putting her own domestic cloths out for fulling, which she had either purchased crude from a weaver or made herself. But more likely, in view of the number of cloths, she was actively engaged in cloth production, possibly as an entrepreneur putting out cloths to be fulled or as a weaver of cloths herself. It is interesting also that Yockes, not Alice, took the case up in court.

The next process after the cloth had been fulled would be shearing and there was at least one woman, Isabella le Bruster, who in 1341 was fined for shearing cloth without licence from the bailiffs of the town.[22] But as far as the more prestigious and, in the early fourteenth century, more numerous, finishing crafts of dyeing and tailoring were concerned there are no references whatsoever to female participation.

These were, in fact, the two wealthiest textile crafts in Shrewsbury. Many dyers and tailors became entrepreneurs putting out work to those engaged in the lesser trades of spinning, weaving, fulling and shearing. By the end of the fourteenth century many dyers and tailors may have ceased craft labour altogether to concentrate on the more mercantile activities of buying wool or yarn and selling cloth or garments.

Since they were wealthy, dyers and tailors were much more likely to have been taxed and could afford recourse to litigation. So the absence of female dyers and tailors from the sources could be a significant indication that women were actively excluded from participation in such profitable crafts. Perhaps it was not deemed seemly for the wives of dyers or tailors, being respectable middle class townswomen, to engage in industrial or trading activities.

It is especially significant that whilst there were no

female tailors, there were probably countless women as seamstresses and indeed one or two of them appear in the records even though they were probably very poor.[23] Obviously whilst women in fourteenth century Shrewsbury had no access to the more prestigious craft of tailoring, they were allowed to put their sewing skills to work for, presumably, much lower pay.

So a clear pattern emerges as far as the sexual division of labour in the textile industry is concerned. With the exclusion of carding, women were chiefly engaged in the preparation of the raw wool and spinning yarn, mainly as a supplement to their husbands' incomes or to support themselves as single women. The work would have been mainly provided by wealthy merchant-entrepreneurs and executed in the home. There are very few instances of female participation in other aspects of commercial cloth production and as far as the two wealthiest finishing crafts were concerned the male monopoly was clearly established by the fourteenth century. Wives of dyers and tailors, if they acquired any craft skill at all from helping out at home, were never allowed to use this skill to earn an income after the death of their husbands. This picture of the Shrewsbury cloth industry is fairly similar to that usually presented by historians. Eileen Power found that 'cloth remained one of the chief occupations of women until it passed into factories at the end of the eighteenth century'.[24] She found examples of 'women employed in almost all the stages of cloth production', but especially in the preliminary processes and spinning, although weaving was mainly done by men.

In the early fourteenth century, however, the leather industry was by far the most important manufacturing industry in Shrewsbury and there are one or two interesting examples of female participation in leather working. Although all the shoemakers and saddlers were men, women could be found working as tanners, glovers and skinners. There is a very good example of a widow taking over her husband's tanning business; although there are also examples of widows of tanners who did not continue to have leather and equipment necessary for tanning amongst their movable possessions. William Balle, tanner, regularly appeared in the lay subsidy returns from 1306 to 1313. After he died it would appear that Petronilla, his widow, continued the family business, at least until 1315. In the subsidy of that year she had tanned skins, a tanning vat and tanning bark worth forty shillings.[25]

It was probably more common for women to work in the skinners' craft. Skinners, or parmenters, were primarily engaged in preparing and stitching skins or trimming garments with furs. So the very nature of their work required the manual dexterity of nimble fingers. It is obvious from the poll tax that skinners had large numbers of maid servants living in, and sometimes had no male servants at all.[26] Similarly an example could be quoted of at least one skinner's widow with furs amongst her taxable goods and would therefore appear to be continuing her husband's business.[27] There was also one female skinner listed amongst the tensers of 1351.[28]

So in fourteenth century Shrewsbury, women occasionally participated in the leather industry, which is not traditionally an industry associated with women's work. One might expect to find women stitching skins and furs or making gloves, as Juliana de Coleham did in 1351, but the evidence of a wife engaging in tanning is more surprising.[29] Not even Eileen Power found evidence of female tanners. It is also interesting that she does not include potters amongst her long list of crafts in which women could be found working,[30] for there was certainly one widow in Shrewsbury, at the start of the fourteenth century, making pots several years after the death of her husband, Peter the Potter.[31]

So all in all, apart from the more traditional occupations of wool preparation, spinning, sewing, stitching furs and possibly also weaving, there are very few other references to women working in manufacturing and none whatsoever in the heavier crafts, such as metallurgy, building or woodworking, nor even in the most numerous craft of all – shoemaking. Perhaps this lack of evidence for women participating in manufacturing was to be expected.

Traditionally medieval women were much more likely to engage in retailing and fourteenth century Shrewsbury was no exception. There are countless examples, especially in the latter part of the century, of female regrators. To take the view of frankpledge of March 1400 as an example, twenty-two out of the thirty-five regrators named were women and of the thirteen males six were fishers.[32]

Many of these female regrators would appear to have been single, and most of their surnames are unique in the Shrewsbury records. This would seem to indicate that they originated from outside the town. Possibly they had been unable to marry in their native village, due to lack of men or money, and had therefore come to the town to try their luck. They were supporting themselves from buying up grain, vegetables and fish as it entered the town and also bread baked in the town, and by retailing such victuals in the streets and market places for a meagre profit. It was a practice much frowned upon by the authorities, anxious to keep food prices down, but one which they found difficult to stamp out.

It is interesting to note, though, that while women quite often sold bread in the streets very few were actually involved in the craft of baking. In the 1402 view of frankpledge the bakers were punished for making excessive profit and all nineteen bakers named were male.[33] This is not to say that women were completely excluded from the bakers' craft. There are a few examples of female bakers, some of whom were wives or widows of bakers. Walter de Ingelwardyn, baker, registered as a tenser in 1351 but it was his wife who takes his place in the 1361 list.[34]

Married women involved in retailing were often helping their husbands, especially if their husbands happened to be butchers or fishers. Butchers' wives were constantly being punished for leaving dung and entrails in the streets. Curiously enough, in view of the probable absence of *femme sole* status, even while the husband was still alive it was often the wife who was fined in court for such offences. It was also quite common for butchers' widows to continue the family business after their husbands' deaths – often until the son could take over. In fact, in Shrewsbury butchering seems to have been an hereditary occupation, since the same surnames, and especially that of 'Blake', appear as working in the craft throughout the entire fourteenth century. It is known that in Paris the craft of butcher was also an hereditary one.[35]

Many of the women punished for forestalling and regrating fish were wives of fishers. Likewise, one or two male cooks appear to have been assisted by their wives, although there were also many single female cooks.

Brewing, however, and to some extent retailing ale and keeping taverns, was virtually a female monopoly and was very often accepted as such by the authorities. Much of this brewing was done as a side industry in the home. In March 1400, forty-eight brewstresses were punished for brewing and retailing.[36] Many a medieval housewife, accustomed to making beer for her own household, must have been tempted to earn a few extra pennies by selling a little ale. If she did this too often without a licence she was liable to be punished by the authorities.

Some of this brewing, although done in the home, was done on a fairly large scale and certainly the vats were large enough to hold a human body as the sad tale of Agnes de Hagemon shows.[37] One Saturday in November 1296 Agnes was brewing beer in her house in the Frankwell suburb of the town. As she poured a tub full of hot liquor into the vat, she slipped and fell into the vat herself and was badly scalded. While she managed to climb out, her burns were too severe and she died. The case has been recorded in the coroners' rolls and the beer was sold off, raising $2\frac{1}{2}$d profit for the crown.

Finally there are also some interesting examples of women taking part in mercantile activities as haberdashers, chandlers, spicers, mercers and vintners. Not all these women were widows simply taking over their husbands' goods. Elena la Peyntor, Alice le Peyntor and Tibota de Byford all had tallow and candles amongst their moveable goods in the early fourteenth century subsidy rolls but their surnames were unique in the Shrewsbury records.[38] They could all have been single women, who had settled in the town, earning their living as chandlers.

Certainly the evidence for female participation in the medieval urban economy is not great; but this is more a reflection of the sexual bias of the surviving data. Even references to women engaging in the more 'traditional' female occupations, such as the textile industry and petty retail, are not very numerous.

As far as it has been possible to tell, however, there was certainly no 'rough and ready equality' between men and women working in fourteenth century Shrewsbury, despite Eileen Power's assertion to the contrary.[39] In fact, a clear sexual division of labour can be seen in operation. Women were only to be found working in certain occupations, mainly those closely associated with domestic labour, such as the preliminary stages of the textile industry, brewing, petty retail and, of course, domestic service. While there is no concrete evidence that women were actively excluded from the heavy crafts, such as metallurgy, woodworking and building, they certainly did not participate actively in such industries, according to the evidence at our disposal. They played little or no part in the more prestigious and profitable occupations, thus being forced into the lesser paid and low status tasks.

Furthermore, even if women did help out in certain crafts they were never accorded equal status with their male counterparts, at least as far as the civic authorities were concerned. Many wives who helped out in their husbands' domestic workshops did not continue the family business for very long once they became widows, presumably because they were not allowed to do so. Here, of course, there was a clear distinction between the wives of journeymen, who left the family home to walk to work in someone else's domestic workshop every day, and the wives of master craftsmen, who owned these domestic workshops. In the case of the latter, there must have been a considerable interchange between the unpaid domestic labour of the wife and the commercial activities of the husband, particularly if the craft itself called upon the skills of a medieval housewife, for example baking, weaving and even stitching skins. Wives of masters must have frequently helped out in the domestic workshop, especially if the workshop was situated in the family home.

Wives of journeymen, however, must have either spent their day doing unremunerated housework or, more likely, supplementing the family income from the profits of their own labour, mainly by taking in spinning from a merchant-entrepreneur, petty retail or brewing. Women quite often engaged in a combination of all three activities simultaneously. Single women, of course, frequently had to support themselves in various ways, including prostitution, since they were excluded from the benefits of apprenticeships and skilled craft labour.

During the course of such an investigation of the sexual division of labour in the late medieval town, however, it is not enough simply to look for ways in which women participated in male activities. It is wrong to try to contrast and compare their experience with that of men. For indeed women made a major contribution in their own right towards the medieval economy. Within the urban household, the work which women performed, either in the workshop itself or in their own separate industry, provided a very important supplement to the family income and may have made the difference between starvation and subsistence.

On a wider scale, the medieval cloth industry was founded upon the hard toil of innumerable women of both town and countryside alike, without whose poorly paid labour the costs of preparing wool and producing yarn would have been considerably higher. It has often been said that the fortunes of the English economy were founded on the export of cloth from the fourteenth century onwards. Certainly the profits amassed by the proto-capitalists of the medieval textile trade would not have been so great without this cheap female labour.

Similarly the urban economy would have collapsed without the efforts of vast numbers of female hucksters, regrators and brewstresses maintaining the food supply to the manufacturing population. Medieval marketing was essentially fragmented and decentralised. So, even though regrating had acquired a bad name and was classified as a marginal activity by hostile regulations, the urban and, indeed, the rural economy was dependent on the key role played by countless women who bought up local produce from the peasants bringing their surplus into the town for sale.

Such women must have experienced moments of frustration at their exclusion from access to the civic hierarchy, particularly when those males who held the

power tried to interfere with the ways in which women
earned their living. It is no wonder that there were so
many scolds in the medieval town. Women such as Sibilla
Smith, who was charged with being a common scold
(litigatrix) and blocking the King's highway with dung in
1400, quite frequently appear in the court rolls.[40] It was
often the only outlet these women had for their
grievances.

Notes

1. See especially: C. Middleton, 'The Sexual Division
   of Labour in Feudal England', *New Left Review,*
   Vol. 113-4, (Jan./Apr. 1979), pp.147-168.
   M. Roberts, 'Sickles and Scythes: Women's Work and
   Men's Work at Harvest Time', *History Workshop
   Journal,* Vol.7 (1979), pp.3-28. R.H. Hilton, 'Women
   in the Village' in *The English Peasantry in the Later
   Middle Ages,* Oxford, Clarendon Press (1975),
   pp.95-110.
2. E. Power, *Medieval Women,* Cambridge, Cambridge
   University Press (1975).
3. C.V. Phythian-Adams, *Desolation of a City,*
   Cambridge, Cambridge University Press (1979), p.87.
4. Shropshire County Record Office, Shrewsbury Borough
   Records (S.B.R.) 151-160.
5. S.B.R. 158, Taxation of Town and Hamlets for the
   twenty-fifth part (? Edward II) m.2.
6. S.B.R. 758 et. seq.
7. Power, *Medieval Women,* p.59.
8. S.B.R. 766 Roll II, Tensarii 35 Edward III (1361-2).
   S.B.R. 780, Tensarii 25 Edward III (1351).
9. Public Record Office (P.R.O.) E179/166/27,
   Shrewsbury Poll Tax (4 Richard II).
10. W.G. Hoskins, *Local History in England,*
    London, Longmans (2nd edn., 1972), p.238.
11. ibid.
12. S.B.R. 156, Taxation of the Liberties for the fifteenth
    granted to the King 7 Edward II (1313) m.1.
13. S.B.R. 788, Court Roll 1, 6-7 Richard II (1377-1383),
    m.2, m.4.
    S.B.R. 793, Court Roll 6 Richard II (1382-3), m.3,
    m.1d.
14. G. Espinas, *Les Origines du Capitalisme*
    Vol.I, Lille (1933).
15. S.B.R. 784, Curia Generalis 46 Edward III - 7
    Richard II (1372-1384), m.3d.
    S.B.R. 789, Court Roll 1-2 Richard II (1378-9), m.3d.
16. S.B.R. 794, Court Roll 7 Richard II (1383-4), m.2d.
17. Power, *Medieval Women,* p.60.

Also: J. O'Faolin and L. Martines (ed.),
Not in God's Image, London, Virago (1973), p.170.

18. S.B.R. 784, Guria Generalis 46 Edward III - 7
Richard II (1372-1384) m.l. the wife of Hugh le
Webbe retailed ale.
19. S.B.R. 793, m.l.
20. S.B.R. 802, Rot. Mag. Cur.18 Richard II (1394).
S.B.R. 809, Rot. Mag. Cur. 23 Richard II - 1 Henry
IV (1399-1400).
21. S.B.R. 785, Court Roll 47 Edward III (1373-4).
22. S.B.R. 773, Curia Generalis 11-21 Edward III (1337-
1348).
23. P.R.O., E179/166/27: Agnes Sewster and Agnes le
Sower.
24. Power, *Medieval Women*, p.66.
25. S.B.R. 157, Taxation of a fifteenth 9 Edward II
(1315), m.2.
26. P.R.O., E179/166/27.
27. S.B.R. 156, m.5: Mabilla widow of Warin de la Tour
had furs worth 13s. 4d.
28. S.B.R. 780, Tensarii 25 Edward III (1351).
29. ibid.
30. Power, *Medieval Women*, p.59-60.
31. S.B.R. 156, m.l.
32. S.B.R. 809.
33. S.B.R. 812, Curia Magna 3 Henry IV (1401-2).
34. S.B.R. 780 and S.B.R. 766 Roll II.
35. G. Fagniez, *Etudes sur l'Industrie et la Classe
Industrielle a Paris au XIIIe et au XIVe siecles*,
New York (1877, reprinted 1970), pp.103-4.
36. S.B.R. 809.
37. S.B.R. 2689, Coroners' Roll 24-34 Edward I
(1295-1306), m.l.
38. S.B.R. 152, Tax of a twentieth of goods (? Edward
I), m.6, m.ll.
S.B.R. 153, Taxation of the Liberties (? Edward I),
m.4, m.7.
39. Power, *Medieval Women*, p.34.
40. S.B.R. 809.

3 'CHURMAIDS, HUSWYFES AND HUCKSTERS': THE EMPLOYMENT OF WOMEN IN TUDOR AND STUART SALISBURY

Sue Wright

Anyone who has studied a small section of an Early Modern community such as women, children or servants, will know something of the problems of trying to find adequate documentary evidence. Faced with a dearth of material we are in danger of falling into one of two traps; the first of seizing upon every reference and exaggerating the group's importance, the second of assuming that because they were so rarely mentioned they could not have had a significant history. In the case of women, in particular, we should be wary of taking the careers of the one or two successful business-women who appear in so many towns as a model for the female population in general.[1] It is unfortunate that, apart from these 'quasi-men', the majority of urban records are remarkably silent about women. We are hampered in part by the fact that much of the available documentary evidence concerns the formal craft world. Within the carefully regulated guild hierarchy women apparently played their least significant role. But there also existed a world of casual and seasonal employment in which women were able to compete as equals with men.

One of my concerns in this paper is to compare the opportunities available for women in both environments. Whilst it was exceptional for a woman to be accepted as a member of a craft guild, there must have been many women who took on temporary work, perhaps as hucksters or as domestic helps or charmaids, but who never appear in our records. Although it is unlikely that more than a small proportion would have been involved in trade at any one time, a far greater proportion would have had experience of work at some stage during their careers. Bearing this in mind, my second concern is therefore, to pinpoint some of the employments available to women as they passed through the different stages of the life-cycle.

The evidence used in this study is drawn principally from the archives of the city of Salisbury, a town

which ranked fifth in wealth amongst English provincial
towns in the 1520s, but which had dropped to thirteenth
or fourteenth in the urban hierarchy by 1576. During the
Middle Ages Salisbury's importance rested on its dual role
as a cloth manufacturing town and a distributive centre.
By the late sixteenth century its fortunes had begun to
wane. The cloth industry suffered a series of crises from
the 1550s onwards and never recovered its earlier
predominance. Contemporaries also complained of a
decline in the city's other crafts and of growing
competition for work as 'outsiders' set up shop in the
town. The authorities were faced, meanwhile, with a
number of civic disputes, with mounting poverty and with
two serious outbreaks of plague in 1604 and 1627.
Although the citizens were able to obtain a charter of
incorporation in 1612, a measure which they had hoped
would revitalise the town government and stimulate the
growth of local trade, Salisbury never regained its former
pre-eminence and had already begun to change in
character from an industrial to a social centre.[2]

The incorporation of the city is important in the
present context for it led to the reorganisation of the
craft fraternities and to the issuing of a series of new
craft ordinances from which can be gained some impression
of contemporary attitudes towards the employment of
women. Prior to 1612 the evidence is limited. Detailed
minute books have only survived for the Tailors' Guild
and the ledgers of the town corporation contain no general
statements about the role of women in trade. Nevertheless,
a certain amount of information concerning the careers of
individual women can be obtained using wills and court
records. It is unfortunate that very few documents
relating to the Salisbury town courts and none of the
earliest Quarter Sessions records for the city have
survived. However, valuable material is to be found in
the accounts or depositions of the witnesses who appeared
in the local ecclesiastical courts. On the quantitative
side, meanwhile, the size and mobility of the female
population can be assessed by using a series of
population listings known as Easter Books. In essence
the Easter Book was a ledger in which were recorded the
names of all parishioners of communicable age who
contributed towards a parish tithe at Easter. Fourteen
such lists survive for the parish of St Thomas between
1574 and 1607, each of which was compiled on a household
by household basis. Gaps between some of the books
cause inevitable problems, but the five years between
1592 and 1596 are all covered so that, for a short period
at least, we can witness changes taking place year by
year.

It seems logical to start our discussion of the role

of women in trade by briefly considering what type of work was available for children. Evidence from a number of sources makes it clear that many girls would have begun work at an early age. Whilst we can only guess what errands children may have been given by their parents, positive evidence concerning the employment of poor children exists for a number of towns. In Salisbury, as part of the corporation's attempt to alleviate the problem of poverty it was ordered in 1626 that,

> No child be suffered to beg but that all the children of the poor that are not able to relieve them be set to sewing, knitting, bone-lace making, spinning of woollen or linen yarn, pin making, card making, spooling, button making or some other handiwork,

a list which incidentally includes most of the main occupations of poor women.[3]

The age at which it was first thought suitable to start training children seems to have been about six or seven. An ordinance made a year earlier stated that clothiers and spinners were to declare how many children of seven and over they could set on work, and in two censuses of the poor taken in 1625 and 1635 there are several examples of children of six or even younger being given work.[4]

In the first of these censuses details are given of length of time children were to serve, what wages they were to receive and sometimes, how much they were to produce each week. Whilst training may in some cases have entailed actually leaving home, most of the younger children listed probably still dwelt at home. Certainly one of the ordinances initiating the scheme stated that during the first year 6d was to be allowed for the maintenance of each child and they were to board and lodge with their parents.[5]

Although child labour was only organised when the pressure of the poor forced urban authorities to find masters for poor children, one would assume that most children from poorer families would have undertaken some form of work long before leaving home. Girls from the middling ranks of society may, meanwhile, have received a rudimentary education although in common with their poorer fellows they too may well have faced a period of domestic service between leaving home and marriage. In considering the role of women as servants we must rid ourselves of the modern conception of domestic help as a luxury. In an age when domestic tasks were heavy and time consuming and when the mistress of the house was frequently incapacitated by child birth additional help, temporary or otherwise, was vital and even some of the humblest households contained servants.

As a maid servant a girl would gain experience of the arts of 'housewifery' and possibly some knowledge of a trade as well. Again from the modern viewpoint we tend to see domestic and craft labour as two entirely separate entities. In the early modern period however, there was a good deal of interaction between kitchen and workshop. Some of the male servants and apprentices who appeared in the ecclesiastical courts described themselves, not simply as weavers or pewterers, but also significantly as domestic servants. Just as they presumably did certain domestic tasks, so maidservants could become involved in the workshop.

Female assistance would have been particularly important in the victualling trades. Drawing beer, serving food and selling bread are all mentioned in court records. But men other than victuallers also employed maids in the retailing side of their businesses. In the account of his days as an apprentice to a Salisbury merchant, Simon Forman related how, on one occasion when his Master and Mistress were absent, the kitchen maid was willed 'to looke into the shope and helpe yf occasion served'.[6] A small number of girls were formally apprenticed and indentures occasionally mentioned that they were to be taught a trade besides the domestic arts. In January 1612, for instance, Elizabeth Deacon was bound to a Salisbury tailor and his wife in the 'mistery and sciencs of huswyfrye and flexdressing', whilst two months later Mary Gunter was apprenticed in the art of 'le huswyfrye and knittinge'.[7] The number of girls who were actually apprenticed was always low. In Salisbury only 5 of the 138 agreements made between 1603 and 1614 concerned girls, whilst in Bristol just under 3% of all apprentices listed between 1542 and 1552 were female.[8] However, the enrolment of girls was possibly laxer than for boys and the number of apprenticeship agreements may in reality have been slightly higher.

Given the high mobility of servants it was possible for a girl to obtain indirect knowledge of several different trades before she married.[9] It is not possible to trace the detailed careers of more than a handful of Salisbury girls. However, in St Thomas's, one of the three Salisbury parishes, one can gain some idea of the length of time servants spent in individual households by comparing the names recorded in the late sixteenth century Easter Books.[10] Due to the flexibility of the age of first communion and also to the high mobility of servants it is quite possible that the latter were under-registered, although the results obtained are in fact, high when compared with several other studies.[11] Taking simply the 1590s, when there was a series of consecutive books, it appears that nearly half the servants listed were present for more than one year. However, very few stayed in one household for longer than four years and terms of one or two years do seem to have been the norm. [12]

Often when a girl disappeared from the lists it was to get married. Of 82 female servants present in 1592 but missing by 1593, nine are known to have married within a year, another eight within three years, whilst a number more would presumably have married outside the town. However, whilst marriage certainly terminated the careers of many maidservants it would be wrong to assume that service was an option for the young alone. The ages of a group of 26 maidservants who appeared as witnesses in the Salisbury church courts between 1560 and 1650 ranged from 16 to 50, although the average age was 24, slightly below the mean age of marriage established in recent family reconstitution studies.[13] Some of the older women formed part of a small group of what might be described as permanent servants. Included in this group were women who moved around from one household to another. Temperance Taylor, for instance, dwelt with John Eyre in 1593, with his neighbour Giles Tucker for the next two years and with William Becke in Oatmeal Row in 1596. Other women, like Mary Saunders who at fifty had served her mistress for well over ten years and Emme Burell, the servant of John Odell for over twenty, became the permanent employees of one particular family.

Besides the small group of permanent resident servants there existed a group of older domestics who escape record because they did not actually reside with their masters. Casual service would have been particularly important for married women who wished to supplement the family income or widows unable to support themselves. To some extent daily helps, or 'charmaids' as they were known, were frowned upon by the authorities for, existing outside the normal framework of covenanted service, they could easily find themselves without employment and with no income other than parish relief. In Southampton at the end of the sixteenth century presentments ordering women to find themselves permanent employ or to leave the town occurred with regularity. Complaint was actually made in 1597 that,

> theare arr in this towne dyvers young women and maidens w(h)ich kepe themselves out of s(er)vice and worcke for themselves in dyv(er)s mens houses contrary to the statute w(hi)ch we dess(ire) may be considered of and reformacon thereof to be had.[14]

In Portsmouth the attitude may have been more liberal for a list of wage rates dating from 1643 distinguished between servants paid by the year and servants paid by the day.[15] The official civic records are silent on the subject in Salisbury, possibly because so few court records exist, but charwomen were obviously not unknown. In his 'Declaration' about poverty in 1661, John Ivie mentioned women known as 'chewrers' whose tasks included lighting fires in the morning and washing the children and who apparently depended in part upon parish relief.[16]

Obviously, given the existence of a fluctuating group of casual servants and the fact that high mobility may have prevented complete enumeration in the population listings, it is impossible to give an exact figure for the proportion of women engaged in service. But it was clearly far from negligible. In St Thomas's just over a quarter of the households mentioned in the Easter Books contained female servants, a figure contrasting with roughly 15% for male servants and 20% for apprentices. About 80% of these homes, some of which lay in the poorer back streets, apparently contained one maid only. However, in reality solitary maids were perhaps less common than this would suggest, for a number of people must have employed girls who were below communicable age. The actual proportion of the adult female population known to live in as servants was about 20%. As the wealthiest of the three Salisbury parishes, St Thomas's may have contained a slightly higher number of resident servants than the other two parishes. But St Edmund's and St Martin's would possibly have included more of the casual servants. Whatever the exact figure, however, it is clear that a far larger percentage of women would have had some experience of service during their lifetime and that domestic service is an aspect of womens' work deserving of far more detailed study.[17]

Having suggested that a girl could gain some basic knowledge of a trade during her years as a servant, we need to consider what opportunities she would have had to use her skills in later life. As a *femme couvert*, for instance, did she become involved in her spouse's trade or was she able to take up some other occupation? A few will-makers hinted at the fact that their wives had been more than mere housewives and mothers. In 1600 Thomas Reade left all his property to his loving wife who, 'by her joint care, travell and industry hath supported and augmented mine estate'.[18] Another man, an innkeeper, made his wife his sole beneficiary 'for she hath ben marryed vnto me theise three and twentie yeres and worked when I have played'.[19] How many women though, would actually have 'got their fingers dirty' rather than simply overseeing the servants. More importantly, considering the exacting demands of running a home, how many would have had time to play any role other than that of a housewife during the peak years of childbirth?[20]

The degree to which a woman could physically assist in the shop would depend on the nature of her spouse's work and to some extent on the prosperity or otherwise of his trade. In the wealthier household she might assist on the retailing side of the business. Thus, Mrs Boston, the wife of a Salisbury brewer, helped to sell ale and to hire labour.[21] Poorer men engaged in petty retail may also have involved their wives. In 1585 Henry Stocker testified that he 'chiefly liveth by selling and vttering ale wherein hee imploeth his wife'.[22] The wife's labour would have been especially important in the home of the humbler craftsman who employed little extra labour. Of the householders of known occupation who appeared in the Easter Books it is notable that the weavers, tailors and shoemakers in particular, had few resident servants and it is in crafts such as these, involving little equipment and demanding skill rather than strength, that female participation is likely to have been most common.

Some evidence of the role of married women can be obtained from guild records. However, in using such records one should take note of the context in which the various ordinances and minutes were made. Wives may have been encouraged to work when trade was good and discouraged when conditions were bad. In Bristol, for instance, complaints were made in 1461 of a decline in trade and of unemployment amongst the city's weavers. As a result men were ordered not to set their wives, daughters or maids to work, either for themselves or for any other men.[23] Two years later, however, conditions had evidently improved for women were specifically advised to 'help and labour with hir housband for thair boothe sustynaunce and thair childryn thair encrease'.[24]

A further problem in using guild records is that one must be careful not to confuse social and economic roles. Although some crafts included both Brothers and Sisters, the latter may only have belonged as social members. The Salisbury Tailors' Guild is a case in point. It originated as a socio-religious guild rather than simply as a craft fraternity and in its earliest ordinances women were clearly expected to attend such functions as the annual feast and the funerals of departed brethren.[25] Indeed, periodic references to the charges to be levied for the Midsummer Feast make it clear that this was something of a family occasion to be attended by each brother with his wife, children and servants. However, in neither these nor in later ordinances were women ever mentioned in any economic capacity.

Lack of evidence does not, of course, imply a complete lack of involvement. In the Tailors' minute books a couple of memoranda suggest that women probably did assist in an informal capacity. In 1567, for instance, it was agreed that, 'neither Anthony Lambert, his wife, nor any servant shall exercise the craft of furring any garment other than for their provision',[26] and in 1613 a man who had not served a full apprenticeship was admitted to the guild on charitable grounds, but was ordered to keep 'neither servant nor apprentice except his wife'.[27] However, whether the Tailors were typical in their attitude towards women is impossible to judge without similar records for the other Salisbury crafts. The material that does exist generally provides more evidence of married womens' involvement in independent occupations than of husbands and wives working together and, whilst there are no examples of married women acting as *femmes soles* in any of the city's more formal crafts, women from poorer households, and particularly from those in which the husband worked away for a major part of the day, seem to have taken part in a variety of occupations ranging from domestic service and nursing to spinning and huckstering.

It has already been mentioned that, although domestic service was primarily an occupation for the young and the unmarried, it was also important for the *femme couvert* who could only work on a temporary basis. Evidence for casual work of this kind occurs in the Norwich census of the poor dating from 1570.[28] As many as 36 of the wives and 15 of the widows listed in the census (roughly 7% in both cases), were noted for 'washing and skouring', 'helping women to wash', or simply 'helping others'. These activities were often done in conjunction with another occupation such as spinning. Laundering, a common method of supplementing the family income, sometimes necessitated taking in work, as did Agnes Jervis, the wife of a Salisbury tailor.[29] Occasionally it meant permanent employment, a small number of women being officially appointed to serve particular institutions. Thus, when William Waterman was made keeper of the workhouse in 1623 his wife was nominated as 'laundress and nurse of the house and to be at the steward's command for the cleanly keeping and usage of those in the house.'[30]

To some extent nursing was even more casual than domestic work and often entailed no more than one neighbour helping another during a period of illness. Thus, when Mrs Boston lay sick 'for six weekes space' her next door neighbour, the wife of a bottlemaker, attended her daily and was given in return an old cloth gown.[31] In a similar fashion one finds examples of will-makers leaving small gifts to the 'women that kept me during my sickness' and of women being temporarily employed by the overseers of the poor to attend the sick. For the younger woman there was always the possibility of earning a little extra money by acting as a wet-nurse. Joan Hewland, a poor woman from St Martin's, apparently lived by 'nursing of children'.[32] Another woman, Elizabeth Symonds was 'norse to Henry Parry the naturall son of Henry Parry chancellor, when she had had her first child'.[33] In times of plague and other epidemics women were in particular demand, sometimes as nurses, sometimes to take on the unpleasant task of searching the dead in order to verify that they had actually died of the plague. We know, for instance, that Ursula, the wife of Frances Burnet, and Margery, wife of John Guphill, were searchers during the outbreaks of plague in 1604 and 1627, the former still employed despite allegations that she had caused a child to be buried alive during the earlier epidemic.[34]

In addition to the women who could be called on in an emergency, there were some for whom nursing may have been a more permanent activity. This would include the small group of midwives who appear in every town, as well as those women who became reputed for their skills and would have been turned to whenever particular cures were required. The skilful nurse derived a certain social standing from her abilities. Something of the respect with which midwives in particular were held can be gauged from an incident in Southampton in 1601 when a man was admitted to the freedom because his wife 'is of verie good opinion amongst the whole inhabitants and hath manie yeres past bene and yet is the coman and chiefe middwife of thie Towne and hath taken great paines and honest care in her function as perteyneth'.[35] Although midwives had supposedly obtained some elementary training, nursing was still largely dependent on folk remedies rather than on scientific skills and, as the Salisbury Barber-surgeons complained in 1614 'there are divers women and others within this citie altogeather unskilfull in the Arte of chirurgeries (which) due often tymes take cures on them to the greate danger of the patient.'[36]

Another area of female employment which would have been important for the poorer married woman and even more so for the widow was that of petty retail. Fish-wives, ale-wives and hucksters of bread and of a variety of small wares appear in the records of most sixteenth century towns, although it is generally impossible to estimate the numbers involved at any one time. One Salisbury goodwife claimed to be the servant of Goody Penny and her daughter 'and doth sell cowheeles for them when she is at home'.[37] Other by-products of the butcher's trade were dealt with by the aptly named 'pudding wives'.[38] In the early seventeenth century a number of local women were presented for buying faggots in the market and selling them again 'by the penny', whilst in 1638 an ordinance specifically licenced four men and five women to act as coal bearers.[39] Occasionally references occur to women who travelled further afield to sell goods. A spinster named Elisabeth Skeate testified that for eight years she was the servant of Alice Temple of St Edmund's 'who, being a petichapman and selling small wares, she ... as her servant and by her appointment did carry the same in pack over the country to sell'.[40] Another woman, this time the widow of a carrier, sought the approval of the corporation in 1631 to carry wares from Salisbury to London.[41]

Huckstering was an activity which would have fluctuated according to season and demand and which may have taken the woman away from home for long periods. The other traditional area of female employment, in the textile industry, may have been easier to combine with running a home and family and thus have been more attractive to the married woman.[42] There are no references to female weavers in Salisbury, but during the fourteenth and fifteenth centuries, when Salisbury was at its height as a cloth producing centre, spinning had been particularly important. Although by the sixteenth century the slump in the cloth trade must have considerably reduced the amount of work available, a large part of the wool distributed for carding and spinning was still given to women who worked at home for piece-rates.

In a report to the Wiltshire Quarter Sessions in 1633 reference was made to 'ye poorer sort of people who spinne theyr wooll in theyr owne houses', and another report that year mentioned fine yarns 'spun by farmers wifes and others of the better sort' for between 17d and 2s 4d the pound and lower sorts of yarn spun at between 9d and 17d the pound.[43] Apart from spinning, lacemaking, buttonmaking and knitting were occupations traditionally associated with the poor. The 1625 census of the poor is valuable in giving the names of a number of women who actually taught these crafts to poor children, along with the names of other poor women employed by local clothiers. Of thirty such mistresses, sixteen of whom are known to have been married and five widowed, twenty-two taught bonelace making, four spinning and three knitting. The majority employed only one child, but a few had comparatively larger workshops. The wife of Lancelot Russell, for example, taught six children to make lace, whilst Alice Swift had three servants and six apprentices.

The predominance of bonelace-makers amongst the mistresses suggests that this may have been an industry

centred principally around the home and run entirely by
women.   Spinning, on the other hand, was engaged in by
both men and women and was normally linked with the
activities of large scale clothiers and market spinners. Of
the women in the census who were set on work, ten were
listed as spinning, five as carding and spinning and four
as knitting.   Where ages are given they normally seem to
have been older women; Widow Baldwyn, for example, who
at 70 span for Thomas Ray, or the wife of John Kengington, a woman of 56.   Significantly it was specifically
noted that the youngest woman recorded, aged 32, was to
be allowed to attend her children.   Was it in fact rare
for women with very young children to take up such
occupations?[44]   In a few cases, when the children were
older the whole family seems to have been engaged in the
enterprise.   Audrey, the wife of Hugh Eliot was to spin
ten pounds a week with her ten year old daughter Joan;
Katherine Crocher and her two daughters span and carded
eighteen pounds a week for Bartholomew Tooky and, whilst
John Kengington and his wife span, their son was trained
in the art of quilling.

Although all the occupations mentioned so far were
performed by widows as well as by married women, the
area of 'informal' trade with which the widow was
particularly associated was victualling.   To sell ale and
various food stuffs was a recognised means of subsistence
for the poor.   In a letter to the Privy Council in 1608 it
was noted that alehouse keepers were, 'generally for the
most p(ar)te verie auged and poore people whose labours
are past and have no other means of lyving',[45]   and
during the late 1620s and 1630s a number of petitions from
poor tradesmen and widows requested licences to victual.
Alice Webster, for instance, asked to sell bread, drink
and similar provisions, 'being nowe aged, not being able
to imploye her selfe to her bodie for her releefe and
comforte'.[46]

As a result of official attempts to regulate drinking,
particularly from the 1620s onwards, a number of lists of
tipplers and alehouse keepers exist.[47]   It is apparent
that, whilst the numbers of women involved were never
very large, they were by no means insignificant, although
of course in a town the size of Salisbury it is quite
likely that many widows would have managed to sell
victuals without becoming licensed.   In the lists of
victuallers recognisances made between 1627 and 1635 the
number of women never rose above 14 a year. Nevertheless, they still formed over a third of the total and, in
1634 and 1635, nearly half.   Another list made in 1630
listed 43 alehouse keepers of whom 15 were women, with a
further four women noted as cooks and three as innkeepers.   The contrast between the numbers of female inn-

keepers, only 7.5% of the total, and the number keeping alehouses demonstrates that it was chiefly at the poorer end of the market that women operated.[48]

Some widows, amongst whom one might expect to find a number of alehousekeepers and innkeepers, were in a position to act as pawn-brokers and money lenders to their poorer neighbours. Lists of goods held as pawns are occasionally found in widows' inventories. Edith Bide, for instance, was owed over fifteen pounds 'upon pawnes' when she died in 1625, whilst poorer women, for whom broking may have been their chief means of gaining a livelihood, were presented in court from time to time for selling stolen goods.[49] In 1631, for example, Agnes Masters, a butcher's widow, was questioned for her part in selling a stolen apron and a neckerchief. She was referred to in the case as 'a coman carrier of cloathes and other things about the towne to sell and to pawne'.[50] The network of individuals mentioned in the case for buying or pawning goods consisted entirely of poor women, for whom such an informal system was possibly the only means of obtaining 'new' clothes or household goods.[51]

Theoretically, besides being involved in retail, in casual service and in the textile industry, the widow had scope to work in a much wider range of crafts and, unlike the majority of married women, to venture into the more formal, hierarchical world of the guilds. However, there is little evidence for women working in this sphere, either during the sixteenth century or after 1612 when, according to the ordinances issued as the crafts were reorganised into companies, the widow was permitted to trade until she remarried.[52]

Doubtless a number of women who traded in the city would have escaped all record. But the general lack of evidence also raises two other possibilities, namely that the majority of widows either remarried or that they became involved in the less formal areas of trade already discussed. Evidence from the parish of St Martin's suggests that at least a third of the women bereaved between 1570 and 1599 remarried.[53] Although the average interval between bereavement and remarriage was slightly longer for women than for men, most of the known examples had only a year or two of solitary existence, a period so short that if a woman had temporarily continued her husband's business it is quite feasible that she would have escaped all record.

How far second marriage was entered into out of pure necessity is a debatable question. But it does seem likely that many widows would have found it difficult to maintain a shop or indeed to find adequate means of support for their families. To appreciate why remarriage may have been preferable to trading as a *femme sole* we need to consider some of the practicalities involved. The widow who wished to trade independently needed firstly tools and a place in which to work; secondly a labour force and thirdly some previous experience of business. Of these the third would obviously have depended on whether the woman had actually assisted her husband, a matter about which, as we have seen, it is difficult to do more than speculate. The other two main requirements, if we can rely on testamentary evidence, may have been passed on to the widow with less frequency than might be expected.

Apart from occasional references to dyehouses and tanhouses, places of work are rarely mentioned in wills. However, given the fact that industry was still domestically orientated, it is possible to make certain assumptions about the proportion of women who may have inherited a workshop by considering the descent of the marital home. At first sight it seems that the proportion may have been high, for in as many as two-thirds of a group of wills made between 1500 and 1640 in which a married testator specifically mentioned his dwelling house, the latter descended to the widow. Yet for every testator who made known his wishes about the house, another two failed to mention it. Did they make some prior arrangements or did they leave the division of the estate to the workings of the common law? A more serious problem lies in the fact that only a very small proportion of the total adult population actually made wills and, being mainly drawn from the elite, these men would have been more likely to own their home and thus, relatively free to determine its descent. [54]

Bearing these problems in mind I would suggest that it may be optimistic to assume that some two-thirds of all widows would have inherited a home and workshop. Certainly, even if the proportion was this high, many women seem to have moved quickly from their old marital home. In St Thomas's, where it has been possible to trace the continuity of property between man and wife, roughly half the women bereaved during the late sixteenth century had disappeared from their marital home in under a year after their spouse's death, whilst many more moved away, often to remarry, after only a year of independence. [55] When one adds to this the fact that a number of the occupiers in the parish would have been wage-earners with no workshop, and that sometimes, even when the wife gained possession of the house, a son or kinsman took charge of the shop, it seems fair to conclude that only a small minority of widows would ever have taken charge of a workshop for more than a very short period.

Evidence for the inheritance of stock and equipment

is even harder to find than evidence concerning the workshop. In one or two wills the testator clearly intended that his tools should pass to his wife. In 1610, for instance, George Davis left his apprentice a pair of shears and 'four course of handles ... within one month after my wife shall leave of the trade which i dowe nowe use',[56] whilst another testator, Nicholas Atkinson, left all his embroiderer's tools to his son, 'which I will my wife shall keepe and use as long as she doth use my trade'.[57] But there are just as many examples of tools being given to a child or to a servant in preference to the widow. In fact tools are only mentioned in 42 of the 438 wills made by married men between 1500 and 1640. It may simply have been the rule that stock passed automatically to the executor, but comparison between the inventories of man and wife suggests that this was not always the case.[58] Indeed tools are only listed in four of the 116 widows' wills examined between 1590 and 1640 and eleven of the 55 inventories, (3.4% and 20% respectively).

Clearly more information is needed about the circumstances of individual families and, given the fact that some crafts would demand far more equipment than others, about the requirements of different trades. Dyeing and brewing, for instance, were particularly capital intensive. The tailor, meanwhile, needed only a pair of shears and a pressing iron. Thus, whilst it is clear that tools and equipments were by no means the inevitable prerogative of the widow, it cannot be automatically assumed that if she appeared to be left without tools she would have been unable to trade. On the other hand, even the woman who inherited an apparently prospering workshop may have been rapidly forced to sell its contents. One testator lamented that 'I have given away soe much that I shall leave my wief but a poore woman and my cloth is not sold yet nor my children are not yet bred'.[59] In order to maintain the children his wife was forced to sell the stock at a loss. Another woman, the widow of a pewterer, had inherited stock worth £48, but would have had to dispose of this in order to settle her spouse's debts and legacies amounting to £68.[60]

The other major requirement if the widow was to continue her spouse's business was to have a sufficient labour force. As with tools, needs varied according to different trades. Metal workers and builders were particularly dependent on adult male servants; tailors and shoemakers could suffice with apprentice labour. With a woman heading the shop the support of male servants would have been even more important. Yet, in the analysis of the number of servants per household in St Thomas's, it appears that surprisingly few women had any servants at all, let alone male servants.

Taking simply the years 1585, 1593 and 1594, 22.3% of all female headed households contained servants in contrast to 45.3% of all male households. 12.5% of the women had maids, 6.5% male servants and 8.7% apprentices. Obviously with no evidence of the proportion of servants who lived out these figures are an inadequate guide to the degree of female involvement in trade. But if a significant number of women did trade for more than a short period after their husband's death then one might expect to find a slightly higher proportion with residential male servants.

To confirm the impression that comparatively few women took over their spouse's business it is interesting to note that of the minority of women with male servants, a number also housed another adult male, such as a son or kinsman, who perhaps took effective charge of the shop. Joan Bricket, for instance, had a man servant in 1590, shortly after her husband's death, but none thereafter until 1601 when her son came to share the house. In 1574 another woman actually lodged her son's man, whilst in 1601 Walter Ashley and his man resided with Widow Dyer and Edward Lye and his man with Widow Lobbe, his future wife. In a number of other cases male servants were only noted shortly after the husband's death, and it seems more likely that they were simply serving out their covenanted time than that they had been appointed by the widow in her own right.[61]

The presence of apprentices in a number of female headed households may be similarly explained. The Butchers are representative of all the Salisbury trades reorganised in 1622 in stating that, 'the apprentices of the husband of suche widdowe and other apprentices she shall take shall serve her as apprentices soe longe time as she shall kepe her husband's trade and remain a widdowe.'[62] But, although theoretically permitted, it is exceptional to find a woman with an apprentice who had been bereaved for more than a couple of years and who may have taken on the boy herself instead of simply completing his training.[63] Moreover, of the 133 boys who were indentured between 1603 and 1614, 17 were bound to a man and his wife, but not one was formally apprenticed to a widow.[64]

As it was unnecessary to re-enroll boys when their master died we should expect to find few references to women completing the training of their husband's apprentices. But there is evidence to suggest that even this was rare. Only a minority of masters may actually have had an apprentice when they died, for training boys seems to have been far more common during the early years of a man's career. Thus, of a sample of 71 master tailors who disappeared from the guild's records before 1630, only 29 had enrolled a boy within seven years of that date and, on average, there was an interval of just over ten years, longer than the normal apprenticeship term, between the last known enrolment and disappearance.

Whether the tendency for men to take apprentices primarily during the early stages of their careers was common to trades other than the tailors is impossible to judge, but if it was universal then it follows that only those women bereaved shortly after marriage would have been left with apprentices. Even then it seems that they did not necessarily complete the training of the boys, for a number of memoranda in the Tailors' minute books refer to boys transferred to other tailors whilst their former mistress was still alive. The explanation must lie in part in the fact that the younger widows were those most likely to remarry and possibly, those who would have been least competent to train an apprentice.

Whilst the evidence described so far demonstrates that there were a number of practical problems involved in continuing a business, it should not be taken simply to imply that widows never became involved in the Salisbury craft guilds. In the list of Free Citizens compiled in 1612, solitary women were listed amongst the merchants, tanners, butchers, pewterers and innholders and odd examples of female tailors, glovers and maltsters appear in other records.[65] But the number of these women was very small compared to the many married women and widows we hear of in the fields of victualling, casual retail and textiles. It is certainly difficult to point to any business women who stood out and rivalled their fellow tradesmen as they did in certain other towns.

Whilst the guilds theoretically permitted widows to trade it is possible that individual tradesmen may have tried to discourage female participation. One clothier, whilst commenting on a widow who had made a loss selling the cloth she had inherited, remarked that he had suffered greatly as a result of the collapse of the European market during the early seventeenth century, and that she must have fared far worse, 'especially being a widow woman not knowing how to doe the best for herself'.[66] The man's reference to the slump, or as he described it, the 'great dampe of deadnes' in the cloth trade is, I believe, important. As mentioned earlier, the cloth industry was suffering serious problems by the early seventeenth century and the citizens were becoming increasingly alarmed by the effect of outside competition on the town's other crafts. With the danger of unemployment amongst the native male craftsmen is it really to be expected that women would be tolerated in any but the more menial, less organised trades?

There is clearly a need for more research into the

levels of female employment, both for married and for widowed women, in different towns and at different periods in order to see just how far the economic fortunes of a town affected its policy towards women. It has already been mentioned how in 1461, when the Bristol weavers were threatened by an influx of foreigners, they forbade men to give work to their wives and daughters. In contrast, in early sixteenth century York, when the population and, in particular the numbers of freemen were declining, females were positively encouraged.[67]

Too often ordinances encouraging or prohibiting women are cited without consideration of the circumstances in which they were made. Possibly in the later Middle Ages and even in the early years of the sixteenth century, when far less evidence is available, conditions were more favourable for Salisbury women. But certainly by the latter part of the Tudor period very few women entered the world of the guilds. Women's work was principally at the casual, menial end of the market, an area which may not have involved large numbers at any one time, but which must have given employment to a significant number of women at some stage during their life-cycle.

Notes

1. Women like Judith Delamotte of neighbouring Southampton, who took over her husband's dyehouse in 1617, but had been operating as a clothier in her own right long before that date. A.L. Merson, ed. *A Calendar of Southampton Apprentice Registers 1609-1740* (Southampton, 1918) p.lxxv.
2. For details of the economic background see *Victoria County History of Wiltshire, IV* (1959) Chs.5 & 6, *VI* (1962) and G.D. Ramsay, *The Wiltshire Woollen Industry in the Sixteenth and Seventeenth Centuries* (London, 1943).
3. Paul Slack ed., *Poverty in Early Stuart Salisbury*, (Wiltshire Record Society, 1975), p.89.
4. S.C.A., Ledger C fol. 312v; Slack, *op. cit.* pp.65-82.
5. S.C.A., Ledger C fol. 313v.
6. A.L. Rowse, *Simon Forman, Sex and Society in Shakespeare's Age* (London, 1974), pp.267-278.
7. S.C.A., Additamenta Box 1-16, No. 7/1, Add.3.
8. E. Ralph & N.M. Hardwick eds., *Calendar of the Bristol Apprentice Book Part II, 1542-1552,* (Bristol Record Society, 1980), p.x.
9. For details of servant mobility see Ann Kussmaul, *Servants in Husbandry in Early Modern England* (London, 1981), pp.51-67. P. Laslett, *Family Life*

and Illicit Love in Earlier Generations (Cambridge, 1977), p.43.

10. S.C.A., St Thomas Records: 31,33,34,36,37,39,41,42,43, 45,46 & 48. The use of Easter Books as a historical record is discussed in S.J. Wright, 'Easter Books and Parish Rate Books: A New Source for the Urban Historian' (forthcoming).

11. The large number of servants in the parish presumably reflect the fact that we are dealing with an urban community and, within that community, the wealthiest of the three parishes. For the three years when the registration of servants seem to have been most complete, namely 1585, 1593, and 1594, it appears that roughly two-fifths of the households in St Thomas's contained servants (42%), a considerably higher proportion than that obtained by Laslett in his study of 100 pre-industrial communities. Peter Laslett, 'Mean Household Size in England since the Sixteenth Century', in *Household and Family in Past Time*, eds. P. Laslett & R. Wall (Cambridge, 1972), p.148.

12. A sample taken from the years 1592-1596 and 1601-1603 indicates that 44.3% of the male servants and 45.6% of the female were present in the same household for more than one year. It is difficult to test for residence for periods of five or more years as there are gaps between the individual Easter Books. However, the results which have been obtained suggest that this was unlikely to apply to more than about one in every twenty servants.

13. S.D.R., Bishop's Court Depositions, 1550-1650. In seventeenth century England the evidence from reconstitution studies suggests that the mean age of first marriage for men was between 27 and 28 and for women between 25 and 26. (E.A. Wrigley and R.S. Schofield, *The Population History of England, 1541-1871; A Reconstruction*, London 1981). The importance of service as a prelude to household formation in North-West Europe is discussed by John Hajnal in 'Two Kinds of Pre-industrial Household Formation' in R. Wall ed. *Family Forms in Historic Europe* (Cambridge, 1983), pp.65-104.

14. F.J. Hearnshaw, ed., *Court Leet Records, 1578-1602*, (Southampton Record Society, 1906), p.196.

15. R. East ed., *Extracts from the Portsmouth Records*, (Portsmouth, 1891), p.161.

16. P. Slack, *op. cit.*, p.114.

17. Peter Laslett suggests that as many as 40% of all children became servants at some stage in the life-cycle. *Family Life*, p.43.

18. P.R.O., Prob. 11/112/90/249, 1608.

19. P.R.O., Prob. 11/122/108/339, 1613.
20. Although the main concern of this paper is to consider the employment of women outside the home, it should not be forgotten how time consuming and physically taxing normal domestic tasks such as laundering, preparing food and gathering fuel must have been, nor how important was the production for home consumption of items such as clothing and linen.
21. S.D.R., Bishop's Court Deposition Book, No. 9, fol. 189c v.
22. *Ibid.*
23. F.B. Bickley ed., *The Little Red Book of Bristol I*, (Bristol, 1900), p.129.
24. E.W.W. Veale ed., *The Great Red Book of Bristol, Text Part II*, (Bristol, 1933), p.69.
25. S.C.A., Tailors' Guild Act and Memoranda Book, I/245, fols. 8–10.
26. S.C.A., Tailors' Guild Assembly Book I, 1517–1575, I/246/1, fol.59.
27. S.C.A., Tailors' Guild Assembly Book III, 1597–1613, I/246/3, fol.80v.
28. J.F. Pound ed., *The Norwich Census of the Poor*, (Norfolk Record Society XI, 1971).
29. S.D.R., Bishop's Court Deposition Book, No.8, fol.7.
30. P. Slack, *op. cit.*, p.87.
31. S.D.R., Bishop's Court Deposition Book No.9, fol. 189c v.
32. *Ibid.*, No.29, fol.19v.
33. *Ibid.*, No.18, fol.129.
34. S.C.A., Box N101, 82 and 86. Women who normally cared for the sick probably also dealt with the corpse. In the Inventory and Account of Simon Worley, who died in 1627, it is interesting that 6d was set aside for the bearers of the body and for 'the woman that did take paynes about him', whilst a will dating from 1610 stipulated that Goodwife Mytten should 'wrap my body after my decease in a shrowde made of one of my sheets'. W.R.O., Sub-Dean Wills, Simon Worley, 1626. P.R.O., Prob. 11/115/54/402.
35. J.W. Horrocks ed., *Assembly Book VI, 1602–1608*, (Southampton 1917), p.ix.
36. S.C.A., E/I/224/1, Barber-surgeons Ordinances, 1614.
37. S.D.R., Bishop's Court Deposition Book No.11, fol.46, 1589.
38. An ordinance of 1616 mentioned the fact that butchers sold offal to poor women and 'pudding wives' who created a nuisance by emptying 'those bellies in the rivers (and) in the streets'. S.C.A., Corporation Ledger C fol.251v.

39. S.C.A., Q/136/b. and E/I/253, November 1638.
40. S.D.R., Bishop's Court Deposition Book 11, fol.46.
41. S.C.A., Ledger C fol.376v.
42. The evidence from Norwich suggests that this was, in fact, the most important area of female employment. As many as two-thirds of the married women and widows listed in the Norwich census of the poor were noted for spinning. By contrast only about one in twenty-five women were engaged in retail and one in fourteen in domestic service.
43. P.R.O., SP/16/243/23 & SP/16/267/17. The second report, drawn up with the express aim of discrediting the market spinners may not be totally reliable. Tables of wage rates issued by the Quarter Sessions between 1602 and 1605 suggest that these rates may be rather high, the official rates ranging from 1d to 4d a pound according to the quality of the wool. *H.M.C., Various Collections,* (1901), pp.162–168.
44. Amongst the poor in Norwich extra employment seems to have been important both for those with young children and those without.
45. S.C.A., N101/131.
46. S.C.A., N101/100.
47. S.C.A., Searchers and Sealers of Leather Book, 1626–1743, E/I/253.
48. S.C.A., N101/56.
49. W.R.O., Sub-Dean Wills, 1620s.
50. S.D.R., Bishop's Court Deposition Book 11, fol.46.
51. In Leicester complaint was made in 1573 of women known as 'Brogers or pledge women' who 'vsed the trade of sellinge of apparell and howshold stuff' and who 'have disorderlye used the same in hawkinge abrode from howse to howse'. *Leicester Borough Records III,* ed. M. Bateson, (Cambridge, 1905), p.147.
52. S.C.A., E/I/224. Whether this ruling reflected an earlier system or whether the ordinances were modelled upon those of some other town is difficult to establish without records concerning the previous history of the crafts.
53. 33.3% of the women from St. Martin's can be traced remarrying in contrast to 40.2% of the men bereaved in all three Salisbury parishes during this period. However, these only represent minimal figures for no doubt many people would have married outside the town. A more detailed analysis using both the parish registers and the Easter Books, suggests that for men at least the remarriage rate may have been as high as 75%. It is harder to trace the career of the bereaved woman, but from the available evidence

it would appear that she was less likely to remarry than her male counterpart. The preponderance of women in the community (in St. Thomas's, for example, adult women outnumbered men in the ratio of 85 to 100 in the late sixteenth century), meant that the elderly and the poor would have found it particularly difficult to attract a second husband. During the thirty year period between 1570 and 1599 the median interval between bereavement and remarriage was 7 months for men and 16.5 for women.

54. In St. Edmund's during the 1590s under one in ten men recorded in the burial register are known to have made a will.

55. On average 12.9% of all households in St. Thomas's were headed by women, the vast majority of whom can be assumed to be widows, although they probably included a small group of deserted wives and spinsters. Of the 310 women noted as household heads between 1582 and 1607 only 110 (35.5%), are definitely known to have succeeded their spouse. Approaching the question from a different angle meanwhile, of 45 women whose husbands appeared in the Easter lists and whose death can be traced in the year preceding an existing book, two remarried within the year and handed the property to a second spouse, whilst 22 remained at the head of the household, albeit for a short period only in many cases. We know that two of the remaining widows died shortly after their spouse, two went to live with kin and three can be traced as house-holders in another street, but the fate of the rest is uncertain.
For a detailed discussion of the question of continuity between man and wife see S.J. Wright, 'Family Life and Society in Sixteenth and Early Seventeenth Century Salisbury', University of Leicester Ph.D., 1982.

56. P.R.O., Prob. 11/130/97/261, 1617.

57. W.R.O., Sub-Deans Wills, 1618.

58. The executorship was entrusted to over 80% of the widows whose husbands died testate between 1540 and 1639.

59. W.R.O., Bishop's Court Deposition Book No.11, fol.102.

60. W.R.O., Consistory Court Wills, Richard Horner, 1595.

61. This appears to have been an accepted practice for several testators specifically required their servants to remain with the widow for a year after their decease.

62. S.C.A., I/244.

63. It is significant that when the Guild ordinances were reissued in 1676 the clauses mentioning 'such apprentices as she shall take' were either crossed out or omitted altogether.
64. S.C.A., Additamenta Box 1-16, No.7/1, Add.3. We can only speculate whether the 15 individual women mentioned in these indentures, who were incidentally married to a wide variety of tradesmen, did actually help to train the boys or whether their concern was solely with their welfare. It is interesting to note that the apprentice indentures in Bristol almost invariably mentioned the woman as well as her spouse. E. Ralph and N.M. Hardwick, *op. cit.*
65. S.C.A., 1/252.
66. S.D.R., Bishop's Court Deposition Book, No.45, fol.102.
67. Angelo Raine ed., *York Civic Records, III*, (Wakefield, 1942) p.126.

The Salisbury archives have recently been moved to the County Record office at Trowbridge, and the collection is in the process of being relisted under the general class mark of G23. For convenience the original repositories are referred to here using the following abbreviations:-

S.C.A.   Salisbury Corporation Archives

S.D.R.   Salisbury Diocesan Records

W.R.O.   Wiltshire Record Office.

4

'WORDS THEY ARE WOMEN, AND DEEDS THEY ARE MEN'[1]:
IMAGES OF WORK AND GENDER IN EARLY MODERN ENGLAND

Michael Roberts

I want to begin in familiar territory, in the Essex textile town of Colchester.[2] Around the year 1622 an eight year-old girl, having been 'bred up' by a nurse or foster mother, was instructed by the town authorities to enter service. Recalling the event some sixty years later, she recounted her dismay:

> I had a thorough aversion to going to service, as they called it, though I was so young; and I told my nurse, that I believed I could get my living without going to service if she pleased to let me; for she had taught me to work with my needle, and spin worsted, which is the chief trade of that city, and I told her that if she would keep me, I would work for her, and I would work very hard.

The girl's reluctance was initially interpreted by her elders as a child's natural timidity. To her fretful cry that 'I can't work house-work', the nurse replied 'well, child, but though you can't work house-work, you will learn it in time, and they won't put you to hard things at first'. Their dialogue developed into a series of confrontations between the child, with her innocent intentions, and the amused response of women who were more familiar with the constraints on female employment in the adult world. The girl's desire for independence was received with ironic laughter; for poor girls in their view should not normally be expected to shape their own economic destinies. 'Why, what', the nurse was forced to ask, 'is the girl mad? What! would you be a gentle-woman?'. To make her point plain the nurse exposed the economic dangers of the argument:

> 'Well, madam, forsooth, you would be a gentle-woman? What! will you do it by your fingers' ends?
>   ('Yes')

Why, what can you earn; what can you get a day
at your work?
> ('Threepence when I spin, and fourpence when
> I work plain work')

Alas! poor gentlewoman, what will that do for thee?
> 'It will keep me, if you will let me live with
> you')

But that will not keep you and buy you clothes,
too; and who must buy the little gentlewoman
clothes?
> ('I will work harder then, and you shall have
> it all')

Poor child! it won't keep you; it will hardly find
you in victuals.
> ('Then I would have no victuals; let me but
> live with you')

Why, can you live without victuals?
> ('Yes').

It became clear in the encounters between the girl and
adult women which followed that she lacked not only their
sense of economic logic but also their social vocabulary.
She was taken aback when addressed ironically as 'Miss';
'the word miss was a language that had hardly been
heard of in our school, and I wondered what sad name it
was she called me'. Her notion of being a gentlewoman
was more concrete, 'it was one that did not go to service,
to do house-work'. Unaware of the connotations of the
words she was using, the child defined her notion of a
gentlewoman by example: 'for there is such a one', who
mended lace and washed ladies' laced heads. 'She is a
gentlewoman, and they call her madam . . . I am sure
they call her madam, and she does not go to service nor
do house-work'. The women's corrective was swift and
sharp: 'poor child, you may soon be such a gentlewoman
as that, for she is a person of ill fame, and has had two
bastards'. The girl had a clear image of possible dignity
and self-reliance as a woman; her seniors saw a more
complicated world, grounded in biological realities and
riven by differences of status. 'All I understood by being
a gentlewoman', the girl later recalled, 'was to be able
to work for myself, and get enough to keep me without
going to service, whereas they meant to live great and
high, and I know not what'.

For the historian of women's work this dialogue is
tantalisingly full of suggestions. Service was not an
unusual employment for girls of this age and background;
but this particular girl had a thorough aversion to it.
How unusual was she? Her desire was not to avoid work of
all kinds, but to escape the terrors and indignities of

house-work as a servant. Her training as a needle-woman had left her feeling decidedly ill-equipped for service, 'able to do but very little, wherever I was to go, except it was to run errands, and be a drudge to some cook-maid'. She feared a servant's discipline, too; 'if I can't do it they will beat me, and the maids will beat me to do great work, and I am but a little girl'. Her needle-woman's skills had already given her a sense of self-reliance, but both the girl and her advisers assumed a major distinction between this form of employment, living 'by her fingers' ends' as they put it, and the quite different phenomenon of 'house-work', with its drudgery and errand running, and the 'hard things' and 'great work' that would come later. The self-reliance of the one form of work was compromised by the inability to afford the clothing and food of a true gentlewoman, and the like-lihood of future dependence on that rare kindly guardian, or the more probable male seducer. The wisdom, and perhaps resignation, of the girl's adult advisers sought to point her in another direction, towards the security of service, with its greater range of unfamiliar tasks, its occupational hierarchy, and its subordination.

II

The girl, of course, was a fictional character: Moll Flanders.[3] Her experiences offer us a glimpse into the thoughts and feelings of such working girls that we can scarcely expect to obtain from the documentary record. The roles of women in the work-force, the kinds of work they undertook and the wages they were paid, can be studied with comparative ease by the early modern historian. How contemporaries saw such work, and what they felt about it, however, are much more difficult to grasp. This paper attempts to explore the latter questions, albeit indirectly, in the belief that only by reconstructing the meaning which work held for contempo-raries can an adequate account of its significance for women be given.

Defoe's novel is a good starting point, because it introduces us to some of the many ways in which the work of women could be conceived. Its evocation of Moll's childhood[4] was constructed from several components. Much of its content, the practices of fosterage and service, the intervention of the urban authorities in the training of the young poor, the employment offered by needle-work, spinning and washing and their meagre rewards, reflected the circumstances of Defoe's own world of the 1720s, which he described at greater length in his *Tour* and other

works.[5] This material was used to furnish Moll's life,
which was then formally arranged as a specimen of
criminal autobiography, in the manner of the *True
Relation . . . of Mrs. Mary Frith, commonly called Mall
Cutpurse,* or the *Memories of the Life of the Famous
Madam Charlton,* works which were in circulation in
Defoe's youth when he is said to have 'devoured every
scrap of print he could set eyes on'.[6] Some narrative
artifice was required, however, for Defoe to place his
heroine within a social context whilst keeping her free of
any specific social background. Born in Newgate, her
mother transported, she arrived in Colchester with a
gypsy band, whose convenient departure left her isolated,
and without memory of any earlier place of settlement. It
is on this basis that Defoe persuades us she was not
immediately moved on to another parish by the local
overseers:

> for though I was not a parish charge upon this or
> that part of the town by law, yet as my case came
> to be known . . . compassion moved the magistrates
> of the town, to take care of me, and I became one
> of their own as much as if I had been born in the
> place. [7]

A reader familiar with the contemporary settlement
laws and the disputes to which they gave rise cannot
have failed to notice Moll's good fortune in finding
herself in this, rather than another less charitable,
town.[8] This device provides a clue to the moral economy
which lurks beneath the fake criminal autobiography; for
Defoe was interested in the care of children as a subject
in its own right, and very willing to expose the failings
of his fellow-countrymen in this field.[9] Moll's story has
barely begun before we are told, in her third paragraph,
'that in one of our neighbouring nations, whether it be
France or where else I know not', immediate provision
was made for the children of condemned criminals in a
'house of orphans'. Children trained there were all able
to provide for themselves by 'an honest, industrious
behaviour'. Lacking such help, Moll was brought

> even before I was capable of understanding my case
> or how to amend it . . . into a course of life,
> scandalous in itself, and which in its ordinary
> course tended to the swift destruction both of soul
> and body.

Only extraordinary good fortune led to her rescue and
training by a nurse, who 'bred up the children with a
great deal of art, as well as a great deal of care . . .

very religiously also . . . . very housewifely and clean; . . . very mannerly, and with good behaviour'. [10] In this way Defoe, author of *The Family Instructor*, moulded a criminal autobiography which he had already embellished with contemporary economic detail. Moll's story thus became a moral tale implicating the contemporary reader's own willingness to promote a civilised society, as well as Moll's willingness to embrace that society's vices. [11]

III

We began with the artless words with which the young Moll attempted to make sense of the adult world of work. On closer inspection it is clear that her story is a highly complex and artificial creation, despite the simplicity and even popularity of its form and style. A full analysis of its effect on the contemporary reader, and of that reader's contributory response, is beyond the scope of this paper. [12] But even a brief glance at such a book reveals how powerful images of work and gender could become embedded in the least likely productions of contemporary culture. Defoe's artfully constructed story lies at one end of the spectrum of historical evidence. It is explicit and clearly focused, and belongs to a genre which depended for effect on a substantial degree of verisimilitude. Real girls who were reluctant to enter service are not hard to find in the sessions records of the time. [13] Much of our documentation, by comparison, concerns women only incidentally or implicitly, and makes the discovery of their thoughts and feeling about work a question of inference, if not of guesswork. Yet all our sources, novels and sessions rolls alike, are the products of a complicated society that was structured, among other means, by ideas, assumptions, and images of work. It is with that patterning of ideas about work that the rest of this paper is concerned.

Some preliminary remarks about the framework of women's work in this period are required. It should be borne in mind that there were important variations between countryside and town, between cottager or pauper families and those of yeomen or artisans, and between one part of the country and another. For the majority of women below gentry status, life saw a series of transitions; from childhood, through service, into marriage and motherhood, with the possibilities of widowhood and remarriage beyond. Childhood for many girls was already a time of work, which began at the ages of four or five for the very poor. By her seventh year the daughter of one unemployed Norwich labourer could both 'knit and spin'. A fourteen year old girl in the same city was providing the 'chief living' for her forty-six year old father's family in 1570, by knitting 'great hose'.[14] The move from home into service on a farm or in a crafts-man's household was thus not necessarily a move from play into work, although a handful even of the officially designated poor families in Elizabethan Norwich were able to send their daughters to school, at least for a time, and if only to a neighbouring widow who would teach them to spin.[15] Moll would have recognised this environment.

Service provided by far the most common form of education and training for girls in their late teens and early twenties. Of the 20-24 female age group in Ealing, Middlesex, in 1599 some 58% were in service; a similar proportion, 43%, were in service in the Warwickshire village of Chilvers Coton in 1684.[16] Rural girls commonly left home for service about the age of 13 or 14,[17] and service probably began at much the same time in the towns.[18] Migrant girls seeking work in London, many of whom had lost their parents, however, moved at a rather later age in the late sixteenth and early seventeenth centuries, closer to 17 or 18.[19] Where local authorities feared the burden of a rising poor rate, the children of pauper families, or orphans like Moll, might be put out to service or apprenticeship at a much earlier age.[20] Service brought the acquisition of adult skills on the farm or in the household, and rural servants in particular must have built up a varied fund of experience through their annual moves at hiring time from farm to farm.[21]

The age of marriage in this society was late, at a mean age of 26 for seventeenth-century women to judge from family reconstitution studies, though important regional and occupational variations must be kept in mind.[22] The great majority of women married, the propor-tion of the female population remaining unmarried falling from 27% for women in their early 30s to only 7% for those a decade older.[23] The character of a woman's work after marriage was strongly moulded by the age, skills, capital and occupation of her partner; the connections between male and female spheres of activity within marriage were complex and very variable from one household to another. The wife's activity was also affected by the characteris-tics of the local economy, by the nature of its marketing system, the availability of industrial by-employments or casual agricultural work, and by the number of servants and other resources at her command.[24]

Her husband's death freed a woman from the legal constraints on her activity associated with her status as daughter, servant or wife. Between a fifth and a half of all women may have been left in this position in different early modern communities.[25] For those who inherited their husband's workshops widowhood might offer the opportunity of economic independence for the first time, though widowhood could be an unhappy state for the poor. Some forms of work, ale-selling or teaching children to spin, for example, were often informally reserved for such poor women. Remarriage was not infrequent; as many as 30% of marriage partners in the mid-sixteenth century may have been married before.[26] The likelihood of a husband's death, the character of widowhood and the prospects for a widow's remarriage were all affected by her original choice of partner, and by the difference in their ages. Remarriage was also probably linked to the prevailing demand for landholdings, which was high in the populous late sixteenth century, and lower by 1700.[27]

Members of the nobility and gentry probably married earlier than their social inferiors; but among the lower orders, too, there were important variations. Those with a wage income from a craft or farm labour were able to marry earlier than couples hoping to inherit property from their yeomen or husbandmen parents.[28] A recent survey of London brides has suggested that in a metropolitan context the bride's origin – in the city itself, or in a place from which she had migrated – was a more important factor in the determination of marital age differences than the status or occupation of the bride or groom. Migrant women were married later, to men of ages similar to their own, and may have had greater freedom in the choice of spouse and the conduct of the courtship.[29] But how far proximity of age affected a couple's working relationship remains to be investigated. Moreover, this evidence concerns only one sixth of London brides, those who could afford to marry by licence, and the fortunes and behaviour of poorer girls may have been rather different. One of the factors which may be presumed to have affected the approach to marriage at different social levels was the significance which was given to women's work. It is to the patterns of ideas which gave meaning to the various kinds of women's work that we must now turn.

How best to study that patterning of ideas is not clear. We have at our disposal a wide range of evidence, generated by very different processes and requiring more or less distinct methods of interpretation. The most explicit and extended discussions of work are found in the printed texts of preachers, administrators and philanthropists. But much of use can also be found in contemporary jest books, courtesy literature, and tracts detailing the supposed virtues and vices of women; in the poetry, plays and romances which entertained members of both sexes;

and amongst a miscellany of other materials such as almanacs, ballads and collections of proverbial sayings. These 'literary' sources raise a number of questions. Is it legitimate to draw information from texts of different dates, even when these were composed with a common genre? How can we discriminate between the more and the less influential ideas current at the time? What does 'influence' of this kind mean? How reliable are the numbers of published texts as a guide to their readership or popularity?

The interpretation of such sources has generally been undertaken in recent years through the study of particular genres of writing, rather than of associated patterns of ideas. This has enabled authors' intentions and the characters of their audience to be mapped out in some cases at least,[30] but it has also meant that we still lack an account of contemporary attitudes towards work which could match those available for ideas about politics or religion.[31] Without such an account, even one founded only on extant printed sources, such documentary evidence as we have of popular reactions to work and to women's involvement in it is difficult to interpret. The source of any changes in attitude, and the relationship between plebeian and elite conceptions of work must also remain mysterious. In writing about attitudes to women's work, therefore, we are inevitably exploring on two fronts: into the field of women's history on the one hand, and into the history of 'work' on the other.

As a step in the latter direction we might begin by identifying a number of approaches towards work which recur in the printed evidence. These characterised it respectively as vocation, art, employment, occupation, or pastoral escape from care. Each of these perspectives was widely disseminated in print during the sixteenth and seventeenth centuries, though not always among the same groups of readers. Together, they provide a provisional framework within which we may subsequently be able to locate notions of work expressed in other sources, and against which it may ultimately prove possible to chart the differences of approach to work between one social group, or one period, and another. It must be stressed that in the space available only a preliminary sketch of these ideas and their implications can be offered, and that on the connections between specific social groups and particular ways of thinking much still needs to be done. Some small progress can perhaps be made, however, by situating Defoe's evocation of a girl's view of work within a broader context of ideas, both to illuminate a relatively neglected aspect of contemporary 'service', and to explore the comparative strengths and weaknesses of 'literary' and documentary evidence.

IV

Among the intellectual creations commonly attributed to sixteenth-century Protestant reformers is the concept of calling or vocation, 'a certain kind of life ordained and imposed upon man by God for the common good'.[32] It provided a means of conceptualising the activities of all social groups in the same terms, as so many examples of divinely ordained, purposeful, behaviour.[33] The idea drew much from earlier, pre-Reformation, attempts to view the social and occupational structure in the round. Such was the theory of the three orders (of priests, warriors and labourers), which by the fourteenth century, and perhaps earlier, was being adapted to account for a greater variety of social roles, comprehending the student, craftsman, servant, merchant and judge 'so every man travail in his degree'.[34] Organic explanations of differing social roles, as propounded by Plato or Aquinas, were likewise influential in forming the idea of a calling. William Perkins' detailed classification of general and particular callings, written c. 1600 and widely influential thereafter, compared the distribution of callings within society to the form of the human body, wherein 'there be sundry parts and members, and every one hath his several use and office, which it performeth not for it self, but for the good of the whole body; as the office of the eye is to see, the ear to hear, and the foot to go'.[35] Such an approach to work could be lent an egalitarian emphasis:

> Every man, of every degree, as well rich as poor, as well mighty as mean, as well noble as base, must know that he is born for some employment to the good of his brethren, if he will acknowledge himself to be a member, and not an ulcer, in the body of mankind.[36]

It also permitted the fusing of divine purpose with the urgings of ordinary secular appetites. John Donne explained that

> to go on industriously in an honest calling, and giving God his portion all the way, in tithes, and in alms, and then, still to lay up something for posterity, is that which God does not only permit and accept from us, but command to us, and reward in us.[37]

Seventeenth-century exponents of this view addressed themselves directly to those engaged in honest work, to *The Religious Weaver*, or to expound on *Husbandry Spiritualised, or the Tradesman's Calling.*[38]

The significance of this view of work for women, however, was ambiguous. The tendency to elevate even the humblest manual labour as a calling certainly offered to place the work of women servants on a par with that of men. 'If we compare work to work', explained William Perkins, 'there is a difference betwixt washing of dishes, and preaching the word of God: but as touching to please God none at all'. Luther had earlier concluded that 'the works of monks and priests, be they never as holy and arduous, differ no whit in the sight of God from the works of the rustic toiling in the field or the woman going about her household tasks'.[39] The idea of a calling thus offered a way of looking at female work which took account of its low social status without postulating any radical distinction between male and female activities. For the pursuit of a calling was to be followed, according to Robert Bolton, 'in conscience and obedience to that common charge, laid upon all the sons and daughters of Adam to the world's end'.[40] Gallants were to be condemned, thought Robert Sanderson, because 'they neither labour nor spin'. 'God doth call every man and woman', wrote Richard Steele.[41] Taken to one conclusion, the doctrine permitted the untutored, with women in their ranks, to preach.[42]

But the linking of vocation to the social order also implied a need for conformity to established values. Viewed in this light, as may have become more common by the end of the second half of the seventeenth century, [43] the doctrine provided for women merely a redescription of their existing occupational subordination. The Christian industriously following a calling with a view to the inheritance of posterity tended to be a man who, in Donne's words, 'shall not stand so right in God's eye at the last day, that leaves his children to the parish, as he that leaves the parish to his children . . .'[44] The most extended treatment of female activities within the vocational framework came indeed not in the discussion of such callings as those of the merchant or husbandman, 'as serve only for the good . . . estate of society', but in the consideration of the personal callings of husband and wife, master and servant, magistrate and subject, which were 'of the essence and foundation of any society, without which the society cannot be'.[45] By embracing both occupations and more general social roles, such as that of the wife, within one view of social activity vocational theorists thus made possible the elevation of household tasks to a certain dignity. The author of *The Ladies Calling* recommended even the woman of a 'great family' to undertake this role, not least since

> her more constant residence gives her more opportun-
> ity of it, then the frequent avocations of the

husband will perhaps allow him. St. Paul sets it as the calling, and the indispensible duty of the married women, that they guide the house, 1 Tim. 5.18. not thinking it a point of greatness to remit the manage of all domestic concerns to a mercenary house-keeper.[46]

But the assumed inter-changeability of the wife's role in such a family with the work of her servant, together with the transparently utilitarian motives for the suggestion in an age when 'mercenary' servants were thought to be both expensive and unruly, can have done little for the lady's dignity.[47]

V

A second approach to work conceived of it not so much as the basis of social relationships which were maintained through the interaction of callings, as rather the process whereby mankind interacted with nature, by means of art or skill. The distinction between 'art', as skill and cunning, and nature had been familiar enough to Chaucer. In the fourteenth century the realm of art already extended from the learning of the schoolmen on the one hand, to the work of Gower's artificers on the other, 'which use crafts and mysteries, whose art is called mechanique'.[48] The key to this view of work lay in its emphasis on the use of artfulness and skill to transcend the demeaning confines of mere manual labour. This emphasis justified the recognition of a hierarchy of work which could in turn be associated with the existing social order. The approach may have drawn something from the pride and exclusiveness of the gilds, and from the medieval upper-class contempt for manual labour which persisted into the sixteenth and seventeenth centuries. [49] Unlike the vocational approach, this view of work did little to elevate the status of humbler occupations, even though it subsumed all work under the common yardstick of degrees of art. The first English dictionary definitions of work were written from this point of view. 'Labour' consisted of 'pains, toil and work', the labourer being one 'that does drudgery work'. 'Drudgery' was in turn defined as 'dirty laborious work, slavery', and the slave was 'a perpetual servant, a drudge'. Such painful and ignoble activity was contrasted with art, 'all that which is performed by the wit and industry of man'. The arts were divisible along lines laid down by Bacon into 'liberal' and 'mechanic' pursuits. The former were such as 'are noble and genteel, viz. grammar, rhetoric, music, physic, the mathematics, &c.', whilst the mechanic arts were such 'as require more of the labour of the hand and body, than of the mind; as carpenters, carvers, gravers, statuaries, &c.'.[50] This scheme, loosely applied, might still give dignity to mundane occupations such as the *Art of Water-Drawing*, the *Art of Pruning*, the *Art of Simpling* or the *Art of Good Husbandry*,[51] but it left many working activities in a lower sphere of servitude or even slavery. Wage-work, in particular, was often regarded as a servile activity, both because it was performed under the direction of a master, and because much of it was carried out by the young, working as servants for example, whose own status and respectability were in contemporary terms low.[52]

The characterisation of work as a productive wrestling with nature, either through laborious toil, or through the agency of instruments as a mechanic art, had complex implications for the evaluation of women's work. On one level, the institutionalised controls on access to mechanic arts might prove disadvantageous to women. Alice Clark's influential account of seventeenth-century working women, for example, stressed the closing of opportunities to work as skilled artisans or tradeswomen with control over their own workshops and equipment.[53] At another level, the role of strenuous effort in defining gender had the effect of limiting the appreciation of activities which women were able to carry out. Though the sixteenth century saw the transformation of the inherited notion of woman in several respects, including the medical, her assumed physical frailty and mental instability remained fundamental to intellectual views of women, and to the treatment of women more generally.[54] The implications of these assumptions were felt with varying degrees of severity. In the physically testing environment of harvest work they helped to sustain a particular sexual division of labour.[55] The assumed centrality of a woman's reproductive function might enable her legitimate activity to be confined, at least in print, to the home and what was described as 'an easy life'.[56] Within the household menstruation might further circumscribe her her activity.[57] Arduous efforts were confined to the male sphere of work. The heraldic device symbolising labour and industry was a masculine arm, 'fortified . . . with strong arteries, nerves, muscles and sinews'. Femininity, by contrast, was a kind of natural idleness, corrupting the ability and will to work like too much prosperity or love of worldly beauty which, thought John Downame, 'hurteth ourselves both in our bodies, soules and names; our bodies thereby are made more tender soft and effeminate, yea also more weak and sickly . . .'[58]

Yet the metaphorical view of feminine characteristics

had also to be reconciled with the work which women actually did perform. When English writers considered the social structure of the North American Indians, the only aspect they unanimously condemned was its implicit affront to English priorities in allocating labour, so that, as John Smith put it in 1612, 'the women be very painful and the men often idle'.[59] In England itself the notion of feminine incapacity was likewise challenged by the evident participation of women in many kinds of strenuous work. One solution lay in postulating socially divergent feminine capacities. It was suggested, for example, that country women whose work brought them plenty of exercise menstruated only briefly.[60] Another resolution of the dilemma was achieved admitting the centrality of the female reproductive function, as a form of work, whilst simultaneously dismissing it under the description not of 'art', but of mere bodily 'travail' or 'labour'.[61]

VI

Our third approach to work stressed neither its significance as a godly calling, nor its place in the spectrum of art and labour, but its value as employment. This was characteristically the preoccupation of councillors and magistrates, of projectors and pamphleteers, and of church ministers and overseers of the poor. Tudor MPs inherited a concern for the regulation of employment conditions from their medieval predecessors,[62] a concern which was intensified by the impoverishment brought by demographic growth and inflation during the sixteenth and early seventeenth centuries.[63] These pressures engendered an approach to work which coupled moral disapproval of idleness, with a practical zeal to win the pauperised and under-employed to regular, self-sustaining work. Added to the praise of industry and denunciation of idleness, was an emphasis on the effective employment of one's time. This was no new phenomenon; it can be traced well back into the Middle Ages.[64] But the emphasis was particularly characteristic of vocational doctrine, and increasingly so during the course of the seventeenth century.[65] These various influences were fused into a remarkable body of writing on the employment of the poor which characterised the decades after 1660.[66] 'People are the wealth of the nation', it was argued towards the end of the century, – by which 'it is only meant, laborious and industrial people, and not such as are wholly unemployed, as gentry, clergy, lawyers, servingmen and beggars, etc.'.[67] Though drawing on vocational thinking, the philosophy of employment at the same time diminished unproductive social roles, echoing an old distaste for 'caterpillars' on the body of the commonweal which had been familiar in the sixteenth century when the first employment schemes were launched.

This approach to work took for granted the low social standing of much laborious or repetitive work whilst nonetheless recognising its economic potential. The schemes which were devised to employ the poor and halt the squandering of God-given resources had important implications for women.[68] For a writer such as Thomas Firmin, in 1678, the poor lacked the domestic resources to offer the wife a full-scale calling.

As, suppose a poor woman that goes three days a week to wash or scour abroad, or one that is employed in nurse-keeping three or four months in a year, or a poor market-woman, who attends three or four mornings in a week with her basket, and all the rest of the time these folks have little or nothing to do.

Some of the work such women found themselves, moreover, resembled the pseudo-employments common among modern immigrants to third world towns. Daniel Defoe described how even the more demeaning services of the urban apprentice, such as cleaning his master's shoes, were taken over in this way, as 'there are poor women generally at the shop-doors, to do those things, as well as for the apprentices as for the masters, and they are paid for it'.[69]

Firmin's solution was to eradicate reliance on intermittent work by providing regular spinning employment, through which means the women 'are not only kept within doors . . . but made much more happy and cheerful'. The emphasis on confinement 'within doors' was possibly a reaction to the fact that poorer women, lacking capital and other scope for domestic production, were noticeably more mobile than the wives of yeomen or tradesmen. Even when engaged in industrial work they might still be difficult to pin down. A traveller in Suffolk in the early 1680s saw women 'go spinning up and down the way as I went with a rack and distaff in their hands', and like Firmin, he assumed that such employment must make the women more cheerful. For 'if a comparison were to be made between the ploughmen and the good wives of these parts, their life were more pleasant, for they can go with their work to good company, and the poor ploughman must do his work alone'.[70]

In its most successful form, however, it was intended that employment for women should bring them more than cheerfulness. 'For there are several mysteries and employments', explained Carew Reynell in 1674 'that even women, nay children of eight or nine years old, would earn more money [in] than they spend'. Walter Blith hoped to see 'the poor in every parish, maintained, both comfortably in a calling and livelihood, especially all women kind, and children . . . fitted and brought up to a trade and way, that may render them publicly useful to the nation'.[71] Vocational thinking thus encouraged an interest in seeking out, and even originating, employment. Concern to utilise female resources even extended to the wives of middling families, whose work is thought to have grown increasingly circumscribed in this period.[72] Defoe was to condemn the reluctance of businessmen's wives 'to be seen in the counting house'. Writing for gentlewomen in the 1670s, Richard Allestree likewise argued that 'he that shall consider the description which Solomon gives of a virtuous wife, Prov[erbs], 31, will be apt to think her province is not so narrow and confined, as the humour of the age would represent it'.[73] The trades in which poorer girls were to be inducted by employment schemes, however, were predictably limited; to 'spinning, carding, sewing, weaving lace, ribbon, tape, and other things; in setting of cushions, carpets, hangings, and other things fit for the work of women', as one writer put it in 1659. Poverty and the humble employments of poor women were indeed symbolically intertwined in the seventeenth century through the use of images of their work, as spinsters, washerwomen and the like, to indicate the purpose of the small change tokens that were minted to facilitate payment to, and purchases by, the poor.[74]

VII

Continuous employment in a form of work endowed the worker with a recognisable 'occupation'. This way of conceiving work had long preceded the emphasis on callings which characterised the sermons of the late sixteenth and seventeenth centuries. The medieval gilds had shown how work could be bound up together with a whole way of life through a specific craft training, with its own tools and technical vocabulary, provision for the welfare of the entire family, and festive or religious ceremonies and symbols. A similarly close relationship between family and occupation was sustained by those dynasties of craftsmen whose tools and experience were passed down through the generations. Occupations had long since given rise to permanent surnames. Work conducted in these terms had an apparent solidity which resisted the mutability of everyday life. When William

Perkins came to explain the strengths of pursuing a single calling he turned easily to this sense of security, expressed in the popular adage that 'an occupation is as good as land': 'because land may be lost, but skill and labour in a good occupation is profitable to the end because it will help at need when land and all things fail'.[75]

The solidity of an 'occupation' in this period of economic change was indeed often more apparent than real; employment for many was an intermittent experience, and several kinds of work had often to be combined to make a living. Yet the discussion of work in terms of a range of distinct 'occupations' did not wane, and may even have grown in frequency during this period.[76] There were many reasons for this. Growing landlessness made the work of the rural poor more visible as they turned from working their own holding to selling their labour on the open market. The 'cottager' or 'husbandman' was thus transformed into a 'labourer'. In a society with considerable geographical mobility, with an increasingly large metropolis drawing many hundreds of migrants to it each year, there was also much to be said for replacing location by occupation as a means of casual identification. At the same time an increasingly sophisticated administration capitalised on growing literacy to record and classify the population in greater detail, using a record of occupation to enable it to identify those best able to fill its needs: for more taxation or fighting men, or for lower poor rates and fewer wandering vagrants. Some ministers even extended the practice to their parish register. At this more intimate level, as in the similar case of the testator and appraisers of a will, an occupational designation provided an opportunity for those with perhaps complex sources of income to choose their preferred identity, and for their neighbours to exercise their own judgement on the matter.[77] The use of occupational labels, then, need not have been very closely connected with developments in the world of work to achieve popularity. In the case of writers attempting a rounded description of their society, however, an increased awareness of the value of the working population probably did encourage the greater sensitivity to occupational distinctions which characterised their works in the later seventeenth and eighteenth centuries, when compared with those of their sixteenth-century forebears.[78]

The survival of occupational designations in our sources can be very beguiling for the historian of labour. They enable us to construct pictures of the contemporary 'occupational structure' in great detail, to compare one locality with another, and to trace the impact of change

over time.[79] However, for the historian of women's work
their usefulness is more limited, and they may indeed be
seriously misleading. It is generally assumed that the
occupational designations which appear in our records
reflect the association of the individuals concerned with
work of some specialisation and continuity. Women were
much less frequently identified by these means than were
men, more commonly being distinguished in parish
registers and the like in terms of marital status.[80] This
practice has been attributed to the comparatively
restricted range of occupations followed by women, which
made this a less useful form of identification than the use
of marital status, or the husband's name and occupation.[81]
Other historians have concluded from similar evidence that
'women were presumably engaged for the most part either
in domestic work or in unspecified agricultural labour'. [82]
How convincing is the assumption that this distinct use
of occupational designations reflected a real difference in
the character of work undertaken by the two sexes?

Were we to define the pursuit of an occupation as
the regular, daily undertaking of the same kind of work,
exercising skills learnt and rights to trade obtained
through a lengthy apprenticeship, there is no doubt that
we should have to conclude that the great majority of the
women of early modern England were not, in this sense,
'occupied'. It is clear, too, however, that a great many
men would also fail to qualify by these criteria. Seasonal
or sporadic unemployment; the combination of one trade
with another, or with husbandry; the pursuit of a 'trade'
without serving apprenticeship; each of these factors
blurred the 'occupational commitment' of many men.[83] Evidence of multiple employment, or of the combination of a
trade with farming, is sufficiently extensive to have
cautioned historians against accepting the occupational
information concerning men in our records at face value. [84]
But the implications for the study of women's work seem
to have been overlooked. We need to ask why, if
occupational designations for men conceal a sometimes very
complex working lifestyle, they were nonetheless still used
extensively in contemporary documents, whereas their
female equivalents were not. It is arguable that the
explanation lies not in the character of the work undertaken, but in the different relationships to authority of
contemporary men and women. As heads of their households
husbands were given priority by record-keepers over
women; their names were listed first, and their activities
recorded in greater detail. Insofar as officials communi-
cated an interest in the occupational status of individuals
this, again, impinged on men before it affected women. As
the active, representative, and outward-going head of his
family, moreover, the male was assumed to possess an

occupational identity far stronger than anything experienced by women. In many cases, of course, the husband's occupational identity served for the whole family, his wife and children assisting him at his work.[85] But even where this was not the case, as with many of the poorer families in Elizabethan Norwich, record-keepers persisted in assuming that women merely 'did' various kinds of work, whereas their husbands were identified by them. The Norwich authorities consistently referred to men in occupational terms, as 'John Brother, knacker', but to their wives as women 'that spin white warp', 'that knit & wash & help others' or 'that soweth & make bone lace'. [86] This was done even where the men, but not their wives, were unemployed, and even where the men followed two occupations or had changed from one to another, such as Thomas Fraunces 'a smith & boatman', or John Yonges, 'cordwainer journeyman & now a waterman'.[87] Women were not completely excluded from this kind of description; John Yonges' wife was indeed listed as 'a spinner of webbing wool'. But this equality of treatment was unusual, and largely confined to spinners of this kind. Throughout the 1570 Norwich census it was to the husband's name that the phrase 'in work', or 'not in work' was attached, and in some cases employment was even expressed by a soon to be obsolete word derived from the idea of occupation; John Davi was described as a 'baker, of 40 years, that occupy labouring'; Robert Polter as 'of 30 years, a keelman that occupy'; and John Browne as 'of 50 years, a baker, & occupy to gather cony skins'. Women were not stated to 'occupy' their lives in this way.[88]

Occupational designations, then, did not bear a direct relationship to the character of work actually undertaken by the people so described. They served, particularly in towns with elaborate gild structures, to confer a legal and fiscal identity as much as an economic one. In London between the fourteenth and the sixteenth centuries 'occupational ascriptions came to mean no more than gild and company membership, which might or might not provide some indication of occupation. The great variety of activities of the City's freemen was, as it were, drawn superficially within a straitjacket which served to channel political and social aspirations and helped to solve some of the problems of municipal control of trade'. [89] London may have been an extreme case, but changes in the work performed by individual members of a gild or 'occupation' are familiar enough from other towns. In the records of early modern Leicester it has been concluded that 'style was no guide to occupation and no sure guide to class'.[90] It would seem, from the above discussion, to be also a misleading indicator of differences in the continuity and specialisation of work between the sexes. The consignment of so much of women's work to a residual sphere of activity, occupationally unlabelled, and outside the well-documented male 'occupational structure' needs to be carefully reconsidered. 'The male weaver', we are told of eighteenth-century industry, 'took the name of the trade and for the most part did perform the core craft operation, but the family was necessary to perform the many subsidiary but essential operations in the making of cloth'.[91] The history of women's work in this period is very much the history of how such 'trades' and supposedly 'core craft operations' were defined, and allocated between the sexes.

We have examined some of the implications for women's work and its evaluation of the development of a more extensive occupational vocabulary in this period. It remains to be seen how far the formal constitution of occupations affected women's working lives. Early modern women participated in a wide range of trades numerically dominated by male labour, but their roles were often circumscribed by the institutional forms taken by crafts, arts and mysteries.[92] The availability of the necessary tools and training was limited by the treatment of these as forms of property, to be bequeathed where possible to a son.[93] Capital, too, was bequeathed away from women in this way. Hugh Peters was one of several reformers who argued that 'if daughters were ingenious and would work they ought to have equal portions with sons'.[94] The importance of 'breeding' in the transference of craft skills was further emphasised by the methods used to introduce foreign production techniques into England; individuals, and sometimes whole communities of craftsmen, including refugees, were settled to pass on their skills, and ultimately to intermarry with the local population.[95] Women, of course, inherited their own peculiar skills, such as dairying, from their mothers.[96]

Though a woman might on occasion inherit trading privileges from a husband or father, her subordinate status within the gild could still be ritually confirmed. Fellow craftsmen attended the marriages of Coventry gild members, and the funeral of a craftsman was a craft occasion at which the widow's inheritance of occupational privileges was legitimised.[97] Though not all such widows remarried, and some continued their husbands' businesses unaided,[98] their dependence on men was popularly supposed to have continued, exemplified in the image of the widow as a lusty woman, her sexual appetites awakened, eager to remarry.[99] 'The widow weeps with one eye', ran the adage, 'and casts glances with the other'.[100]

A whole set of assumptions of this kind, tied up not simply with notions of work, but also with conceptions of womanhood and the household, served to maintain a situation in which, to borrow the description used by Natalie Davis of sixteenth-century France, the occupational identity of women 'was thin, their productive energies available to be shifted into other work channels if circumstances demanded it'.[101] The same flexibility of female work has also been observed in eighteenth-century France by Olwen Hufton, whose analysis has seen poor women as the principal sustainers of a precarious 'economy of make-shifts'.[102] But how far are such conclusions applicable to early modern England? It is one thing to identify differences in the terms in which male and female workers were described, and another to conclude that such distinctions represented real differences in the 'shape' of the work they undertook, differences in its continuity, specialisation, or complexity. For while the public presence and continuity of male trades were sustained by their institutional forms, their official recognition, and their popular reputations, continuous and exclusive employment in a single occupation was not guaranteed even for men in a society of multiple employments, frequent natural disasters, and recurrent dislocations of trade.[103] Moreover, there were certain kinds of work which were undertaken by women with sufficient regularity for them to have been recognised as 'women's' or 'housewives' trades'.

The way in which these terms were used, however, surreptitiously confirmed the transient character of feminine 'occupations'. One early seventeenth-century commentator advised men to avoid what he described as 'housewives' trades (as brewer, baker, cook, and the like) because they be the skill of women as well as of men and common to both'.[104] 'Men's trades' were not, of course, normally regarded as equally available to women. In other cases, women's occupational statuses were fused with their marital standing, as 'herb wives, tripe wives, and the like'.[105] In this way their somewhat insubstantial occupational status was maintained. In turn, men assumed a real weakness in women's occupational commitments. 'Their employments', wrote one who compared their work with men's, '(for the most part) may better admit of intermission for them to go out to Church twice a day'.[106] At the same time, women's presumed reluctance to make a way of life of their occupations freed them to make up for the deficiencies of men in this respect. A proposal of 1739 advocated the transfer to women of several sections of the retail trade:

> There are few trades in which women cannot weigh and measure as well as men, and are so capable of selling as they, and I am sure will buy as cheap, and perhaps cheaper: For they can go to the whole-

141

sale merchant's house, and purchase their goods; whereas the men generally transact all business of this kind in taverns and coffee-houses, at great additional expence, and the loss of much time . . .[107]

Proposals for the formal admission of women to trades were necessary because women were so often excluded from independent participation by the institutions of apprenticeship and 'freedom', which conferred gild membership and the right to trade. The proportion of female apprentices recorded in surviving indentures from a wide range of locations was normally smaller than 10% of the total.[108] Where this proportion rose, to around 23% in seventeenth-century Southampton, or to 33% in Eaton Socon, Bedfordshire, during 1693-1731, it did so because apprenticeship was being used by local authorities as a vehicle for the settling and employing of pauper children.[109] How far the normally small numbers of girls who were apprenticed actually learnt the trade of their masters is uncertain. More than a third of the 106 girls apprenticed in Bristol during 1532-52 were to be trained in the 'art of the housewife', or 'in occupation of housewifeship'. Another 30 girls were to learn the skills of the shepster (tailoring) or seamstress. None of the girls were to be given tools at the end of their terms, a practice common enough among the Bristol boys, though several were to be given a cash sum which would have served well as a dowry, and others were to receive some clothes.[110] Female apprenticeships to housewifery were entered in other places, and many of those girls indentured to unspecific occupations may have been intended for work of similar character.[111] 'Housewifery', of course, itself encompassed a number of skills. A Bedfordshire girl was apprenticed to 'good housewifery, and to sew, knit and spin and other such like works fitting for her' in the 1630s. Susan Godwyne of Kingston-on-Thames was bound in 1648 'to be taught to spin, card, knit and other things belonging to housekeeping'. Agnes Veale had earlier been bound to be taught 'all things that belong to the maid servant of a husbandman' in 1610.[112] The very many girls who were apprenticed to mantua-makers, lace-makers or seamstresses may thus have led very similar lives to those of the girls apprenticed to 'housewifery' and employed in domestic industry. The acquisition of industrial skills, by one means or another, was certainly of importance to women, as Moll Flanders knew. It drew a girl back from reliance on unskilled, and poorly paid, labouring, and was a valuable marital asset. Sarah Gibson, apprenticed to a Holborn widow as a mantua-maker, was released from her mistress in 1715 because she had encountered the kind of harsh house-work that the young Moll feared: 'instead of

learning the trade of a mantua-maker she had been
employed in common household work, cleansing and
washing lodgers' rooms and had been immoderately beaten
and not allowed sufficient food'.[113]
     In most cases, however, the precise relationship
between girl apprentices and their masters and mistresses
is obscured by the practice of recording apprenticeships
in the name of a couple, or of the husband alone.[114] The
number of female 'masters' recorded in indentures is
small,[115] though there are many signs that a wife would
have participated, or even taken the lead in training
such a girl. In certain Surrey indentures the positioning
of the trade to be learnt after the husband's name (in
the case of a goldsmith or fisherman) or the wife's (in
the case of mantua-makers, coat-makers or tailors) may
indicate who was regarded as taking the principal
responsibility for training the apprentice.[116] The occupational terminology imposed on work by the gild structure
can in such cases be a poor guide to the work actually
being conducted, as in the case of the girl presented at
the Pewterers' Hall in London by a master pewterer 'to
learn the art of child's coat-making which his wife now
followeth'. Whichever skills female apprentices learnt,
however, few of them proceeded to take up their freedom
and to trade independently on that basis, even where, as
in sixteenth-century Bristol, their indentures had obliged
their masters to defray the necessary costs.[117] The skills
that were learnt were primarily deployed, and no doubt
further refined, within marriage, an institution which
diffused and diluted a woman's 'occupational' identity
among the many varied 'things belonging to housekeeping'.[118]
     In conceiving of work as divisible into a range of
'occupations', therefore, contemporaries generally assumed
that men rather than women would undertake a family's
defining occupation. There were some occasions on which
the existence of distinctively female trades was recognised, and this allowed the dominance of certain retail,
textile and food processing activities by women to be
conceived as an occupational phenomenon comparable with
that experienced by men. In the case of apprenticeships
to 'good housewifery' even the housewife's calling appears
to have been conceived in occupational terms. But this
approach to work was generally difficult to fuse with
other ways of thinking about women which concern themselves with delineating their position in the household.
The management of the domestic arrangements of a farm or
workshop, the tending of cattle, pigs or poultry, and the
feeding and clothing of servants, were activities as
complex and demanding as any man's occupation,
particularly when linked with the concomitant marketing of

143

produce, shop-work or part-time industrial production. Yet these were primarily viewed as the social obligations of a wife rather than as the 'occupation' of a married woman. The pastoral poet saw the woman's role in a different way again.

VIII

In the views of work which we have so far examined observation, evaluation, and exhortation were mixed in different measures. Our fifth and final contemporary perspective, the pastoral tradition, presents us with a view which seems the least exhortatory and the most idealised. Within the conventions of this ancient artistic genre, however, poets and painters wrestled with the same assumptions and contradictions which beset the preacher and pamphleteer when treating the question of women's work. The tradition offered the reader of poetry or spectator of painting a vivid image of work as antithesis or antidote to the stifling complexities of urban or courtly life. Its relationship to the actualities of working life was a shifting one, the blend of observation and ideali-sation in the composition of the rural idyll changing from one decade to another.[119] A prominent protagonist, the shepherdess, for example, was dispensible when a new figure, the milkmaid was thought to offer a more convincing picture to the poetry-reading audience of what rural life was actually like.[120]

In its treatment of rural work, the pastoral tradition provided its own distinctive images of rustic simplicity whilst drawing on other ways of apprehending the phenomenon of labour. Its impact as a reversal of the sophisticated values of its readers depended in part on the reversal of their conventional views of work. The pastoral poet was thus able to draw on, and poetically to overturn, the conventionally polite disdain for mere, artless, bodily labour.[121] Such idealisation of 'the simple life' was not, of course, the poet's sole prerogative; other writers used the same means to justify the lowly stations to which some workers had been called. 'Those who live softlier than others', advised Anthony Ascham,

> their natures receive no advantage by it; nay they are unhappier than the poor, because they cannot want so many things as the other can, and are more sharply punished for their delicateness; ploughmen being rarely racked with gouts, tormented with petulant consumptions, the stone, or the like.[122]

'Be thankful to God', Richard Baxter urged the labourer accordingly, 'who for a little bodily labour, doth free you from the burden of all these cares'. The melancholic law student John Manningham confided to his diary at the end of Elizabeth's reign that 'to keep sheep' was 'the best life'. 'Wilt thou be king?', he mused, 'Be a shepherd, thou hast subjects, thou hast abundant subjects, thou hast sheep, thou hast a sceptre, thou hast a crook'.[123]

If its preoccupation with the world of rural work sometimes gave a substantial dignity to the labourer, the pastoral tradition did little to reverse the conventional division of work between the labourer and his wife. Robert Herrick's poem, 'The Hock Cart', for example, places harvest work on the spectrum of art and labour from its opening lines. This harvest is a strenuous exercise of the male physique on the part of the sturdy 'sons of summer', 'By whose rough labours, and rough hands, We rip up first, then reap our lands'. The centrality of the male contribution to this work is later affirmed by the invitation to these 'harvest swains' to drink, to their lord, their tools, 'then to the maids with wheaten hats'.[124] Emphasis on the strenuous male contribution to harvest labour survived even the transformation of pastoral into anti-pastoral verse in the early eighteenth century at the hands of the thresher poet Stephen Duck. His account has been commended for its acknowledgement of the hardships of farm work; but its view of the woman's contribution to such work is, of course, a narrow one.[125] Duck's women are loyal housewives and childminders, who await their husbands' return from work:

> When sooty pease we thresh, you scarce can know
> Our native colour, as from work we go:
> The sweat, the dust, and suffocating smoke,
> Make us so much like Ethiopians look,
> We scare our wives, when evening brings us home;
> And frightened infants think the bugbear come.

The poet's account of cutting the grass stresses the artfulness and skill of those who wield the scythe, adding an heroic quality to their endeavours:

> And now the field, designed to try our might,
> At length appears, and meets our longing sight.
> The grass and ground we view with careful eyes,
> To see which way the best advantage lies;
> And, hero-like, each claims the foremost place.

This noble activity is sustained by the evening's welcoming domestic idyll:

> Homewards we move, but spent so much with toil,
> We slowly walk, and rest at every stile.
> Our good expecting wives, who think we stay,
> Got to the door, soon eye us in the way.
> Then from the pot the dumpling's catched in haste,
> And homely by its side the bacon placed. [126]

Duck's account of harvest work gives dignity and depth to some of the lowliest activities in the contemporary world of work. But he sustained his sense of work by associating it with the conventional image of a married male as head, and sustainer, of his household. His harvest has few women workers. We may be tempted to see in this a reflection, or premonition, of changes in the sexual division of harvest labour which were to become more apparent later in the century, with increasing specialisation in grain particularly in eastern England bringing a greater concentration on male as opposed to female harvest labour.[127] But Duck's casual treatment of women is more likely simply to have reflected his own assumptions as a somewhat negligent male breadwinner,[128] together with the conventions of the pastoral genre. His success in winning the patronage of Queen Caroline created a controversial vogue for plebeian poetry which saw the publication of verses by a bricklayer, footman, miller and weaver in the years 1731-34.[129] Out of this wave of writing came a point-for-point rejoinder to Duck's account of work, from the Hampshire washer-woman Mary Collier. This 17-page poem meticulously demonstrated the interlocking of male and female activities in a labourers' marriage.[130] Her description covers the following course of female work: at hay time raking and turning the hay, cooking, bed-making, feeding pigs, setting the table, serving meals, dressing and feeding the children, and mending their clothes; at harvest time reaping the wheat or gleaning whilst minding the youngest children, gathering the cut corn, and cutting peas; and after the harvest when men are threshing, charring or cleaning pewter and kitchen utensils, and brewing for neighbouring gentlewomen at daily wages, [131] the latter work often being performed at night. Collier deliberately countered the hardships of male work one by one, stressing women's contribution to cutting the wheat, their encounters with tight-fisted employers, the sheer number of their routine tasks, and their physical hardships. They pursued their night-time charring work

> Until with heat and work, 'tis often known,
> Not only sweat, but blood runs trickling down
> Our wrists and fingers; still our work demands
> The constant action of our labouring hands.

At the same time, however, the poem appears to claim for women's work a generally less heroic status than that claimed by Duck for the work of men; women figure prominently in the poem, alongside children, as gleaners; they 'help to reap the wheat', and 'take up the corn that you [the men] do now'. Though women are said to be 'always ready . . . in every work to take our proper share', it is clear that the boundaries of their 'proper' work extend to depths below those normally reached by men:

> No labour scorning, be it e'er so mean . . .
> So many hardships daily we go through,
> I boldly say, the like *you* never knew.[132]

The exchange between Duck and Collier drew some of its interest from the re-enactment in somewhat different form of a long-standing literary debate about the nature of marriage. This had been conducted in a wide range of publications from the most elaborate works of courtesy to the humblest chapbook,[133] and to judge from the prominence of advice on the topic in contemporary collections of proverbs,[134] the debate had also formed an important part of colloquial conversation. Work, and the contribution of each partner to its completion, were recurring themes in this debate, and the orderliness or otherwise of the marriages described was often determined on this basis. Misogynist writers systematically emphasised the husband's working efforts as the background against which he bore additional burdens created by an indolent or shrewish wife. On returning from a country visit such a husband 'settles to work, endeavours to set all things to rights, takes a great deal of pains', while his wife goes a-visiting to 'chat with her gossips'. On the birth of their first child she lies a-bed as he undergoes 'the drudgery of the day with care and pains'.[135] 'In the day, the husband must labour abroad', but with a shrew for a wife 'in the night at home, strife and contention is in his bed'.[136] The talkative wife of another man 'used to keep him waking past midnight, when the poor honest man, who had travelled [sc. worked] hard all day, had rather been at rest'.[137]

In these writings marriage was discouraged not because it lacked a conventional division of labour between the partners, but because the conventions were frequently undermined by the scheming or wilfulness of the wife. The woman's point of view was treated with varying degrees of sympathy. These may have corresponded to the hoped-for composition of the reading audience.[138] It was possible both to present a wifely case, and to undermine it through slight exaggeration. In one vignette a husband returning home tired and hungry from a business trip was told by his wife that

> I have lost more by my hemp and flax since your absence than you will get these five years, by taking your man along with you, so that I had no body to help to soak, or whiten it; besides . . . you did not stop the holes in the hen-house; for the stinking pole-cat hath eaten three of my best laying hens, whose loss is not so inconsiderable as you imagine . . . [139]

The sense of grievance here is convincing, but its impact lessened by a context which gives the male the reader's sympathy. In another instance a husband's offer to intervene to save his child from a beating is met with his wife's retort that 'you are not at the trouble of bringing them up, or looking after them; that is my drudgery, night and day, as long as I am able to stand upon my legs'.[140] The character of the husband's working activities is taken for granted in such instances, and by defending her own efforts the wife is made to lose our sympathy through the appearance of special pleading: 'I am up early, and down late, feeding your poultry, looking after your domestic affairs, spinning, carding, and what not, never idle, I am sure the care I take will shorten my days . . .'[141]

In the seventeenth century, however, the female audience for printed discussions of marriage was sufficiently large for some sustained sympathetic writing to be possible.[142] As with misogyny, this took a variety of forms, some highly stylised others apparently more 'realistic'. Of these the printed ballad was perhaps the form most calculated to appeal to a female audience.[143] The balladmaker was described by one character-writer as 'in pay by the country wenches, to write love stories to lamentable tunes, which they sing to the cows, and make them weep milky tears to hear them'.[144] Several seventeenth-century broadside ballads, however, recounted more down-to-earth female concerns. The *Careful Wife's Good Counsel* exhorted an erring husband to provident ways 'against a rainy day':

> I in thy yoke will draw with you,
> And what I can will freely do,
> If you the like will do again,
> Our charge I'm sure we may maintain;
> Thus by our labour then we may
> Save something for a rainy day.[145]

The same tale was told in the husband's voice by *A*

Caveat for Young Men, wherein a wife and her children
leave their home in protest against a husband's drinking:

> Half that you spend in vain,
>   and merely throw away,
> Our family would maintain,
>   and our house-rent it would pay.

The men in both cases end by acknowledging their wives'
advice, the second adding the warning:

> Now I all men advise,
>   this caveat think upon,
> Be ruled by your wives,
>   for old age it will come.[146]

Nor was this recognition of feminine sense exceptional. It
formed a prominent part of contemporary proverbial
wisdom, which averred that 'he that will thrive must ask
leave of his wife'; 'a good wife makes a good husband';
and 'a woman's advice is a poor thing, but he is a fool
who does not take it'.[147] Respect for wifely skills and
experience was also the theme of a rather different ballad
called *The Woman to the Plow.* In this a couple vexed
with each other's failings embark on an experiment in
role-reversal, with predictable and hilarious results, the
husband proving quite incapable of rivalling his wife's
experienced hand with a child or at the milking. The
concluding moral restores the conventional working roles,
but with enhanced credit for the woman:

> Take heed of this you husband-men,
> Let wives alone to grope the hen,
> And meddle you with the horse and ox,
> And keep your lambs safe from the fox,
> So shall you live contented lives,
> And take sweet pleasure in your wives.[148]

Hilarity was one means of coping with the tensions
within the existing sexual division of labour. But it is
worth remembering that the association of a particular
allocation of tasks with the existing social order made
some contemporaries react to any threatened change in
male and female roles with deadly seriousness. An early
English critic of Lutheran teaching claimed that in
Germany they

> confound and deface all good order of divine and
> humane things, allowing the women to serve the
> altar, and to say mass while the men tarry at
> home, and keep the children and wash their rags

149

and clothes: and as well they might allow the women
to be captains of their wars and to lead and guide
an army of men in battle, while their husbands
tarry at home to milk the cow, and serve the sow,
and spin and card.[149]

The spectacle of 'woman on top' was, of course, a
familiar theme of contemporary literature and ritual.[150]
Unlike certain chapbooks and ballads, however, most
pastoral poetry reversed only the conventional disdain for
labour, and retained the existing sexual division of
labour intact. The tone in which that division was
portrayed was capable of some modulation. Thomas
Campion's poem 'Jack and Jane' presented a pastoralised
image of domestic Christian harmony:

Jane can call by name her cows,
And deck her windows with green boughs;
She can wreaths and tutties make
And trim with plume a bridal cake.
Jack knows what brings gain and loss,
And his long flail can stoutly toss;
Make the hedge, which others break,
And ever thinks what he doth speak.

This couple pursued a godly division of time as well as
of labour. They

Do their week-days' work and pray
Devoutly on the holy day;

and even their love of children is shared:

Tib is all the father's joy,
And little Tom the mother's boy.

The absence of tension in the couple's relationship is
perhaps sustained by their fortunate economic position.
Unlike the labouring families portrayed by Stephen Duck
and Mary Collier, this household, depicted over a century
earlier, was blessed with the possession of an enclosed
rented holding, which was endowed with orchards, corn
and cows. [151]
Campion's vision of domestic harmony rested not only
on the plausibility of its economic basis, however, but
also on its deliberate contrast to the 'strange delights'
of 'courtly dames and knights'. These latter were
Campion's audience, whom he flattered with the bitter
knowledge that

Yet for all your pomp and train,
Securer lives the silly swain. [152]

A similar combination of sentiments informed another literary genre prominent in Campion's day, the 'character'.[153] These brief sketches of familiar social types, virtues and vices, compressed the exercise of wit, moral instruction and recreation into a single paragraph. Their social vision was limited by a concentration on certain stock themes, a tendency most marked in the treatment of women. The great majority of 'characters' depicted men. The virtues and vices of the female personality were squeezed into a mere handful of stereotypes: the chambermaid, milkmaid and hostess; the virgin, woman, and wife; the widow, the wanton, and the scold. These limitations may tell us something of how the seventeenth-century gentleman viewed the options open to less gentle women. Some were treated with barely concealed sarcasm, as was the chambermaid: 'her industry is upstairs and downstairs, like a drawer; and by her dry hand you may know she is a sore starcher...' and the Handsome Hostess who 'is the fairer commendation of an inn, above the fair sign, or fair lodgings. She is the loadstone that attracts men of iron, gallants and roarers, where they cleave sometimes long, and are not easily got off'.[154] Others were idealised in a pastoral setting, where the pains of farm work and domestic industry were transcended, at least for the gentleman observer, by a kind of psychic innocence. Such was, for example, 'A Fair and Happy Milkmaid':

> The golden ears of corn fall and kiss her feet when she reaps them, as if they wished to be bound and led prisoners by the same hand that felled them ... She makes her hand hard with labour, and her heart soft with pity; and when winter's evenings fall early (sitting at her merry wheel) she sings a defiance to the giddy wheel of fortune. ... She bestows her year's wages at next fair ... she is never alone for she is still accompanied with old songs, honest thoughts, and prayers ...[155]

How far such reading matter affected the approach of gentlemen magistrates to the regulation of women's work we may never be able to ascertain with much precision. The possibility that their actions were influenced by assumptions draw from such sources, however, and that literature helped maintain a perceptual screen between the gentle and the worker's view of work surely needs to be entertained, not least because so much of our evidence of the conduct of work comes from gentle pens.

IX

The preceding discussion has shown that even among the literate minority in early modern English society there was no single, uniform concept of 'work'. The experience of working, and of watching or dealing with working people, was conceived and interpreted in a number of ways, with correspondingly different implications for women. How far did these views affect the experience of working itself, and how far were women free to choose between them and other ways of thinking? Historians have grown cautious of tracing straightforward links between literary statements and social practice.[156] But as the works of Mary Collier and Stephen Duck indicate, the worlds of the pen and the plough were not closed to each other in this period. Several of the views of work we have examined were propounded to influence the behaviour of working people or the authorities responsible for their regulation, and all of them, from the milkmaid's ballad to the courtier's pastoral ode, bore witness to the considerable impact of varied notions of work in contemporary culture.[157]

The proverb collections of the time suggest that many of the assumptions underpinning literary views of work also formed part of common speech.[158] Caution is required in handling such a source, since the proverb collectors were themselves literary figures whose compilations may well have been selected in accordance with their own assumptions. Nor do we know very much about the contexts in which the proverbs would actually have been used.[159] Within these limits, however, the collections do provide a glimpse of the terms in which work was described in ordinary conversation. The assumptions of writers about work, that work was a largely arduous experience, whose undertaking had to be justified as an obligation to God or society, and distinguished from pleasure and relaxation, were indeed proverbial.[160] At the same time there are some indications of a less reverent attitude. It was thought 'better [to] sit idle than work for nothing', and 'as good [to] play for nought as work for nought'. 'If anything stay', proverbial wisdom advised, 'let work stay'. It was admitted, too, however, that 'a good paymaster never wants workmen'; and that 'he that hath some land must have some labour.' Good payment, then, rather than a sense of vocation, might be a spur. Hardship and fear tended this way, too: 'they must hunger in frost that will not work in heat'. For the self-employed other motivations were perhaps more effective: 'a work ill done must be done twice'; 'he who does not rise early never does a good day's work'; 'fools and bairns should not see half-done work'.[161]

Is it possible to establish the part played by such adages at the village level? The influence of communal sentiment on the definition and performance of work is most familiar in the context of the manorial court, and there are also indications that communal pressures were brought to bear in other ways.[162] But the demographic and economic changes of the sixteenth and seventeenth centuries with their accompanying process of social differentiation made the maintenance of a common approach to work throughout a town or village an impossibility.[163] The plurality of approaches to work in print was a reflection of this fact.

In the case of women's work, the impact of economic change was felt within a context of more slowly changing views of women's status and the proper forms of marriage.[164] The tensions between an enduring marriage pattern and changes in the opportunities for female employment were expressed both at the level of marital theory, in the debate about the nature of marriage for example, and in other more diffuse forms. Male reactions to female activity in the market are particularly interesting in this context. For here women's activities most clearly contradicted male assumptions about what the scope of female work should be. Marketing women were visible, talkative, and competent. The sale of produce from workshop or farm, and the purchase of foodstuffs or raw materials, was frequently a female preserve, and to achieve a successful bargain must have required a considerable fund of experience and knowledge of market conditions. Some women developed their expertise here in particular ways, as did the women of sixteenth-century Nuremberg,[165] to offer additional services such as the running of employment exchanges, or the distribution of farthing tokens.[166] Yet this business was evaluated in terms of its numerous threats and dangers more than as a form of work, and perhaps because of this very expertise marketing women were regarded by men with suspicion. Their work was tainted with a popular distrust of all dealing,[167] which was compounded by women's involvement in the counterfeiting of coins or the receipt of stolen property.[168] The multiplicity of women dealers also appeared to threaten official restraints on trade, and their names figure prominently in prosecutions of regrators and the like.[169] At the same time, the prominence of women in the defence of customary price levels by riot exposed them to another kind of official censure.[170]

At the individual level, however invaluable her activities outside the home, a woman's visits to the market brought dangers. By deserting her 'natural' sphere for the streets and lanes a woman put the reputation of her entire family at risk, through the network of

gossip.[171] A fund of proverbial wisdom closely linked the
market with such talk. 'Three women and a goose make a
market', ran an Italian proverb well-known in England,
for 'where there are women and geese there wants no
noise'. 'A journeying woman speaks much of all, and all
of her', ran another adage, and 'the goodman is the last
who knows what's amiss at home' observed a third. 'A
rouk-town's seldom a good house-wife at home' averred a
Yorkshire saying, and it was more widely feared that
'women and hens by too much gadding are lost'.[172] The
bartering of reputations in which gossiping women were
thought to engage was closely associated with the noise
and bustle of the market; 'they scold', ran one expression, 'like so many butter-whores, or oyster-women at
Billingsgate'.[173] The association was in turn used to
belittle the dignity of a more important labour. A
husband's stock response to his wife's cries in childbirth
might well be simply that 'my wife cries five loaves a
penny'.[174]

The skilled and frequently vexing work of attending
a market with scarce resources was thus met with a
mixture of fear, suspicion and contempt by many male
observers. Their reactions were undoubtedly complex and
require more careful examination before we can be sure
exactly how far such attitudes were directed towards
women alone.[175] In marketing, however, women do seem to
have run up against some of the more enduring
assumptions underpinning the conventional sexual division
of labour. Their 'gadding', unattended, set inquisitive
minds a-wondering; their work lacked the productive
character of a craftsman's or a farmer's labours; it
sustained no gild or professional training; its bartering
noise flew in the face of conventional wisdom ('least talk,
most work');[176] and its pursuit by even the humblest of
poor women further reduced its social status.[177]

Marketing was only one of many functions undertaken by women which were only vestigially dignified as
work. Much of this activity, wet-nursing or child-
minding,[178] healing the sick or mourning the dead,[179] was
fundamental to the maintenance of social well-being. Both
gossip and riot also served important roles in the reproduction of communal values, as did the tales told to
children by women in the fields or at the fireside.[180] Some
writers recognised the importance of this 'work of
custom'.[181] The author of *The Woman's Advocate* expressed
dismay at a husband's dislike of women's traditional
celebration after a new birth:

> Then for gossips to meet, nay to meet at a lying in,
> and not to talk, you may as well dam up the arches
> of London Bridge, as stop their mouths at such a
> time. 'Tis a time of freedom, when women, like

Parliament-men, have a privilege to talk Petty
Treason ... Women are sociable creatures as well as
men; and if they can't talk philosophy, they must
talk of that which they better understand ... Men
must acknowledge that women have done them a most
extraordinary kindness, to ease them of that
ponderous weight of infant-carriage.[182]

The tone is condescending, but the note of recognition
seems real enough. In general, however, the sixteenth and
seventeenth centuries saw a declining respect for the
'easy and slothful observances' of magic and ritual with
which women were particularly associated.[183] These were
contrasted with a more physically strenuous, and perhaps
given contemporary assumptions about work, implicitly
more masculine, image of life as a round of industry and
pains.[184]

X

Marketing and magic were particular areas of conflict
between the activities of women and conventional definitions of their role. Historians have recently become better
equipped to interpret the more general interaction between
theories of the marital division of labour and actual
marriage practices through the publication of a major
study of English population history.[185] This has already
formed the basis for a study of service in husbandry, an
important employer of female labour in this period.[186]
Through the examination of the process by which new
households were formed, particularly by young couples
leaving service, these studies have opened up a valuable
field of enquiry which may ultimately enable us to clarify
some of the more difficult questions connecting age, sex
and employment. The circumstances in which new households were established and the motives and aspirations of
betrothed couples, are a crucial part of any explanation
of the sexual division of labour in this period. It has
recently been argued, too, that in explaining those
fundamental shifts of population growth which moulded the
economic fortunes of early modern society it is to these
same cultural determinants of household formation that we
must now turn; those attitudes towards work, marriage
and respectability that we have just been examining.[187] A
similar explanatory emphasis on household formation has
also characterised recent writing on 'proto-industrialisation', - whereby rural industry provided additional
employment and a paid income for work at home, thus
facilitating changed consumption and working patterns in

such households and promises to give much greater clarity to our picture of 'popular' attitudes towards work.[188]

Demographic history may also help to explain the changing character of some of the printed works we have examined. Rosemary Masek has suggested that writers' hostility to shrewish or scolding wives grew in intensity during the first half of the seventeenth century, and that this 'attack' slowed after 1660.[189] A number of factors may account for such a change, including the changing character of the Stuart court.[190] It is noteworthy, however, that a dismal view of marriage, from the male viewpoint at least, grew more pervasive as the level of population itself rose towards its seventeenth-century peak, with all that such growth implied for the availability of resources for newly-married couples.[191] During the later seventeenth and early eighteenth centuries, when population growth was extremely limited, literary hostility to married women appears to have waned,[192] concern was expressed for the fortunes of the 'old maid',[193] and 'there are many signs in the culture at this time of the pressure for marrying'.[194]

It is against such a background of changes in the balance between population and employment opportunities that the dilemma of Moll Flanders and her real-life sisters can best be understood. In the early eighteenth century when Defoe was writing, inherited attitudes to work were being gradually re-cast to the accompaniment of substantial economic change. The growth of 'consumer occupations' and of proto-industrialisation offered new forms of employment, which did not require a lengthy preparation via service or apprenticeship to be undertaken. Economic expansion at a time of only sluggish demographic growth meant that different employers competed for the same labour, and for the labourer there was greater choice of work, and perhaps greater choice in the distribution of time between work and leisure.[195] It would be wrong to romanticise this period of change as one of wholesale improvement for the working population; many earned incomes were still pitifully low, and the pattern of change was very regionally and chronologically uneven. But there are signs of a shift in the relative fortunes of employers and labour, which needs to be noted alongside the more pessimistic picture of proletarianisation and its effects on women presented by Alice Clark.[196]

Reactions to these economic changes were various. Some commentators urged the abandonment of employers' traditional penchant for low wages so as to spur workers on, and the economy forward, through high wages and increased consumer expenditure.[197] But for the employers of servants, and for moralists concerned with the socialisation of the young, matters were more difficult. Rising real wage-costs made housekeeping more expensive for the employer. Temptations were also created for the young consumers who received those wages. Some young people, moreover, might avoid the discipline of service altogether by relying on the income from industrial work. Defoe's account of Moll's childhood was written with an eye to this moral and economic dilemma. Moll's reluctance to take up the advised service was, of course, a useful narrative device and how much more Defoe intended to convey by these means must remain open to doubt. But Moll's behaviour is certainly explicable in terms of Defoe's observations of life as well as in those of imagination and narrative planning. Moll's preference for independence 'at her fingers' ends' and her reluctance to heed the advice of local authorities mirrored the actual experience of numerous girls whose motives are now lost to us. Distaste for service, perhaps particularly acute when alternative sources of income provided greater scope for choice between work and leisure, was not confined to such periods. The servant's medieval predecessor, the *famulus*, also required some compulsion to forsake the more leisurely pace of other kinds of work.[198] In the early modern period there was also some articulate resistance. William Gouge, for example, felt obliged in 1622 to counter 'the opinion of Anabaptists' that 'it is against nature for one to be a servant', whilst Defoe's contemporary Bishop William Fleetwood stressed Christian egalitarianism in the same cause:

> This is no little thing for servants to consider, that however mean and despicable their condition may appear in the sight of men, yet that in God's eyes, who understands the value of his creatures best, they are of equal worth with the great and noble ...[199]

There is evidence that a number of potential servants were reluctant to take up such a 'despicable' form of employment.[200] Our most interesting evidence comes from the records of those overseers and magistrates who were actively involved in the attempt to persuade 'idle' sons and daughters to cease living at their own hands. A range of motives prompted them to present individuals to Quarter Sessions on these grounds. For some the fault was simply their being young 'single persons and fit to go to service', such as the 41 girls and 12 boys reported from Bedworth, Warwickshire in 1673.[201] The ages of such culprits might be as low as that of Ann Mann, a 16-year old Bermondsey spinster reported in 1662, and as high as those of the 4 Essex men presented in 1572 for being out of service whilst still under thirty.[202] Two other Essex bachelors presented for the same fault who argued that they were about to marry shortly[203] were probably in their mid twenties.

The 1563 Statute of Artificers provided the legal basis for the presentment of unemployed individuals who were 'compellable to serve',[204] and certain Quarter Sessions cases refer to episodes of this type, where masterless men or women had been instructed to enter service with a specified employer and had refused.[205] The House of Correction was a common next stage in the process of persuasion.[206] Other cases concerned those who were accused of witholding the labour from the community at a crucial time (during the harvest).[207] But the authorities were also concerned about the moral implications of a youthful, masterless life. Offenders were said to be living 'an evil life',[208] or to be reluctant to adopt 'any honest, industrious way of getting their livings'.[209] Some of the consequences were incidentally mentioned: hedge-breaking,[210] theft,[211] pregnancy[212] and not least the setting of an evil example.[213] The Buckinghamshire spinster Mary Science was reported to have 'offered nothing material in her excuse' when presented for refusing to enter the service her local overseers had found for her in 1698, she 'only expressed an unwillingness to labour, which may be of ill example to lazy and thriftless people'.[214] How easily might Moll's innocent desire to be a 'gentlewoman' have been received in the same manner.

The records of their accusers allow us to build up a fragmentary picture of the attitudes towards service of such young people. Not all of them were without employment, as the expression often used by the authorities, that they were 'living at their own hand', implies. Where industrial work was widely available, as in Elizabethan Essex, there was tension between the willingness of weavers to take up casual employment, and the concern of the authorities to prevent their dismissal and mass pauperisation during slumps in the international cloth trade. In 1572 some four dozen men (half from the textile centre of Coggeshall) and eight women were presented for working by the day or month out of service.[215] Contracts of service or apprenticeship obliged the employer to retain the young employee, and generally to provide food and housing, even when work was unavailable, and thus lessened the communal burden of the poor rate and the disruption of the youngster's training. Piece-working or casual work by the young was also restricted in many places as limiting employment opportunities for servants hired by the year and for adult journeymen or smallholders wishing to supplement their incomes. Complaints reached the justices from local inhabitants about such activities,[216] and the matter was also of concern to local overseers,[217] churchwardens[218] and congregations.[219] Intimidation might also be employed. Joan Gynner, who worked for a Kentish employer for around thirty weeks on a weekly basis in 1600 was threatened with a whipping by three local men if she didn't leave the parish.[220]

Youngsters who sought employment outside the framework of annual service might thus face a number of obstacles, which we may feel the engaging young Moll Flanders was lucky to avoid. The hostility of the official or communal reaction no doubt varied considerably from time to time and from one place to another; the details have yet to be established by historians. Nor were communities always united in their hostility; the employers of such young workers were clearly able to satisfy their consciences with the prospect of cheap, and easily dismissed labour. Parents, too, sometimes objected to the loss of their children to service. A Hertford man presented for keeping two daughters of serviceable age at home in 1636 boasted that no Mayor would make him change his mind.[221] Some thirty-eight parents in the town were involved in such cases during the years 1627-41.[222] The institution of service was, as Defoe himself was later to explain, at least partly

> a concern which the law takes for parents, whose circumstances being but mean, and their children lying heavily upon them, are willing to be maintained in idleness and sloth, and refuse either to work for themselves, or go out to service.[223]

But not all parents were able to follow this logic, some preferring to keep their offspring at home and thrusting the calculation of any likely economic disadvantage onto the local community. Thus in 1655 the Wiltshire justices ordered into service all young men and maids whose parents were not 'of ability to keep them', since their preference for working at home was tending to force up the level of servants' wages.[224] Another consequence was detailed for the Buckinghamshire JPs in 1703 whereby 'the children of several poor people in the parish of Brill in this county that are fit and able to go out and hire at service refuse so to do, and do live and cohabit with their parents'. Not only did this cause hardship to the parents, 'who are not of ability to maintain themselves or their said children', but there was also a threat that 'the [poor rate] collection is likely to be increased to the great prejudice of those who are the proprietors and farmers of estates in that parish'.[225] Communities were thus divided by the issue of finding suitable employment for the daughters of the poor. Families, too, might be divided. In 1657 the baptist congregation of Fenstanton, in Huntingdonshire, sent emissaries to the troubled household of Thomas Green and his wife, who were in 'such contention, as that publicly they railed exceedingly, the one against the other, to the great dishonour of God and scandal of his truth'. They found that the dispute

> was occasioned by their daughter, whom they kept
> at home, the man being unwilling to retain [keep]
> her, and the woman not willing to let her go. And
> further it was declared, that their daughter being
> kept at home was a great occasion of offence to
> many; in that she was tolerated to steal wood, etc.
> Which things the congregation taking into considera-
> tion, did resolve that it was unlawful for them to
> keep a daughter at home, maintaining her in idle-
> ness to their own prejudice, who is able to earn her
> living, and to suffer her to do other unlawful
> things. Whereupon the persons being present, they
> were sharply reproved for their sin, and exhorted
> to put their daughter to service.

However, despite the weight of the congregation's full moral pressure the girl's mother refused to be separated from her daughter, and the woman was excluded from the fellowship of the church instead.[226]

In choosing to stay out of service, girls like Moll, whatever their motives, were embarking on a different route to maturity and marriage from the one envisaged for them by many local authorities, and by many of the writers whose views of women's work we have examined. This route lacked the prolonged subordination and training in housewifely arts which were the hallmarks of service in another's household. Although the households formed when such girls married may have resembled those of conventionally trained young women more than Moll's menages ever would, the age of marriage, the marital division of labour, and the social subordination of the wife were all brought into question. Girls like Moll were given their chances of independence by an economy which was providing new forms of work, or which was offering wages for such old domestic skills as spinning, when these were organised in new ways. Dependence on such skills in a market economy was, as Moll's adult friends advised, a precarious course of life. It was to demon-strate the moral, as well as economic, perils of such an independent attitude to life and work that Moll's story was devised.

Notes

1. J. Florio, *A Worlde of Wordes*, London (1598), Epistle, recounting an Italian proverb then apparently well-known in England; cf. *The Oxford Dictionary of English Proverbs*, Oxford, O.U.P. (3rd edn. 1970), p.175.

2. In revising this paper I am much indebted to the response of its original Oxford seminar audience, and to Lindsey Charles and Jane Rowlandson for trying to clear up passages of muddle. Those that remain, and the errors, are all my own work. Much of interest to readers of the present article will be found in two recently published surveys of research: Elizabeth Fox Genovese, 'Placing Women's History in History', *New Left Rev.*, 133 (1982), and Olwen Hufton, 'Women in History: Early Modern Europe', *Past and Present*, 101 (1983).

3. D. Defoe, *The Fortunes and Misfortunes of the Famous Moll Flanders*, Oxford, Shakespeare Head Press (1927; 1st pub. 1722), i. 4-8.

4. Moll's autobiography was supposedly written 'in the year 1683', when its author was 'almost seventy years of age', which would put her eighth year around 1622; Defoe, *Moll Flanders*, ii. 175.

5. D. Defoe, *A Tour Through the Whole Island of Great Britain*, London, (1724-26); P. Earle, *The World of Defoe*, London, Weidenfeld and Nicolson (1976) provides a survey of Defoe's many interests.

6. *The Woman's Champion; Or The Strange Wonder Being a True Relation of the ... Strategems of Mrs. Mary Frith, commonly called Mall Cutpurse*, London (1662); *Memories of the Life of the Famous Madam Charlton; commonly Stiled the German Princess*, London (1673). F.W. Chandler, *The Literature of Roguery*, Boston (1907), ch. iv. deals with the genre as a whole. T. Wright, *The Life of Daniel Defoe*, London (1931 edn.), p.10 for Defoe's reading.

7. Defoe, *Moll Flanders*, i.3; for the legal position see D. Marshall, 'The Old Poor Law, 1662-1795', *Econ. Hist. Rev.*, 1st ser. iii (1937); P. Styles, 'The Evolution of the Law of Settlement', *Univ. Birmingham Hist. Jnl.*, ix (1963-64).

8. Defoe appears to have considered Colchester somewhat exceptional in offering even children as young as 4 or 5 a chance to 'earn their own bread': J.J. Richetti, *Defoe's Narratives*, Oxford, O.U.P. (1975), p.99.

9.   Earle, *World of Defoe*, ch.7.
10. Defoe, *Moll Flanders*, i. 1–4.
11. Richetti, *Defoe's Narratives*, pp.97–100 examines
     the role of these early pages in the context of the
     book's ethical message as a whole. On the theme
     of choosing vice, see also W.A. Speck, 'The
     Harlot's Progress in Eighteenth–Century England',
     British Jnl. for Eighteenth Century Studies,
     iii (1980).
12. For this see J.J. Richetti, *Popular Fiction Before
     Richardson, Narrative Patterns, 1700–1739,*
     Oxford, O.U.P. (1969), esp. ch.2; I. Watt, 'The
     Recent Critical Fortunes of Moll Flanders',
     Eighteenth–Century Studs., i (1967–68);and Ruth Perry,
     Women, Letters, and the Novel, New York, AMS
     Press (1980). I am grateful to Ian Bell for
     guiding me to Richetti.
13. See below, pp.53–57.
14. *The Norwich Census of the Poor 1570,*
     ed. J. Pound (Norfolk Rec. Soc., xl, 1971),
     pp.40, 55.
15. *Norwich Census,* ed. Pound, pp.35, 36, 38. Of 25
     schoolchildren of specified sex, 8 were girls: *ibid.,*
     pp.23–92, *passim.*
16. P. Laslett, *The World We Have Lost,*
     London, Methuen (2nd edn. 1971), p.263; cf. *idem,*
     Family Life and Illicit Love in Earlier Generations,
     Cambridge, C.U.P. (1977), p.34. Table 1.7, showing
     a median of 40% of the female 20–24 age-group
     in service in six pre-industrial settlements; cf.
     R. Wall, 'The age of leaving home', *Jnl. Family
     Hist.,* iii (1978).
17. A. Kussmaul, *Servants in Husbandry in Early
     Modern England,* Cambridge, C.U.P. (1981),
     pp.70–72.
18. C. Phythian–Adams, *Desolation of a City,*
     Cambridge, C.U.P. (1979), pp.229–30.
19. V. Brodsky Elliott, 'Single Women in the London
     Marriage Market: Age, Status and Mobility,
     1598–1619', in R.B. Outhwaite, ed. *Marriage and
     Society,* London, Europa (1981), p.90.
20. *A Calendar of Southampton Apprenticeship
     Registers, 1609–1740,* eds. A.J. Willis and A.L.
     Merson (Southampton Recs. Ser., xii, 1968),
     p.lviii.
21. Kussmaul, *Servants in Husbandry,*
     chs. 3 and 4.
22. E.A. Wrigley and R.S. Schofield, *The Population
     History of England 1541–1871,*
     London, Edward Arnold (1981), p.255, Table 7.26.
23. Laslett, *Family Life,* p.27.

24. For a more extended discussion of some of these issues, see A. Clark, *Working Life of Women in the Seventeenth Century*, London, Routledge (1982 edn., introduced by M. Chaytor and J. Lewis), pp. xxix-xl.
25. Laslett, *Family Life*, p. 27.
26. Wrigley and Schofield, *Population History*,
27. R. Houston and R. Smith, 'A New Approach to Family History?', *History Workshop Jnl.*, xiv (1982), 124.
28. K. Wrightson, *English Society 1580-1680*, London, Hutchinson (1982), p.68.
29. Elliott, 'London Marriage Market', p.89.
30. Most recently, for example, in the works by B. Capp, *Astrology and The Popular Press, English Almanacs 1500-1800*, London, Faber (1979); K.M. Davies, 'Continuity and Change in Literary Advice on Marriage', in Outhwaite, ed. *Marriage and Society*; M. Spufford, *Small Books and Pleasant Histories. Popular Fiction and its Readership in Seventeenth-Century England*, London, Methuen (1981).
31. K. Thomas, 'Work and Leisure in Pre-Industrial Society', *Past and Present,* 29 (1964), remains the most broadly-conceived study. The search for a 'Protestant work ethic' continues: G. Marshall, *Presbyteries and Profits. Calvinism and the Development of Capitalism in Scotland, 1560-1707*, Oxford, O.U.P. (1980); W.U. Solberg, *Redeem the Time. The Puritan Sabbath in Early America*, Cambridge, Mass., Harvard U.P. (1977), pt.I 'The English Background'; cf. also R.L. Greaves, *Society and Religion in Elizabethan England*, Minneapolis, Minnesota U.P. (1981). Other important studies of work and work-motivation are listed in P. Mathias, 'Leisure and Wages in Theory and Practice', in his *The Transformation of England*, London, Methuen (1979), p.165 n.1.
32. *The Works of William Perkins*, ed. I. Breward, Abingdon, Sutton Courteney (1970), pp.446-47.
33. W. Haller, *The Rise of Puritanism*, New York, Harper Torchbooks (1957; 1st pub. 1938), pp.123-25; H.W. Sams, 'Self-love and the Doctrine of Work', *Jnl. Hist. Ideas*, iv (1943); C.H. and K. George, *The Protestant Mind of the English Reformation, 1570-1640*, Princeton, N.J., Princeton U.P. (1961), pt.2, ch.3; C. Hill, *Society and Puritanism in Pre-Revolutionary England*, London, Secker and Warburg (1964), ch.4; C. Constantin, 'The Puritan Ethic

and the Dignity of Labor: Hierarchy vs. Equality', *Jnl. Hist. Ideas*, xl (1979); cf. also E.L. Eisenstein, *The Printing Press as an Agent of Change*, Cambridge C.U.P. (1979), pp.378–84; Solberg, *Redeem the Time*, pp.43–45; R.L. Greaves, 'The Origins of English Sabbatarian Thought', *Sixteenth-Century Jnl.*, xii (1981).

34. G. Duby, *The Three Orders*, Chicago U.P. (1980); G.R. Owst, *Literature and Pulpit in Medieval England*, Cambridge, C.U.P. (1933), pp.550–51, quoting a 1388 sermon of Thomas Wimbledon at St. Paul's Cross, London.

35. W. Perkins, 'A Treatise of the Vocations, Or, Callings of Men', in *The Workes*, London (1603), p.904.

36. J. Dod and R. Cleaver, *A Plaine And Familiar Exposition Of the Eighteenth, Nineteenth, and Twentieth Chapters of the Proverbs of Salomon*, London (1610), p.11.

37. *The Sermons of John Donne*, eds. G.R. Potter and E.M. Simpson, Berkeley, California U.P. (1955), ii. 292.

38. R. Steele, *The Tradesman's Calling*, London (1684); J. Flavell, *Husbandry Spiritualised*, London (1669). For *The Religious Weaver* see R.H. Tawney, *Religion and the Rise of Capitalism*, Harmondsworth, Penguin (1966), p.318 n.85. Tawney observed that such writings offered 'professional education' to figures such as the 'independent shopkeeper', *op. cit.*, p.242.

39. Perkins, 'Treatise of Callings', in *The Workes*, London (1612), i, 391, referring to dish-washing in this instance as the work of a 'kitchen boy'; *The Works of Martin Luther*, Philadelphia (1915), ii. 241.

40. Georges, *The Protestant Mind*, p.130; cf. R. Bolton, *Some Generall Directions For a Comfortable Walking With God*, London (5th edn., 1638), pp.48–49.

41. R. Sanderson, *The Works*, ed. W. Jacobson, Oxford (1854), iii. 109; Steele, *The Tradesman's Calling*, p.1.

42. Haller, *Rise of Puritanism*, p.268; K. Thomas, 'Women and the Civil War Sects', *Past and Present*, 13 (1958), reprinted in T. Aston, ed. *Crisis in Europe 1560–1660*, London, Routledge (1965).

43. R.S. Michaelson, 'Changes in the Puritan Concept of Calling or Vocation', *New England Qtly.*, xxvi (1953), 326–36; cf. C.J. Sommerville, *Popular Religious Literature in Restoration England*, Gainesville, Florida (1977), and J. Sears McGee,

The Godly Man in Stuart England, London, Yale U.P. (1976).

44. *Sermons of John Donne*, ii. 292.
45. Perkins, *Workes* (1603), pp.912-13.
46. [R. Allestree], *The Ladies Calling*, Oxford (1673), p.203.
47. For the coarsening of the vocational ideal in this period, see Michaelson, 'Puritan Concept of Calling', 326-36.
48. *The Text of the Canterbury Tales*, eds. J.M. Manley and E. Ricket, Chicago U.P. (1940), iv, 10 (Squire's Tale, line 197); *The English Works of John Gower*, ed. G.C. MacCaulay (Early Eng. Text. Soc., 1901), ii. 279.
49. Thomas, 'Work and Leisure', 57-58; J. Le Goff, *Time, Work and Culture in the Middle Ages*, Chicago, Chicago U.P. (1980), p.70.
50. All quotations from N. Bailey, *An Universal Etymological English Dictionary*, London (1721). See also E. Chambers, *Cyclopaedia*, London (1728), s.v. 'Art'; T.H. Crocker et al., *The Complete Dictionary of Arts and Sciences*, London (1767), s.v. 'Art'; *Encyclopaedia Britannica*, Edinburgh (3rd edn., 1797), s.v. 'Art', 'Labour', 'Labourer'.
51. *The Art of Water-Drawing*, London (1660); N. Venette, *The Art of Pruning Fruit Trees*, London (1685); W. Coles, *The Art of Simpling*, London (1656); R.T., *The Art of Good Husbandry*, London (1675).
52. C. Hill, 'Pottage for Freeborn Englishmen: Attitudes to Wage Labour in the Sixteenth and Seventeenth Centuries', in his *Change and Continuity in Seventeenth-Century England*, London, Secker and Warburg (1974); M.F. Roberts, 'Wages and Wage-earners in England: The Evidence of the Wage Assessments, 1563-1725', Oxford Univ. D.Phil. thesis (1981), ch.6.
53. Clark, *Working Life of Women;* for some problems with this view see the 1982 edn., intro. Chaytor and Lewis (n.24 above) and Christopher Middleton elsewhere in this volume.
54. I. Maclean, *The Renaissance Notion of Woman*, Cambridge, C.U.P. (1980), pp.44, 46.
55. M. Roberts, 'Sickles and Scythes: Women's work and Men's Work at Harvest Time', *History Workshop Jnl.*, 7 (1979); K.D.M. Snell, 'Agricultural Seasonal Unemployment, the Standard of Living, and Women's Work in the South and East: 1690-1860', *Econ. Hist. Rev.*, 2nd ser. xxxiv (1981).

56. P. Crawford, 'Attitudes to Menstruation in Seventeenth-Century England', *Past and Present*, 91 (1981), 72.

57. Ibid., 54, 60-61; cf. N.Z. Davis, 'Women in the *Arts Mécaniques* in Sixteenth-Century Lyon', in *Lyon et L'Europe, Hommes et Sociétés. Mélanges d'histoire offerts à Richard Gascon*, Université Lyon II - Centre Pierre Léon (1980), p.146.

58. R. Holme, *The Academy of Armory and Blazon*, Chester (1688), Bk.2, p.485; J. Downame, *The Christian Warfare, The Second Part*, London (1633), p.408.

59. K. Ordahl Kupperman, *Settling With the Indians. The Meeting of English and American Cultures in America, 1580-1640*, Cambridge, C.U.P. (1980), p.60, citing John Smith, *A Map of Virginia*.

60. Crawford, 'Attitudes to Menstruation', 68.

61. For one woman's account of her own 'exceeding sharp travail, in great extremity ... upon the rack in bearing my child', see *The Autobiography of Mrs. Alice Thornton*, ed. C. Jackson (Surtees Soc., lxii, 1873), pp.95, 91-92; and *passim*; cf. also P. Crawford, 'Attitudes to Pregnancy from a Woman's Spiritual Diary, 1687-8', *Local Pop. Studs.*, xx (1978). For a male view of childbirth as 'the ordinary effect of nature', no more remarkable than 'the laying of a great egg, by a hen or goose', see *The XV Comforts of Rash and Inconsiderate Marriage*, London (1682), p.54. It has been suggested that the rise of 'mechanical philosophy' diminished the recognition of women's contribution to generation in this period: B. Easlea, *Witch-hunting, Magic, and the New Philosophy*, Brighton, Harvester (1980), pp.151-2; but earlier associations of women with mother earth and fruitfulness were themselves not necessarily advantageous to women: McLean, *Renaissance Notion of Woman*, p.44; nor was 'the natural' a simple concept: *ibid.*, p.45. For thought-provoking suggestions which have yet to be thoroughly applied in this period see E. Ardener, 'Belief and the Problem of Women', and 'The "Problem" Revisited', in S. Ardener, ed. *Perceiving Women*, London, Malaby Press (1975); S.B. Ortner, 'Is Female to Male as Nature is to Culture?', in M. Zimbalist Rosaldo and L. Lamphere, ed. *Woman, Culture and Society*, Stanford, Stanford U.P. (1974). See now also C. Merchant, *The Death of Nature*, London, Wildwood House (1982), and K. Thomas, *Man and the Natural World*, London, Allen Lane (1983).

62. For regulation of wages:Roberts, 'Wages and Wage-earners', ch.1; payments in kind: G.W. Hilton, *The Truck System*, Cambridge, Heffer (1961); hours of work: M.A. Bienefeld, *Working Hours in British Industry*, London, Weidenfeld and Nicolson (1972).

63. J. Thirsk, *Economic Policy and Projects*, Oxford, O.U.P. (1978), chs.1-3.

64. Le Goff, *Time, Work and Culture*, pp.29-52.

65. Michaelson, 'Puritan Concept of Calling', 330-34.

66. J. Oldham Appleby, *Economic Thought and Ideology in Seventeenth-Century England*, Princeton N.J., Princeton U.P. (1978), ch.6.

67. Appleby, *op. cit.*, quoting Sir Thomas Dalby in 1690.

68. Woad cultivation, for example, employed numerous women: Thirsk, *Policy and Projects*, pp.29-30; R.S. Smith, 'A Woad-growing Project at Wollaton in the 1580's', *Trans. Thoroton Soc.*, lxv (1961), 30-31.

69. T. Firmin, *Some Proposals for the imploying of the Poor, Especially in and about London* (1678), p.18; D. Defoe, *The Great Law of Subordination Consider'd*, London(1724), p.13.

70. Firmin, *Some Proposals*, p.19; *Hist. MSS. Comm.*, 13th Rept., Appendix, Pt.2 (Portland MSS.), p.266. On female mobility, see also J. Sharpe, *Defamation and Sexual Slander in Early Modern England: The Church Courts at York*, Borthwick Papers No.58 (1981), pp.18-19.

71. C. Reynell, *The True English Interest*, London (1674), p.53; W. Blith, *The English Improver Improved*, London (1652), p.249.

72. Clark, *Working Life of Women*, p.41; Perry, *Women, Letters, and the Novel*, ch.2; M. George, 'From "Goodwife" to "Mistress": the Transformation of the Female in Bourgeois Culture', *Science and Society*, xxxvii (1973), 157-59.

73. D. Defoe, *The Complete English Tradesman*, London (1726), p.225; [Allestree], *The Ladies Calling*, p.178, and cf. p.150.

74. *Chaos*, London (1659), pp.48-49; T. Snelling, *A View of the Copper Coin and Coinage of England*, London (1766), p.14.

75. Perkins, *Workes* (1603), p.906.

76. The practice of recording occupations alongside names in parish registers was becoming 'fairly frequent' by 1660 according to P.H. Lindert, 'English Occupations, 1670-1811', *Jnl. Econ. Hist.*, xl (1980), 689. The number of studies using such data is large; for instances see J. Patten, *English Towns, 1500-1700*,

Folkestone, Dawson (1978); D. Cressy, *Literacy and
the Social Order,* Cambridge, C.U.P. (1980), ch.6.
For remarks on the complex array of social and
occupational designations current in early modern
England, see also C. Phythian-Adams, 'The Economic
and Social Structure', in *The Fabric of the
Traditional Community,* Milton Keynes, O.U. Arts
Third Level Course, English Urban History 1500-1780,
Unit 5 (1977), esp. pp.33-36.

77.   The proportion of surviving wills and probate
inventories containing occupational designations
gradually increases from the sixteenth to the
eighteenth centuries. These were found in 38% of
Norfolk wills, 1563-66; 69% of Norwich wills and
inventories, 1551-75; 43% of Oxfordshire inventories,
1550-90; and 21% of Worcestershire wills and
inventories, 1451-1600; J. Patten, 'Urban Occupations
in Pre-Industrial England', *Trans. Inst. Brit. Geog.,*
new ser. 2 (1977), 300; J. Pound, 'The Validity of
the Freemen's Lists: Some Norwich Evidence',
Econ. Hist. Rev., 2nd ser., xxxiv (1981), 56;
*Household and Farm Inventories in Oxfordshire,
1550-1590,* ed. M.A. Havinden, Hist. MSS. Comm.,
J.P. 10 (1965), p.3; J. West, *Village Records,*
London, Macmillan (1962), pp.125-27. Comparable
later percentages were 49% for mid-Essex inventories
during 1635-1749; 75% in west Midlands inventories
during 1660-1710; 94% in Norfolk wills during the
1690s; and 65% in Kirdford (Sussex) inventories
during 1611-1776; *Farm and Cottage Inventories of
Mid-Essex 1635-1749,* ed. F.W. Steer, Chelmsford
(1950), percentage calculated from entire collection;
M.B.Rowlands *Masters and Men in the West Midlands
Metalware Trades before the Industrial Revolution,*
Manchester, Manchester U.P. (1975), p.20;
Patten, 'Urban Occupations', 300; G.H. Kenyon,
'Kirdford Inventories, 1611-1776', *Sussex Arch. Colls.,*
xciii (1954), 79-80.

78.   Comparing Sir Thomas Smith, *De Republica Anglorum,*
ed. L. Alston, Cambridge, C.U.P. (1906);
W. Harrison, *Description of England,* ed. G. Edelen,
Ithaca, N.Y., Cornell U.P. (1968); and 'The State
of England (1600). By Sir Thomas Wilson, ed.
F.J. Fisher, *Camden Miscellany* xvi (Camden Soc.,
3rd ser., lii, 1936), with Gregory King's famous
social table and its accompanying documentation,
much of it reprinted in *17th-Century Economic
Documents,* eds. J. Thirsk and J.P. Cooper, Oxford,
O.U.P. (1972), pp.770-90; the social estimates
made by Edward Chamberlayne in the numerous
editions of his *Angliae Notitia,* London (1669-1702),

and the calculations of Joseph Massie: P. Mathias, 'The Social Structure in the Eighteenth Century: A Calculation by Joseph Massie', *Econ. Hist. Rev.*, 2nd ser., x (1957).

79. For a useful survey of some of the problems, though wholly concerned with male experience, see Patten, 'Urban Occupations'; and Pound, 'Freeman's Lists'.

80. In a sample of 1494 female taxpayers from the 1692 London poll tax listings for example, only 39 were identified by an occupation other than service: D.V. Glass, 'Socio-economic Status and Occupations in the City of London at the end of the Seventeenth Century', in A.E.J. Hollaender and W. Kellaway, eds., *Studies in London History*, London, Hodder (1969), pp.384-85.

81. Lindert, 'English Occupations', 691-92.

82. K. Wrightson and D. Levine, *Poverty and Piety in an English village: Terling 1525-1700*, London, Academic Press (1979), pp.21-22, where the absence even of any reference to spinning in the surviving documentation is also noted.

83. J. Thirsk, 'Industries in the Countryside', in F.J. Fisher, ed., *Essays in the Economic and Social History of Tudor and Stuart England*, Cambridge, C.U.P. (1961) is a classic study of such occupational variety.

84. e.g. Patten, 'Urban Occupations', 301-5; Pound, 'Freemen's Lists'.

85. In records of payments made to harvest workers, for instance, the work of women and children in raking and gathering was often disguised by a single payment to the male 'mower' or 'harvester'.

86. *Norwich Census*, ed. Pound, p.31. A few spouses' employments were directly inter-linked: as with the Beckets, he a tailor, she a button-maker; or the Brownes, he a slaughterman, she selling flesh: *ibid.*, pp.35,39.

87. *Ibid.*, pp.24, 30. One husband helped his wife at *her* trade: *ibid.*, p.34; cf. Clark, *Working Life of Women*, pp.175-78.

88. *Norwich Census*, ed. Pound, pp.27, 26. The last use of the work 'occupy' in this sense cited in *O.E.D.* dates from 1653.

89. E.M. Veale, 'Craftsmen in the Economy of London in the Fourteenth Century', in *Studies in London History* (note 79, above), p.138.

90. E. Kerridge, 'Social and Economic History 1509-1660', *V.C.H. Leics.*, iv, ed. R.A. McKinley (1958), 77.

91. J. Rule, *The Experience of Labour in Eighteenth-*

Century Industry, London, Croom Helm (1981), p.41.

92. Clark, *Working Life of Women,* remains the fullest account of women's involvement in such trades, esp. ch.5. She notes, on pp.212-13, that the domestic use of a trade such as baking rendered institutional restraints more difficult to enforce.

93. Rowlands, *Masters and Men,* p.40.

94. Thomas, 'Women and the Civil War Sects', p.338, n.109.

95. Thirsk, *Policy and Projects,* pp.51,83; the transfer of alien skills to English workers via apprenticeship was crucial to this process; cf. *17th-Century Economic Documents,* eds. Thirsk and Cooper, p.713.

96. I. Pinchbeck, *Women Workers and the Industrial Revolution, 1750-1850,* London, Virago (1981; 1st edn. 1930), p.123. Inheritance arrangements might still deprive women of such tools as spinning wheels: M. Chaytor, 'Household and Kinship: Ryton in the late sixteenth and early seventeenth centuries', *History Workshop Jnl.,* 10 (1980), 45.

97. Phythian-Adams, *Desolation of a City,* p.91; *idem,* 'Ceremony and the Citizen: the communal year at Coventry 1450-1550', in P. Clark and P. Slack, eds., *Crisis and Order in English Towns,* London, Routledge (1972), p.107.

98. For example as printers and publishers: *A Transcript of the Register of the Company of Stationers of London: 1554-1640 A.D.,* ed. E. Arber, Birmingham (1894), vol.5, pp.lxxxi-cxi, listing 79 widows in a total of 847 publishers from the period 1553-1640; see also Davis, 'Women in the *Arts Mécaniques',* 147-48 for the position in sixteenth-century Lyon printing shops.

99. C. Carlton, 'The Widow's Tale: Male Myths and Female Reality in 16th and 17th Century England', *Albion,* x (1978); cf. Chaytor, 'Household and Kinship', 43-44.

100. M.P. Tilley, *Dictionary of the Proverbs in England in the Sixteenth and Seventeenth Centuries,* Ann Arbor, Michigan U.P. (1950), proverb W 340.

101. Davis, 'Women in the *Arts Mécaniques',* 140.

102. O. Hufton, *The Poor of Eighteenth-Century France, 1750-1789,* Oxford, O.U.P. (1974), esp. chs. 3-4; cf. *eadem,* 'Women and the Family Economy in Eighteenth-Century France', *French Hist. Studies,* ix (1975-76).

103. It is likely, indeed, that 'occupational flexibility' was a characteristic of both sexes at the lowest social levels. John Patten suggests that as many as 30 or 40% of the urban population may have

been engaged in 'spasmodic day-to-day employ':
Patten, 'Urban Occupations', 297.

104. C. Bridenbaugh, *Vexed and Troubled Englishmen*,
Oxford, O.U.P. (1976) p.169, citing Thomas Powell.

105. Clark, *Working Life of Women*, p.202, citing a
Common Council Act of 1631.

106. E. Stephens, *The More Excellent Way; Or a Proposal
of a Compleat Way of Charity*, London (? 1696).

107. Perry, *Women, Letters, and the Novel*, pp.29–30
quoting *The Gentleman's Magazine* for 1739.

108. 4% in the *Calendar of the Bristol Apprentice Book
1532-1565*, pt.1, *1532-1542*, ed. D. Hollis (Bristol
Rec. Soc., xiv, 1948); 3% in *ibid.*, pt.2, *1542-52*,
eds. E. Ralph and N.M. Hardwick (Bristol Rec.
Soc., xxxiii, 1980), p.x; none in Coventry in the
early sixteenth century and only a 'tiny number'
later in the century: Phythian-Adams, *Desolation
of a City*, pp.87, 272-73; less than 1% (7 of 1561)
in the *Kingston Upon Thames Register of Apprentices
1563-1713*, ed. A. Daly (Surrey Rec. Soc., xxviii,
1974), p.xi; 5% of *Surrey Apprenticeships from the
Registers in the Public Record Office, 1711-1731*, ed.
H. Jenkinson (Surrey Rec. Soc., x, 1921); 8% of
Wiltshire Apprentices and their Masters 1710-1760,
ed. C. Dale (Wilts. Arch. and Nat. Hist. Soc.,
xvii, 1961); 3% of *Sussex Apprentices and Masters,
1710 to 1752*, ed. R. Garroway Rice (Sussex Rec.
Soc., xxxviii, 1924); 5% in H. Jenkinson, 'A List
of Bedfordshire Apprentices, 1711-20', *Beds. Hist.
Rec. Soc.*, ix (1925); and 4% of *Warwickshire
Apprentices and their Masters 1710-1760*, ed. J.K.
Smith (Dugdale Soc., xxix, 1975). Calculations are my
own where no page reference is given.

109. *Southampton Apprenticeship Registers*, eds., Willis
and Merson (note 20 above): female pauper
apprentices, 1609-1708; F.G. Emmison, 'The Relief
of the Poor at Eaton Socon, 1706-1834', *Beds. Hist.
Rec. Soc.*, xv (1933), p.67.

110. *Bristol Apprentice Book*, pts. 1 and 2, *passim*.

111. e.g. *Wiltshire Apprentices*, nos. 457, 894, 2380;
Sussex Apprentices, pp.42, 112, 210; three girls
apprenticed to women described as 'housewife';
'Bedfordshire Apprentices': Coats (1727), Longshurst
(1728), Wingfield (1731), all apprenticed to
housewives. A number of girls were also simply
apprenticed to 'yeomen', 'husbandmen' or 'widows'.

112. Emmison, 'Eaton Socon', p.67; *Kingston ...
Register of Apprentices*, nos. 187, 681.

113. M.D. George, *London Life in the Eighteenth
Century*, Harmondsworth, Penguin (1965; 1st edn.,
1925), p.416, no.3.

114. This London practice was also thought appropriate
for sixteenth-century Bristol: R. Ricart,
The Maire of Bristowe is Kalendar,
ed. L.T. Smith (Camden Soc., new ser., v, 1872),
p.102.

115. e.g. 120 as compared with 2200 men training
Wiltshire Apprentices, ed. Dale, p.xv;
Kingston ... Register of Apprentices, nos.258, 356,
418, 616; only 26 female 'masters' are recorded
in the 2454 indentures of *Warwickshire Apprentices
... 1710-60,* p.xv.

116. *Surrey Apprenticeships,* ed. Jenkinson, nos. 467,
1400, 1472, 1601, 1730, 2056, 2252.

117. O.J. Dunlop, *English Apprenticeship and Child Labour,*
London, Unwin (1912), pp.153-54; *Bristol Apprentice
Book,* pt.2, ed.Ralph and Hardwick, p.x.

118. Wives might even be taught their skills only
after marriage, when effectively working as their
husbands' servants: Phythian-Adams, *Desolation
of a City,* p.87; Davis, 'Women in the Arts
Mécaniques' explores the various possibilities.
For a rather different view of the scale of female
apprenticeship, see Keith Snell, 'The Standard
of Living, Social Relations, the Family and
Labour Mobility in south-eastern and western
counties, 1700-1860', Cambridge Univ. Ph.D. 1979,
ch.v.

119. Well illustrated in the commentary to *The Penguin
Book of English Pastoral Verse,* eds. J. Barrell
and J. Ball, Harmondsworth, Penguin (1982).

120. J. Barrell, *The Dark Side of the Landscape.
The Rural Poor in English Painting. 1730-1840,*
Cambridge, C.U.P. (1980), p.51.

121. The removal of 'real' work from seventeenth-
century poems is well described in J. Turner,
The Politics of Landscape, Oxford, Blackwell
(1979), ch.6.

122. A. Ascham, *Of the Confusions and Revolutions of
Governments,* London (1649), p.25.

123. Baxter quoted in R.B. Schlatter, *The Social Ideas
of Religious Leaders, 1660-1688,* London, O.U.P.
(1940), p.67; *The Diary of John Manningham,*
ed. J. Bruce (Camden Soc., old ser., xcix, 1868),
135.

124. Barrell and Bull, eds., *English Pastoral Verse,*
pp.166-68.

125. E.P. Thompson, 'Time, Work Discipline and
Industrial Capitalism', *Past and Present,*
38 (1967), 61-63; cf. 79.

126. S. Duck, *Poems on Several Occasions,* London
(1736) contains 'The Thresher's Labour' at p.10;

much of the poem is reprinted in Barrell and Bull, eds. *English Pastoral Verse*, pp.385–90. For neo-classical literary influences in the poem see R.M. Davis, *Stephen Duck, The Thresher Poet*, Univ. Maine Studs., 2nd ser., viii (1926), 132–34.

127. Snell, 'Agricultural Seasonal Unemployment', 425–26; Roberts, 'Sickles and Scythes', 16–19.

128. cf. the poem attributed to Duck, 'On Providence' printed in Davis, *Stephen Duck*, pp.9–10:
> 'The wife would say, how can you be content?
> I know not how to pay your quarter's rent.
> I bid her look on birds in bushes there,
> And see the little silly insects here ...'

129. Davis, *Stephen Duck*, pp.61–65.

130. Mary Collier, *The Woman's Labour: An Epistle to Mr. Stephen Duck; In Answer to his late poem, called The Thresher's Labour*, London (1739).

131. For brewing on this basis, see Clark, *Working Life of Women*, pp.229–30.

132. Collier, *Woman's Labour*, p.12.

133. R. Masek, 'Women in an Age of Transition 1485–1714', in B. Kanner, ed. *The Women of England from Anglo-Saxon Times to the Present. Interpretive Bibliographical Essays*, London, Mansell (1980), pp.146–52, for a survey; cf. also I. MacLean, *Woman Triumphant. Feminism in French Literature 1610–1652*, Oxford, O.U.P. (1977), esp. ch.2.

134. Most readily demonstrated by examining the entries for 'woman', 'wife' and 'widow' in Tilley, *Dictionary of the Proverbs in England*. Advice on marriage was thought to be peculiarly fitted for proverbial expression by the compilers of these collections; cf. J. Heywood, *A Dialogue conteinyng the nomber in effect of all the prouerbes in the englishe tongue, compacte in a matter concernyng two manner of marriages*, London (1546); J. Howell, *Proverbs, or, old Sayed Sawes and Adages*, London (1659), containing *inter alia*, 'A Letter of Advice, Consisting all of Proverbs, (Running in one congruous and concurrent sense) to one that was towards Marriage', together with, at p.22, 'Some of Old John Heiwoods Rhimes' in proverb form, concerning marriage; J. Ray, *A Collection of English Proverbs*, Cambridge (1670), including 'Proverbs and Proverbial Observations referring to Love, Wedlock and Women' (some 95 in all) at pp.46–54. Ray observed of the adage 'England is the Paradise of Women' (p.54) that 'it is worth the noting, that though in no country of the world, the men

are so fond of, so much governed by, so wedded to their wives, yet hath no language so many proverbial invectives against women'. At least one writer, the French author of *The Woman as Good as Good as the Man*, London (1677) felt the impact of popular sentiments about marriage to be great; he complained (p.76) of the confirmation of anti-feminist prejudice in the common people through their respect for philosophers, who in this matter merely obtained their ideas from the same common fund of prejudice. For this author's Cartesian background, see P. Darmon, *Mythologie de la femme dans L'Ancien France*, Paris, Seuil (1983), pp.70-73.

135. *The XV Comforts of Rash and Inconsiderate Marriage*, London (1682), pp.63, 22.
136. *A Discourse of the Married and Single Life*, London (1621), p.66.
137. T.H. *A Curtaine Lecture*, London (1637), p.152.
138. For an attempt to delineate the sexes' different tastes, see Spufford, *Small Books and Pleasant Histories*, pp.62-65.
139. *The XV Comforts*, p.30.
140. *Ibid.*, p.31.
141. *Ibid.*, p.53.
142. Spufford, *Small Books*, ch.2.
143. *Ibid.*, p.14.
144. J.H., *Two Essays of Love and Marriage*, London (1657), pp.91-92; cf. *The Letters of Dorothy Osborne to William Temple*, ed. G. C. Moore Smith, Oxford (1928), p.51.
145. *The Carefull Wife's Good Counsel*, London (c. 1685-92).
146. *A Caveat for Young Men. Or, The Bad Husband turn'd Thrifty*, London (c.1670-77).
147. First recorded, respectively, in c. 1470, 1557 and 1620: *Oxford Dictionary of English Proverbs*, pp.819, 326, 909.
148. *The Woman to the Plow and the Man to the Hen-Roost*, London (c.1670-82): to 'grope the hen' was to seek out its eggs.
149. J.W. Blench, *Preaching in England in the late Fifteenth and Sixteenth Centuries*, Oxford, U.P. (1964), p.248.
150. e.g. N.Z. Davies, 'Women on Top' in her *Society and Culture in Early Modern France*, London, Duckworth (1975).
151. *The Penguin Book of Everyday Verse*, ed. D. Wright, Harmondsworth, Penguin (1976), pp.223-24; on the impact of agricultural change on the pastoral tradition see R. Williams, *The Country and*

The City, London, Chatto (1973), esp. ch.3.

152. Campion, 'Jack and Joan'.
153. cf. Masek, 'Women in an Age of Transition', pp.148–49.
154. *Character Writings of the Seventeenth Century*, ed. H. Morley, London (1891), pp.59, 210.
155. *Ibid.*, p.70.
156. The links between printed works and 'popular culture' are particularly problematic; for a recent discussion of some of the difficulties, and some proffered solutions, see C. Ginzburg, *The Cheese and the Worms*, London, Routledge (1980), pp.xiii–xxvi.
157. How far was there a greater interest in, and appreciation of, labour and its social value in this period? Greater attention has been noted by Thomas, 'Work and Leisure'; but how do we weigh the preoccupations of one age with those of another, particularly when the invention of printing distinguishes the early modern period from its predecessor? It is important to bear in mind the importance of slavery, serfdom and villeinage in medieval society: 'all three were ways and means of persuading reluctant workers to work', B. Harvey, 'Work and *Fosta Ferianda* in Medieval England', *Jnl. Eccles. Hist.*, xxiii (1972), 289.
158. In addition to the works cited in note 132 above see also J. Clarke, *Paromiologia Anglo-Latina*, London (1639); G. Herbert, *Jacula Prudentum Or, Outlandish Proverbs, Sentences, &c.*, London (1657); 1st edn., 1640); J. Kelly, *A Complete Collection of Scottish Proverbs Explained and made intelligible to the English Reader*, London (1721); T. Fuller, *Gnomologia*, London (1632).
159. The editing is most evident in the second edition of Ray, *A Collection of English Proverbs*, Cambridge (2nd edn., 1678), whose Preface explains the omission of some examples which 'have given offence to sober and pious persons, as savouring too much of obscenity'. Howell, *Proverbs*, Introduction 'To the knowingest kind of philosophers', describes his subject as 'the philosophy of the common people', and defends their use of 'down-right, and homely terms, with wanton natural expressions', which 'cannot be taxed with beastliness, or bawdry'. Later, Kelly noted the continued use of proverbs in Scotland 'especially among the better sort of the commonalty', *A Complete Collection*, Sig. A3[v].

For cautionary words about the use of proverbial
evidence, see N.Z. Davis, 'Proverbial Wisdom and
Popular Errors', in her *Society and Culture*
(note 148 above), esp. pp.243–53; cf. the use of
19th-century French proverbs, including over 1000
relating to marriage, in Martine Segalen,
Love and Power in the Peasant Family, Oxford,
Blackwell (1983).

160. 'The day is short but the work is long';
'Think of ease but work on'; 'The labour of a
husbandman returns in a ring'; 'I will not make
a toil of a pleasure'; 'Labour as long-lived,
pray as ever dying'; 'If the devil find a man
idle he'll set him to work'; 'He who does not
rise early never does good day's work'; 'Slow
at meat, slow at work'; 'Seek till you find,
and you'll not lose your labour'; all listed
in Tilley, *Dictionary of the Proverbs in England*.

161. Proverbs from various sources, listed in Tilley,
op. cit.

162. Through use of procedures enforcing labour under
the Statute of Artificers, and through the poor
relief and settlement systems; see below,
pp.53–57.

163. For an excellent account of this process, and of
its impact on relations between the 'better sort'
and the labouring poor, see Wrightson and Levine,
Poverty and Piety.

164. The decidedly non-revolutionary character of
most Puritan writing on the subject is
demonstrated in Davies, 'Continuity and Change
in Literary Advice on Marriage'; cf. also
Wrightson, *English Society*, pp.103–4.

165. M.W. Wood, 'Paltry Pedlars or Essential
Merchants? Women in the Distributive Trades in
Early Modern Nuremberg', *Sixteenth-Century Jnl.*,
xii (1981), 7–10.

166. Clark, *Working Life of Women*, pp.25–26, on
Bessey Welling, and p.33 for Dorothy Petty; for
the use of poor women to distribute farthing
tokens, see *A Remedie against the losse of the
Subject, by Farthing-Tokens*, London (1644), p.4.

167. Again, proverbial expressions indicate such
distrust, 'to play the merchant' with someone was
to cheat them; it was thought that 'a merchant
that gains not, loses', and that 'he that deals in
the world needs four sieves'. Distrust was
expressed in more formal fashion in the seventeenth
century on the subject of proliferating hawkers
and pedlars: *17th-Century Economic Documents*,
eds. Thirsk and Cooper, section 4, *passim*.

168. J.M. Beattie, 'The Criminality of Women in Eighteenth-Century England', *Jnl. Social Hist.*, viii (1975), 80-81 for counterfeiting; for shoplifters and pickpockets, *ibid.*, 94; C.Z. Wiener, 'Sex Roles and Crime in late Elizabethan Hertfordshire', *Jnl. Soc. Hist.*, viii (1975), 42.

169. Clark, *Working Life of Women*, pp.197-209, 218-21.

170. E.P. Thompson, 'The Moral Economy of the English Crowd in the Eighteenth Century', *Past and Present*, 50 (1971); cf. the particularly well-documented involvement of Ann Carter in 1629: J. Walter, 'Grain Riots and Popular Attitudes to the Law: Maldon and the Crisis of 1629', in J. Brewer and J. Styles, eds. *An Ungovernable People. The English and their Law in the Seventeenth and Eighteenth Centuries*, London, Hutchinson (1980).

171. Sharpe, *Defamation and Sexual Slander*, discussing the normative restriction of female activity on pp.20-21.

172. Proverbs from various sources, all listed in *Oxford Dictionary of English Proverbs*, except 'a journeying woman...', in Tilley, *Dictionary of the Proverbs in England*, no. W. 633. A 'rouk-toun' made a habit of wandering round her village.

173. Howell, *Proverbs*, p.20.

174. Ray, *English Proverbs* (2nd edn.), p.71.

175. It is clear, for example, that in the struggle against male corn-dealers, women were frequently popular heroines.

176. Tilley, *Dictionary of the Proverbs of England*.

177. Phythian-Adams, *Desolation of a City*, p.88: Coventry bakers' wives officially required to *conceal* any loaves they might be delivering to drinking establishments.

178. R. Jarvis Scott, 'Women in the Stuart Economy', London Univ. M. Phil thesis (1973), pp.64-74 discusses the problems of minding young children.

179. 'A description of Cleveland (c.1603-7)', *The Topographer and Genealogist*, ed. J.G. Nichols, ii (1853), 429: 'when any dieth, certain women sing a song to the dead body, reciting the journey that the party deceased must go'.

180. For the transmission of popular songs and stories by women, see Spufford, *Small Books and Pleasant Histories*, pp.4,12; J. Aubrey, *Brief Lives*, ed. O. Lawson Dick, Harmondsworth, Penguin (1972), p.29, describing how 'before the civil wars...

the fashion was for old women and maids to tell
fabulous stories nightimes, of sprights and
walking ghosts, &c. This was derived down from
mother to daughter ...'

181. The importance of 'maintenance labour' in
sustaining social relationships and values is
discussed in A.P. Cohen, 'The Whalsay Croft :
Traditional Work and Customary Identity in Modern
Times', in S. Wallman, ed. *The Social Anthropology
of Work*, London, Academic Press:A.S.A. Monograph
19 (1979), pp.262-65; cf. also *ibid.*, pp.348-55.

182. *The Womens Advocate : Or, Fifteen Real Comforts
of Matrimony*, London (1683), p.24.

183. K. Thomas, *Religion and the Decline of Magic*,
London, Weidenfeld (1971), p.278; women feature
prominently in this account as both witches and
prophets. cf. also the Protestant attack on
Mariolatry: Clark, *Working Life of Women*,
pp.238-39.

184. Easlea, *Witch-hunting*, pp.151-52; cf. Merchant,
Death of Nature, (note 60 above).

185. Wrigley and Schofield, *Population History*.

186. Kussmaul, *Servants in Husbandry*. For work in
progress in this field see the notes to P. Laslett,
The World We Have Lost-further explored,
London, Methuen (1983).

187. R.M. Smith, 'Fertility, Economy, and Household
Formation in England over Three Centuries',
Population and Development Rev., vii (1981),
615-19.

188. Most recently surveyed in P. Kriedte *et al.*,
Industrialisation Before Industrialisation,
Cambridge, C.U.P. (1981), esp. pp.38-93; cf.
also D. Levine, *Family Formation in an Age of
Nascent Capitalism*, London, Academic Press (1977);
and other works cited in M. Anderson,
*Approaches to the History of the Western Family
1500-1914*, London, Macmillan (1980), pp.92-93;
M. Berg et al., ed. *Manufacture in Town and
Country Before the Factory*, Cambridge, C.U.P.
(1983). But see also D.C. Coleman, 'Proto-
Industrialisation: A Concept Too Many?',
Econ. Hist. Rev., 2nd ser., xxxvi, 3 (1983),
434-48.

189. Masek, 'Women in an age of Transition', pp.150-51.

190. The Overbury murder scandal appears to have
focused misogynist sentiment under James I;
it was followed by a succession of anti-female
tracts, of which the most influential was J. Swetnam,
*The Arraignment of Lewd, Idle, Forward, and
Inconstant Women*, London (1615); Masek, 'Women',

p.149. But this period requires more detailed investigation; the years 1616–17 were also a period of anti-feminist literary activity in France, apparently associated with the burning of a prominent witch, and there was a 'cascade of denunciation' against women in 1618 and after: Maclean, *Woman Triumphant,* pp.31–33.

191. Wrigley and Schofield, *Population History,* pp.207–15; Kussmaul, *Servants in Husbandry,* ch.6. It has also been suggested, however, that population growth in Coventry from the 1560s onwards may have loosened, rather than tightened, restrictions on female activity in that town: Phythian-Adams, *Desolation of a City,* p.272.
192. Masek, 'Women in an Age of Transition', p.148.
193. [Allestree], *The Ladies Calling,* p.146, referring to the 'vulgar contempt under which that state lies'.
194. Parry, *Women, Letters and the Novel,* pp.34–35. Spufford, *Small Books and Pleasant Histories,* p.143 suggests that a new wave of courtship chapbooks emerging in the century before the 1680s reflected a 'new fashion, and perhaps a new preoccupation'.
195. Mathias, 'Leisure and Wages' (note 30, above); Kussmaul, *Servants in Husbandry,* p.103.
196. Clark, *Working Life of Women,* p.149 and *passim.* See also B.A. Holderness, *Pre-Industrial England,* London, Dent (1975), pp.203–4 for the changing economic pattern, which meant that things were 'notably better' for wage-workers in 1750 than they had been in 1600; real wages had, of course, declined considerably during the sixteenth century; cf. also Wrigley and Schofield, *Population History,* Appendix 9.
197. R.C. Wiles, 'The Theory of Wages in Later English Mercantilism', *Econ. Hist. Rev.,* 2nd ser., xxi (1968); Appleby, *Economic Thought and Ideology,* pp.181–85.
198. Harvey, 'Work and *Festa Ferianda',* 306.
199. W. Gouge, *Of Domesticall Duties,* London (1622), pp.592–93. W. Fleetwood, *The Relative Duties of Parents and Children, Husbands and Wives, Masters and Servants,* London (2nd edn., 1716), p.310.
200. In addition to that cited below, see also Chaytor, 'Household and Kinship', 48.
201. *Warwick County Records : Quarter Sessions Order Books,* eds. S.C. Ratcliffe and H.C. Johnson, Warwick (1935–53), v. 212.
202. *Surrey Quarter Sessions Records,* eds. D.L. Powell

and H. Jenkinson (Surrey Rec. Soc., xiv, 1935), ii. 150;   F.G. Emmison, *Elizabethan Life: Home, Work and Land,* Chelmsford, Essex C.C. (1976), p.154.

203. Emmison, *op.cit.,* p.160.
204. 5 Eliz., c.4 (1563).
205. *Minutes of Proceedings in Quarter Sessions ... Kesteven,* ed. S.A. Peyton (Lincs. Rec. Soc., xxvi, 1931), ii. 417.
206. W.E. Minchinton, ed. *Wage Regulation in Pre-Industrial England,* Newton Abbot, David and Charles (1972), p.125;   *County of Buckingham. Calendar to the Sessions Records,* eds. W. Le Hardy and G. Reckitt, Aylesbury (1933–58), i. 234.
207. Minchinton, ed. *Wage Regulation,* pp.124–58.
208. E.G. Dowdwell, *A Hundred Years of Quarter Sessions: The Government of Middlesex from 1660 to 1760,* Cambridge, C.U.P. (1932), p.156, n.5; *Warwicks. County Recs.,* v.212.
209. *Bucks. Sessions Recs.* i. 322.
210. Emmison, *Elizabethan Life,* p.155.
211. *Middlesex County Records,* ed. J.C. Jeaffreson, London (old ser., 1886–92), iii. 372–3.
212. J.A. Picton, *Selections from the Municipal Archives,* Liverpool (1883), p.116.
213. *Bucks. Sessions Recs.,*   ii. 184.
214. *Ibid.*
215. Emmison, *Elizabethan Life,* p.151.
216. *Bucks. Sessions Recs.,* i. 322.
217. *Minutes of Quarter Sessions ... Kesteven,* ii. 417; *Bucks.   Sessions Recs.,* ii. 184.
218. Dowdwell, *Hundred Years of Quarter Sessions,* p.156, n.5.
219. *Records of the Churches of Christ Gathered at Fenstanton, Warboys, and Hexham, 1644–1720,* ed. E.B. Underhill (Hanserd Knollys Soc., 1854), p.210.
220. *Guide to the Kent Archives Office,* Maidstone, Kent C.C. (1958), p.233.
221. Minchinton, ed. *Wage Regulation,* pp.125–26.
222. *Ibid.,*   p.126.
223. Defoe, *Great Law of Subordination,*   pp.86–87.
224. *Hist. MSS. Comm., Various Colls.,* i (1901), 132.
225. *Bucks. Sessions Recs.,*   ii. 399.
226. *Records of the Churches ... at Fenstanton,* p.210.

5 WOMEN'S LABOUR AND THE TRANSITION TO PRE-INDUSTRIAL CAPITALISM [1]

Chris Middleton

This paper deals with changes in the nature and value of women's work that occurred as a result of the development of capitalism in pre-industrial England. In particular, it will concentrate on changes in aspects of the sexual division of labour and in the economic contribution of women's work. These are, to say the least, large subjects and the coverage of them must necessarily be limited in certain ways. I shall therefore restrict this account to a discussion of the labouring classes (and then, principally, to those living and working in a rural setting). I shall also omit any detailed reference to women's involvement in housework and childcare (though, in so doing, I do not intend to imply that such activities have less social or economic significance than other kinds of work; still less that they can be counted among life's 'eternal verities' and hence lacking in essential interest to the historian or sociologist).

Two preliminary points need to be established. First, unlike the other contributors to this volume, I am not a trained historian. My main interest in the historical record is with the light it may shed on questions concerning the nature and origins of women's oppression in contemporary western capitalist societies, and for that reason the study is confined essentially to the perusal and interpretation of secondary literature. The second point to be emphasised is the tentative quality of the ideas presented in the following account. They are not firm conclusions held with iron conviction, though they do in my view make plausible sense of the limited and often contradictory evidence which we possess.

The case I wish to argue may be better appreciated if we consider first certain unsatisfactory features of a number of histories which perceive a relative deterioration in the position of labouring women during the course of the transition from feudalism to industrial capitalism. The accounts I have in mind may be said to form part of a 'critical-pessimistic' tradition insofar as most of their authors have been generally sympathetic to the cause of sex-equality, and owe much to Alice Clark's pioneering effort *Working Life of Women in the Seventeenth Century.* [2] It is a tradition that includes Pinchbeck's *Women Workers and the Industrial Revolution* and Tilly and Scott's *Women, Work and Family* since, whatever their assessment of the ultimately benign effects of industrialisation on women's work, both books share Clark's judgement regarding the harmful impact of its earlier stages. [3] In recent years a number of brief historical surveys including those by Hamilton, Oakley, Lewenhak and Zaretsky (each clearly intended to appeal to a much broader, non-specialist public than the earlier more substantial and careful works of scholarship) have repeated the claim that early capitalism and/or industrialisation restricted women's work opportunities and reduced their economic importance. [4] Indeed, this interpretation has almost acquired the status of a conventional wisdom among people committed to the feminist cause. Yet the argument leaves me unconvinced. At the theoretical level it tends to rely on concepts with a doubtful pedigree (for example, capitalist definitions of economic value have been uncritically adopted and indiscriminately applied); while at the substantive level it rests on several false assumptions about the sexual division of labour and related aspects of economic organisation under the feudal mode of production. Moreover, and this is the main focus of the present paper, I think it can be shown that the effects of the process of transition from feudalism to industrial capitalism were both more complicated and uneven than the 'critical-pessimistic' tradition generally suggests.

The 'Critical-Pessimistic' Tradition

The central theme of this tradition is an account of the loss of women's productive capacity that is thought to have occurred as a result of the rise of industrial-capitalism. One is immediately faced with a problem, however. While some authors attribute this loss principally to the development of capitalism, others attribute it to the spread of factory industry, and still others seem unaware of, or confused about, any distinction that might be made between the two.

Alice Clark's book, for all its many virtues, falls into the final category. Here the concepts of capitalism and industrialism are collapsed into each other as can be seen in her threefold classification of production systems:

(i) Domestic Industry is defined as that form of production in which goods are produced for the exclusive use of the family and, therefore, as not being subject to an exchange or money value;

(ii) Family Industry is that form in which the family becomes the unit of production of goods to be sold or exchanged – a form which, she says, is characterised by the unity of capital and labour and the location of work within the precincts of the home;

(iii) Capitalistic Industry, which she equates with Industrialism, is defined as a form of production where wages are paid to individuals and whose establishment is secured by the departure of the father from the home to work on the capitalist's premises.[5]

As these opening definitions indicate Clark is not at all clear regarding distinctions that might be drawn between capitalism and industrialism. In fact, when it comes to attributing responsibility for the deterioration in women's productive role, her emphasis falls firmly on developments which we should nowadays associate with industrialisation rather than on those earlier changes which are denoted by the phrase 'the rise of capitalism'. These were:

(a) the substitution of an individual for a family wage, enabling men to organise themselves in the competition which ruled the labour market, without sharing with the women of their families all the benefits derived through their combination. [6]

(b) the withdrawal of wage-earners from home-life to work upon the premises of the masters, which prevented the employment of the wage-earner's wife in her husband's occupation.

(c) the rapid increase of wealth which permitted the women of the upper classes to withdraw from all connection with business. [7]

The true significance of Clark's argument is obscured by her equation of all three developments with 'Capitalism'. But the first two changes – the shift to an individual wage, and the withdrawal of wage-earners from home life (not all men, incidentally!) – were not, in fact, typical of capitalist expansion before the onset of industrialisation proper. The third, which was, does not concern us here as it did not involve the labouring classes. Admittedly, Clark does show that the seventeenth century capitalisation of crafts and trades and the simultaneous professionalisation of teaching, nursing and medicine led to the exclusion of women from many productive and skilled employments in which they had previously been engaged, and from which they had often derived a fair measure of personal independence. Yet she is also quite definite that the main thrust of change came after the seventeenth century:

> This depreciation of the woman's productive value to her family did not greatly influence her position in the seventeenth-century, because it was then only visible in the class of wage-earners, and into this position women were forced by poverty alone. The productive efficiency of women's services in domestic industry remained as high as ever, and every family which was possessed of sufficient capital for domestic industry, could provide sufficient profitable occupation for its women without their entry into the labour market. [8]

There are several contentious points in this passage with which one might wish to take issue, but the principal thesis is quite clear. Clark's conclusion is, in fact, remarkably similar to that reached by Ivy Pinchbeck who attributed the loss of women's opportunities for productive work at home to the agrarian revolution, and the loss of employment in the older domestic industries to concurrent changes in industrial organisation. [9]

Thus a meticulous reading of Clark's argument shows her to be of the opinion that the majority of female producers were little affected by the rise of capitalism before the spread of factory industry in the eighteenth and nineteenth centuries. Yet, strangely, this is not the impression that one takes away after a casual reading, and even some of her more careful interpreters have, I think, been misled in this regard (notably Hamilton – see below). In part, no doubt, the ambiguity and confusion stem from her decision to focus on the seventeenth century, with the resultant concentration in detail upon changes which are eventually admitted to have had less significance than subsequent developments. But at a more profound level they surely arise from her choice of conceptual categories. Confusion is unavoidable because Clark's model made no allowance for the capitalistic organisation of industry in the producers' own homes through various forms of the putting-out system. The model's categories move straight from Family Industry to full-blown, capitalistic, factory industry, and so leave in a conceptual limbo that stage of pre-industrial (or, more accurately, proto-industrial) capitalism that was actually so vital both to the process of capital accumulation and to the restructuring of the sexual division of labour.

Given Clark's conflation of Capitalistic Industry and Industrialism it is somewhat surprising to find Roberta Hamilton, who draws a sharp distinction between a capitalist revolution in the seventeenth century and the onset of industrialisation a hundred years later, quoting Clark as an authority in her support.[10] This oddity aside, Hamilton is surely right to stress the importance of such a distinction for the analysis of changes in women's labour before the nineteenth century. Her clarity on this basic issue is perhaps the outstanding merit of a thought-provoking monograph.[11] Yet Hamilton's argument, too, can be challenged on several major points. She argues:

a) that the economic base of the pre-industrial but post-feudal family was the same as that of the industrial family, being totally dependent on the wage-labour of individual family members;

b) that, as a result of the capitalist revolution in production, the family ceased to be the economic unit of production, shattering the interdependent relationship of husband and wife in the process;

c) that, when families were evicted from the land, women lost the means to help provide a living for their families;

d) that, forced to sell their labour-power, women could no longer combine their general labour with the bearing and rearing of children.[12]

The effects of capitalisation were, in reality, much more variable than Hamilton suggests. Her portrayal of the process may describe well enough the experience of some newly-created wage-labourers; but the capitalisation of those industries which employed the largest numbers of workers, especially the textile industries, did not immediately remove production from the home, did not eliminate the married woman's non-domestic contribution to the household budget, and did not altogether render her general labour incompatible with the bearing and rearing of children (though this last point raises awkward issues as we shall see). Moreover, the fact that many pre-industrial and post-industrial families depended on wage-labour is not sufficient grounds for claiming that they shared an identical economic base. The material experience of the working household in the proto-capitalist economy was in fundamental respects quite different from that of the industrial proletarian, even though both depended on wages.

I have now outlined several kinds of difficulty and error that arise from failing to conceptualise adequately the transition from feudalism to industrial capitalism. If we are to avoid these problems in the future we shall need first to identify several kinds of capital-labour relation (as would be associated, for example, with merchant capital, proto-capital, and full-blown industrial capital), and then to investigate the varying nature and extent of capital's interventions in the actual organisation of the labour process that tended to result in each instance. Further, we shall have to become more alive to the fact that the transition from feudalism to industrial capitalism was not one of unilinear progression, but gave rise to new forms of labour-process and organisation that contained within them insoluble contradictions which resulted in their disappearance, or at least their banishment to peripheral sectors of the industrial capitalist economy.

The Sexual Division of Labour

If confusion regarding the significance of changes in the structure of women's labour stems in part from a failure to distinguish different modes of capital accumulation, our understanding is not helped if we also fail to appreciate that the concept of the sexual division of labour is not a simple one, but one compounded of several distinct elements. In the discussion that follows I shall break the concept apart in order to refer to three different kinds of division. These are not intended to constitute a classification of the types of the sexual division of labour (that is to say they are not mutually exclusive, nor do they exhaust all the possibilities), but should rather be regarded as offering analytical orientations to the phenomenon.

(i) Sex-specific aspects of the technical division of labour. This term will be used to refer to the sex-specific allocation of jobs - a process which may be further broken down and considered in terms of two sub-processes: task differentiation and occupational specialisation. Briefly, the term task-differentiation will be used to refer to the decomposition of a particular labour-process (be it harvesting, the manufacture of cloth, the production of canned foods or whatever) into a number of component tasks that may then perhaps be allocated according to the worker's sex (or indeed by any other criteria). Disaggregation of this kind may occasionally allow certain task-specialists to acquire specific new skills (i.e. beyond such fluency as comes from the repetitive performance of some simple and monotonous task), but plainly this is by no means an inevitable outcome, and many labour-processes are undoubtedly dismembered precisely in order to obviate the need to provide workers with costly training in appropriate skills. On the other hand occupational specialisation will be used to refer to a development in the relations between a worker and his or her work that, whilst involving a reduction in the range of activities performed, also leads to the acquisition of an occupational identity. Occupational specialisation will commonly be associated with the acquisition of prestigious skills, enhanced scope for low-level decision-taking in the performance of one's job, and the receipt of other, material rewards.[13]

(ii) The sexual division of necessary labour. Necessary labour is defined here as labour which is necessary for the reproduction of labour-power itself. This may take the form of direct contributions to the producers' household economy, the production of goods and services which are then exchanged for an income, or, in a capitalist wage-sector, labour that is equivalent to the value of the wage.[14] Consideration of the declining 'value' or usefulness of female labour during industrialisation has in fact tended to concentrate heavily on this particular aspect of the sexual division of labour, whereas discussions of men's labour are hardly ever couched preponderantly in these terms. Without wishing to downgrade the importance of necessary labour there are grounds for concern here, for it is all too easy to slide into the false assumption that the 'value' of women's labour can be measured solely in terms of what they provide for their households and families.[15]

Analysis of the sexual division of necessary labour must attend both to the relative weight of the contribution made by each sex and to the mechanics of the process by which that contribution is made. (What are the productive forces involved? Does the performance of necessary labour involve either sex in production for a market or tie them directly into a relation of class exploitation? etc.) Both aspects will obviously be affected by the prevailing pattern according to which jobs are allocated by sex.

(iii) The sexual division of surplus labour. Limitations of space will prevent any empirical treatment of surplus labour in the present article. Nevertheless it is worth outlining some of its general features, not least because they bear upon the way in which we empirically define necessary labour.

Surplus labour is defined in the Marxist sense, i.e. as expropriated labour. The term is not intended to refer to the production of goods or values consumed by the producers and which are judged by some external 'authority' to be surplus to the 'essential' or 'subsistence' needs of the producers. (Surely, as ahistorical a notion as one is ever likely to meet!)

The concept of the sexual division of surplus labour operates on two planes. In the first instance, of course, it relates to traditional Marxist categories of class: we may week to identify the sexual division of that labour which is expropriated by feudal or capitalist classes. (A question that may have some bearing on women's involvement in class-based struggles and in public affairs.) This poses no particular problems conceptually, though disentangling the respective contributions of each sex empirically may be a difficult and occasionally impossible task. Secondly, it is possible for women's labour to be expropriated by their husbands, fathers, brothers and so on. (I have explored some of the theoretical issues raised by this possibility elsewhere).[16] In consequence we must accept that some female labour that has traditionally been conceived of as necessary labour, insofar as it has appeared as a contribution to the household economy, should more properly be analysed as surplus labour expropriated by men, and our assessment of women's contribution to the 'home' re-appraised accordingly. Note, finally, that female and other household labour expropriated by a husband, father etc. could provide an impetus to capital accumulation so uniting class and patriarchal exploitation into a single process.

Sex–Specific Aspects of the Technical Division of Labour

Let us consider first the impact of capitalist development in the countryside on the sexual division of jobs. Contrary to common belief the nature of that impact seems to have been far from uniform, but to have depended in large measure on the kind of capital–labour relation (i.e. the particular form of expropriation) established in different sectors of the rural economy. In the following discussion we shall examine developments in two major sectors: first, changes in the pattern of job–allocation which tended to accompany the capitalisation of large-scale agriculture, and then the repercussions of the spreading capitalistic organisation of domestic industry (which I shall define here, unlike Clark, as handicraft industry performed outside the factory and typically in the producers' own home). [17]

Large-scale capitalist agriculture.

Under feudalism the essential instrument through which lords expropriated the surplus product was a rent calculated according to the size of the peasant holding. This was supplemented by income from a range of taxes and personal dues, the profits of jurisdiction, and various production and market monopolies. It was an arrangement that had made the peasant holding, and the labour force attached to it, the cornerstone of feudal property relations. On the one hand the holding served as the direct source of rental income including, where required, the supply of seasonal and part-time bond-labour to the demesne estate; on the other it enabled tenants to produce marketable surpluses out of whose revenues fines and taxes could be met. It was also, necessarily, the essential basis of the peasant household's own subsistence.

Organisation of the labour force on the basis of the peasant holding meant that in most circumstances there was little opportunity for extensive occupational specialisation among the mass of the labouring population. The relatively small size of each labour unit would prevent any major developments along these lines. There was, of course, a traditional demarcation between 'women's work' and 'men's work' applying to both agricultural and household tasks,[18] but it was a division of labour that must perforce remain flexible, and there is no lack of evidence indicating that peasants often performed work not customarily associated with their particular sex.

There were, however, two notable exceptions to this widespread dearth of specialists: a stratum of skilled craftworkers – smiths, carpenters, thatchers and so on – plying their trades on a permanent or at least seasonal basis; and certain waged, though still unfree, workers among the permanent staff employed on some of the larger manorial estates. These were known as *famuli*. Here, where the grander scale of the enterprise allowed the introduction of a more complex division of labour than was possible elsewhere, certain labourers appear to have been employed more or less exclusively in a specialist capacity. This occurred, for example, on eighteen thirteenth-century estates belonging to the Earls of Cornwall, the Abbots of Crowland and the Bishop of Winchester.[19] It is noticeable that most of the specialist *famuli* on these estates (ploughmen, shepherds, herdsmen, carters, millers etc.) were engaged in activities traditionally carried on by men, and that comparable openings for women (mainly in the dairy and gardens) were relatively few. The great majority of female *famulae* were recorded as 'servants'; and while we may readily acknowledge that many women employed in this capacity would not have been mere household drudges, there is surely some significance in the fact that women were already more likely to be recruited into general rather than specialist occupations, and in the further fact that the label applied to most permanently waged female labourers referred to their subordinate status rather than to the nature of the tasks they performed in that role.

Permanent, waged bond-labourers had been essential figures on many large feudal estates since at least the thirteenth century, yet it remains true that demesne farming relied heavily on the unwaged, obligatory part-time labour of the feudal peasantry. With this background in our minds, we may now ask how the technical division of labour changed once the dependence on obligatory labour began to decline and the landed estates converted gradually into capitalist enterprises.

During the sixteenth, seventeenth and eighteenth centuries the preponderance of the great landed estate in the agrarian economy increased through discontinuous but cumulative processes of dispossession and amalgamation. Over the same period, and apparently associated with this growth, there seems to have been a marked rise in occupational specialisation among agricultural labourers. Evidence from account books and diaries suggests that this development was concentrated on estates given over to arable farming or, to a lesser degree, on lowland sheep farms, i.e. in those sectors where the intrusion of commercial principles was having the greatest impact on farming methods and technology.[20] The technical division of labour on some of these estates attained quite sophisticated heights and the number of specialist labourers employed was often quite remarkable. The spread of occupational specialisation even encouraged the extension of 'craft-like' principles into regular agricultural activity (especially where the labour force was relatively immobile) so that, according to Alan Everitt, 'certain arts become traditional in certain families' and 'labourers could afford to stick to the particular farm-crafts in which they had been trained.'[21]

The salient aspect of these developments from the point of view of the sexual division of jobs was the persistence of that pattern already established on the feudal estates. The spread of occupational specialisation, and with it the enhancement of an individual's occupational identity, was predominantly confined to men. Opportunities for women were still limited to the dairy and market garden. But it is not just a matter of women being debarred from a range of new opportunities; nor even a case of relative decline while their own circumstances remain essentially unaltered. Growing occupational specialisation affects the work-situation of those who remain non-specialists, rendering it less varied. There is an inevitable reduction in the flexibility of task-allocation and the work of non-specialist labourers, among whom women are disproportionately represented, becomes more routine, monotonous and unskilled.

There are several obvious parallels between this development in large-scale agriculture and concurrent changes in the sex-specific technical division of labour in crafts, trades and professions as described by Alice Clark; and this occurred despite substantial differences in their underlying form of organisation. Clark attributed the exclusion of women from skilled work partly to the processes of capitalisation and bureaucratisation, and partly to men organising with each other in ways that excluded women. In agriculture the advent of capitalist farming undoubtedly led to a deterioration in women's position at work, both relatively and absolutely, but capitalism cannot be blamed for the invention of a discriminatory pattern which actually had much earlier origins. I would suggest, rather, that capitalism's responsibility lay, first, in its encouragement of land concentration (since larger farm-units were essential if occupational specialisation was to spread), and second, in its promotion of commercial attitudes which stimulated the more efficient organisation of human resources.

The growth of occupational specialisation among agricultural wage-labourers enabled a certain number of predominantly male workers to form a nascent labour aristocracy. Approaching the issue from this direction draws attention to a rarely considered context for traditional debates on this well-worn subject. Whatever the situation among male workers, eligibility for membership of this marginally privileged group was initially governed by the person's sex, i.e. by reference to ascriptive criteria, and not by any consideration of the individual's capacities or achievements. Moreover, sex was not a characteristic that had intrinsic relevance to the individual's capacity to perform most of the tasks in question (though Michael Roberts has argued that male physical strength was important in determining the male monopoly of mowing.)[22]

What we see here, in fact, is an early example of a segmented capitalist labour market, i.e. one which comprises several co-residing submarkets each recruiting from distinct social groupings, and allowing relatively little movement across their boundaries. Moreover, the similarity in the general contours of segmentation as between early agrarian capitalism and twentieth-century industry is very striking. Not only was sex a major criterion governing access to most positions, but there seem to have been fewer opportunities for wage-work open to women and girls; the range of opportunities offered them was more limited; their pay was generally lower; and they were often employed in personal service occupations.

The implications of this observation are quite extensive. Theories of labour market segmentation have come to provide an essential frame of reference for discussions about female wage-labour in modern capitalist economies, and it has been widely assumed that segmentation was a consequence of capitalist development.[23] It would be premature to assume some unbroken historical chain linking the gender-divided capitalist labour markets of the two periods, but it does strike me as interesting that one of the earliest examples of a gender-divided capitalist labour market was so clearly derived from a pattern found on certain feudal estates – where labour may have been paid but no market in labour was involved.

Capitalist organisation of domestic industry

On the large capitalist farm we have just described, the organisation and direction of the immediate labour process lay in the hands of the capitalist or his agent. The relations of production approximated the classic Marxian model of the capitalist enterprise where the owner of capital invests in the labour-power of the propertyless, and where returns on capital depend in the first instance on the difference between the cost of labour-power and the value added to the product in the course of the labour process. Under these conditions the efficient utilisation of human capital, the productivity of labour, is an imperative feature of the enterprise. The level of surplus extracted will be determined in part by the technical division of labour and the co-ordination of workers within each unit of production.

But if, in the organisation of these farms, we see an intimation of the shape of things to come, we should not let the privilege of hindsight distort our perception of their significance in contemporary society. In many other sectors of the rural economy, especially on the holdings of yeomen and husbandmen and within the domestic system of industry, control over the organisation of the immediate labour process remained in the hands of the producers themselves.

From as early as the fourteenth century the population in the countryside was becoming progressively more involved in rural industries, and especially in market-oriented, handicraft industry in the home.[24] Much of this expansion was due to the growing capitalistic organisation of domestic industry. However, in this sector capital penetration did not have the same kind of impact on the sexual division of labour as it was having within large-scale agriculture. In fact, households engaged in domestic production allocated tasks to each sex in a variety of ways, and there were also marked disparities in the degree to which such households would conform to the particular patterns of sexual differentiation prevailing in their region or industry. Our analysis must therefore attempt to answer two questions. Why, first of all, was such diversity ever allowed? (Why, in other words, did the capitalist merchant or employer not attempt to achieve a closer control over the organisation of the immediate labour process?) Secondly, what kinds of factor governed the emergence of one particular pattern rather than another in different sets of circumstance?

To answer the first question we must recognise that, under the domestic system, capital established relations with labour that were fundamentally different from those developed on the capitalist farm or, later, in the capitalist factory. In relation to domestic production capital functioned essentially either as merchant-capital or as proto-capital, though several variants on these basic themes were also possible. Merchant capital relied on independent artisans who, using their own raw materials and tools, undertook several stages of a production process. The merchants supplied the raw materials and/or purchased the finished products. Proto-capitalism, on the other hand, saw the creation of a class relationship intermediate between those of merchant and industrial capitalism. This is not to say, however, that proto-capitalism served always as a transitional form. As Pat Hudson has observed:

> So-called 'advanced' forms of the putting-out system with well developed regional specialisation of labour, high degree of wage dependency and decreasing divorce of labour from the land often proved to be a dead end developmentally. De-industrialisation often followed.[25]

Proto-capitalism appears as a distinct form when capital begins to organise production on its own account. The wage-relation between the proto-capitalist and the producer is a refinement of the relation between cloth-merchant and producer described by Diane Hutton elsewhere in this volume. There the 'wage' was actually the price-difference between two transactions conducted by the merchant: between the 'sale' price of the raw wool or cloth to the producers and the 'repurchasing' price for the finished product. This modified form of merchant-capitalism shades imperceptibly into proto-capitalism as three interconnected developments take place: producers are deprived of alternative sources of livelihood and become completely dependent on the wage; they lose possession of the means of production – often by falling into debt to the merchant; and (again often through debt) they become forcibly attached to a single employer. Thus the characteristic features of proto-capitalism are (i) capital's ownership of raw materials and, sometimes, the tools of the trade; (ii) the separation of producers from adequate means of subsistence so that they must sell their labour; (iii) the purchase by capital of the worker's labour. It is this final characteristic that distinguishes proto-capitalism from 'fully-fledged' capitalism. Proto-capitalism is based on piece-work rates. The entrepreneur pays his workers not for the right to use their capacity to labour, but for value already added to a finished product (less, of course, retained profits). The commodity bought by the proto-capitalist is dead labour - not labour power. This signifies a fundamental difference in the relation between capital and labour for it means that the capitalist remains essentially indifferent to the productivity of labour. Given readily available and cheap supplies of unemployed or underemployed workers, capital can accumulate by extending (in Mendels' phrase) the productivity of workers rather than the productivity of labour, i.e. by forcing an increase in the number of hours they work.[26]

Thus, domestic production could be related to capital in a variety of ways including simple market production for known markets, production for distant markets through merchant intermediaries, production for merchants where the latter had established monopolies over outlets, and proto-capitalism. But in none of these circumstances were producers typically faced with the threat of direct, conscious and systematic interventions in the organisation of the labour-process.

If that helps to explain why variations in the sexual division of jobs might occur, it does not account for the adoption of a particular pattern in any given circumstance. To answer this second question we shall need to reflect on the wider socio-economic contexts within which rural industrial households were situated.

Apart from the size and structure of the household itself, I would suggest that two interrelated factors had most influence on the allocation of tasks by sex, occupational specialisation, and the rigidity of adherence to prevailing norms: (i) the particular local configuration of employment opportunities and labour supply, and (ii) the particular form of capital-labour relation involved, insofar as this impinged on the organisation of household labour as an exogenous structural constraint rather than through a policy of deliberate intervention by the capitalist.

(i) Local configuration of employment opportunities and labour supply. It is two decades now since Joan Thirsk first suggested that the location of most rural industries was by no means solely or even primarily determined by the technological or geomorphological requirements of the industry in question.[27] Instead she postulated a number of socio-economic conditions, relating especially to the supply of labour, that seemed likely to influence the emergence of industry, and especially of handicraft industry, in any particular rural area. For our purposes the most salient of these conditions were: a

popular community most of whom have secure tenure; a
pastoral rather than an arable economy, resting either on
dairying or breeding and rearing but, in either event,
resulting in the presence of underemployed labour; and a
prevalence of independent farms (either enclosed or having
access to generous commons), rather than powerful
manorial organisation or co-operative husbandry. The
family is the recognised unit of production. On the whole,
subsequent research and the re-evaluation of earlier
studies have tended to confirm the importance of these
factors in the location of rural industries.[28]

But subsequent work on the implications of Thirsk's
hypothesis, and related studies of rural underemployment
such as Coleman's work on labour in the seventeenth
century,[29] have tended to concentrate heavily on the
structure of male underemployment. Bias in the sources
may make such selectivity understandable, but it cannot
be justified theoretically for, where a household's labour-
power was not amply absorbed in time-consuming arable
cultivation, the result was a reduction in the labour
expenditure of the household as a whole and not just that
of its male members. It would be a mistake to analyse
underemployment in individualistic terms. The process was
evidently not one where individual workers, finding
themselves underemployed, turned to rural industry to
earn a supplementary income. Underemployment affected
the labour availability of the whole household, and might
result in a complete re-ordering of the household's labour
resources.

The manner of that re-ordering was, however, highly
variable. The alternatives are perhaps best conceived by
constructing two modal patterns of adaptation, whilst
recognising that in practice these merely provided a basis
for many diverse practices. In the first more common
kind of arrangement the husband-father became a full-time
wage-labourer in industry (for example, in mining or
quarrying as in some parts of Western England, or
framework-knitting as in some Leicestershire villages),[30]
while care of the farm or smallholding and of the animals
was undertaken by his wife or children. In addition the
wife would have been expected to perform household and
caring duties, and might become involved in domestic
industry as well. Where the husband's employment kept
him at home, as among the framework-knitting families of
Shepshed, the domestic industry of other members of the
family might well be connected to his own.[31] One would
expect this pattern generally to have predominated in
dairying areas.

In the other modal arrangement men combined
pastoral farming with some form of domestic industry.
Here, too, wives would combine household duties with some

by-industrial employment (again possibly linked to that of their husbands), but they would tend to withdraw from involvement in agrarian activity. Many examples of this pattern could be found in the hill-farming dale communities of Cumbria and the Northern Pennines. It also, incidentally, appears to have been very common in parts of France — a comparison which obviously invites further investigation. [32]

Given the situation in which rural industrial households found themselves, deviations from the two modal types tended to result in a greater degree of symmetry between the sexes as regards the performance of tasks, as each become engaged in both farming and industrial activities. One is inevitably led to speculate whether men, in this event, ever took on responsibility for a significant amount of housework. It is not something one can be dogmatic about, but certainly I have not yet come across any English evidence to compare with the German experience where 'sex-role reversal' in rural industrial households was noted by several contemporary observers. [33]

(ii) Capital-labour relations. Although, as indicated, there was little deliberate manipulation of the labour-process by capitalists organising domestic industry, the discretion of producers would be limited by structural constraints whose nature and intensity varied according to the type of capital-labour relation involved. Repercussions were likely in two areas: the flexibility of the sex-specific divisions of tasks, and the convenience with which domestic industry could be fitted in with women's responsibilities for child-care and housework (though perhaps, sometimes, these ceased to be women's responsibilities alone).

The effects of the expansion of proto-capital on the sex-specific division of labour have been brilliantly analysed by Hans Medick, and I base my remarks on his work. The family of the rural industrial worker was caught up in a specific family-based mode of production that 'created new preconditions of household formation determined by market conditions on the one hand and by the poverty of rural producers on the other.'[34] A family engaged in rural industry under proto-capitalism found itself on the margins of subsistence and so relied heavily on the earnings of all members of the family. Since the ratio between the earnings-capacity and the consumption-cost of each individual was generally at its most favourable among young couples and grown children, a pattern of early marriage and high fertility became common with the consequence that the proto-proletarian family, although generally nuclear in structure, tended to be significantly larger than that of the sub-peasant or land-poor population. The size-differential was reinforced by the tendency for children to stay in the family home for a longer period. (The seeming paradox of children staying longer at home but marrying earlier than others in order to establish an independent household may be explained by the low proportion of children from these families going into domestic service.)[35]

The proto-proletarian household therefore represents a break from the traditional correlation between the size of household and the degree to which tasks are allocated according to sex. The sexual division of labour appears highly flexible in a household which, by the standards of a propertyless unit in pre-industrial society, was notably large.

However, one major restriction on the flexibility of the sexual division of labour did exist. Since the relations of production set such a high premium on child labour, the wife must partially withdraw from the labour process at frequent intervals to procreate and care for infants. This established the typical life-cycle of the proto-proletarian family. When a newly married couple established an independent household they were poor; with the birth of children they became poorer; with the children's maturation they began to prosper; and with their own children's marriage they became poor again sinking finally into destitution as they aged.

The dilemmas of the life-cycle were accentuated under bad market conditions when even smallholders, not yet in a permanent proto-industrial situation, could be turned into temporary rural artisans. Yet proto-proletarian families did not respond to economic fluctuations in ways that might superficially appear as rational to the uninformed outsider – e.g. by reducing family-size in times of straitened circumstances. Naturally, if fertility-rates remained at a high level their collective situation must eventually be worsened as the supply of labour outstripped demand and wages were pushed down yet further; but from each couple's point of view there was little point in restricting the size of one's own family because adult workers could not maintain themselves on adult wages alone. There was, disastrously, a total contradiction between the rational interests of each individual proto-proletarian household and the economic interests of the class as a whole.

As well as influencing the sexual division of labour, the tightening grip of capitalist relations on domestic industry seems likely to have affected the ease with which industrial activity could be integrated with the care of children and other household responsibilities. Before exploring this, however, let me digress briefly to comment on the way in which historians have often used the presumed fit between women's domestic responsibilities and their other activities as an explanation of the kinds of agricultural or industrial labour that women have typically undertaken, and which come to be identified as 'women's work'. Two qualities in the nature of their work are usually deemed essential: that it should allow children to be kept under close supervision by their mothers or by other older girls and women; and that it should not be seriously disorganised by constant interruptions to the work-flow. (Spinning, for example, has often been regarded as archetypal women's work because of the ease with which it can be turned to in spare moments.) [36]

This kind of argument is wheeled out with monotonous regularity, but has rarely been examined. Yet it is, at best, a partial and incomplete explanation of the sexual allocation of tasks and, at worst, I think it can be positively misleading. First, it tends to assume unquestioningly that women will always be responsible for childcare and servicing functions within the household; second, it fails to say why some home-based activities were typically performed by women while others, no less 'convenient' in this regard, were customarily allocated to men; and third, it fails to explain why women were persistently expected to fill their spare moments with some industrious activity, whereas no comparable expectations were held of men. We may remember an old rhyme that dates back at least to the Middle Ages:

> Some respit to husbands the weather may send
> But huswiues affaires haue neuer an end.[37]

But this quality of women's working experience is not simply 'in the nature of women's work' as though that was all there was to be said about it. After all, what was there to prevent men, as they took their leisure, from taking spindle and distaff in hand and beginning to spin?[38] (Or their modern-day equivalents from sewing or knitting as they sit in front of the television?) Rather, definitions of the kind of work seen as appropriate for women must be seen as deriving, at least in part, from social control mechanisms governing the allocation of women's 'time'. [39]

However, none of the above arguments challenges the premise that by-industrial activity was 'convenient' in the manner claimed. Yet this too is an assumption that surely needs to be looked at. The same kinds of assumption have often been made with respect to modern wives and mothers who engage in homeworking or take up part-time employment. But recent sociological research in this area reveals that far from finding the work convenient, most women complain about the way in which their paid work creates difficulties for the supervision of children, reduces the space available in the home and exposes children to danger, interferes with the smooth running of the household, and forces the women themselves to work appallingly long hours. It is hardly surprising, therefore, that real financial pressures rather than the desire to earn 'pin-money' are given as the commonest reason for undertaking such work, it being the only type available that is even minimally compatible with looking after children.

I am not suggesting that evidence taken from a modern industrial society can be readily transposed to a rural industrial economy, not least because housework and childcare made fewer demands on women's time and effort than they do today. Lindsey Charles points out that in many hard pressed cottage industries children who by our standards were very young were enlisted to work in some capacity in the household's production, so would not need separate minding while they played; and that even babies required less time and attention given lower standards of hygiene. Moreover, with more compact living conditions, fewer pieces of furniture and equipment, and less concern over standards of cleanliness, she suggests that housework too would have been less time-consuming than it has since become, though these 'advantages' may have been offset by a heavier sewing load, spinning for home consumption etc. [40] Nevertheless, it is clear that we cannot blithely assume that women's domestic industrial labour could be readily accommodated to her other functions, and there are indeed indications not only that women's labour in general was more unending than that of men, but also that the amount of women's work could seriously reduce the level of attention received by infant children, sometimes with serious results. [41]

If we can resist the temptation to assume some essential compatibility between women's various labours we may also start to think of the relation between them in historical terms, rather than as the timeless round of activity which is so often implied. It seems reasonable to suppose, for instance, that as households became increasingly dependent on earnings from domestic industry, and especially as they became dependent on monopoly buyers or were turned into employees of proto-capitalists, their industrial activity would have become increasingly geared to fluctuating, unknown markets, making it difficult for them to integrate domestic industry with housework and the care of infants, (though where this process involved the loss of a family smallholding women might experience some relief from time spent caring for livestock, making butter, processing food and so on). It seems that when historians discuss the effects of market fluctuations on the living standards of workers, they tend to think not only in narrow, economistic terms, but also in a medium or long-term time scale of prosperity and hardship. But as domestic industry became more firmly entrenched in capitalist markets the effects of short-term fluctuations on family life cannot be ignored. A sudden upsurge in orders with deadlines to be met, all too probable in industries producing for luxury markets (which were often the most sweated trades), might bring some financial relief but could play havoc with household routines. David Levine has argued that the experience of domestic production differed fundamentally from that of factory production insofar as the former allowed the worker to control the pace of production.[42] He has a point. But we should also recognise that control over the pace of domestic production must at times have been subject to extremely severe constraints. I doubt whether domestic industry was ever quite so convenient as is usually implied, but as proto-capitalism developed its demands must have become increasingly disruptive of home-life.

The Productiveness of Women Workers

It is one of the curiosities of historiography that, like the reputedly chronic state of insolvency among farmers or the permanent decline in middle class prosperity, women's contribution to economic life appears to be perpetually on the wane. Historians of every period (at least until the present century) depict women as undergoing a process of rapidly advancing economic marginality, yet those of subsequent periods attest with equal conviction to women's economic vigour and importance at the start of their own age. We are faced then with apparently contradictory statements, only some of which can be attributed to the fact that different scholars may have focussed on dissimilar aspects or classes of women's labour. In this section we shall consider, however briefly and summarily, whether women workers in the countryside really did suffer a loss of productive functions as a result of the rise of pre-industrial capitalism.

Considering first the relation of female labour to developments in the productive forces (that is, advances in technology, the technical organisation of labour, and the state of scientific knowledge as applied to production), there can be little doubt but that rural women workers like their town counterparts, were gradually being squeezed out of those sectors of the economy which were seeing the greatest progress in terms of productive efficiency and potential. As we have already seen, some of the most important of contemporary advances were those being made in large-scale agrarian capitalism, and these

owed as much to the more efficient organisation of human
capital resources as it did to technological innovation.
But women were generally excluded from the growing band
of occupational specialists, being confined instead to
household service or unskilled day wage-labour. Similarly,
the capitalisation of many rural industries tended to
result in their removal from organisational roles and from
the skilled branches of production (e.g. in weaving,
brewing and probably pottery too). On the other hand,
the sphere where the productivity of women's labour
remained generally as high as and often inseparable from
that of men, i.e. in domestic industry, was the very
sector where fewest advances in the productivity of labour
were being made. Whether one regards that as ironic or
as significant will depend on the kind of theory one
develops by way of explanation. My own view is that it
is still too early to make an informed judgement.

As regards women's contribution to the economy of
their own households, however, the picture is much more
varied as different criteria for measuring use-value come
into play. Certainly, there are no grounds for supporting
Clark's bald claim, often repeated since, that the shift
to wage-labour undermined women's contribution to their
families.[43] Whether it did so or not depended on the
nature of the specific capital-labour relation involved,
and on the internal organisation of the household's labour
resources.

Under agrarian capitalism the contribution that a
woman could make to the necessary product generally did
decline in both an absolute and relative sense. The loss
of a smallholding and its associated resources reduced her
capacity to provide for her family without entering market
relations, and the loss would not be compensated by
earnings from wage-labour which were pitifully small,
often insufficient even for her own maintenance, and
considerably lower than a man could secure.[44] But in other
sectors of the rural economy her contribution remained
vital despite the transition to wage-labour, and may in
some circumstances even have increased in its relative
importance. It has been estimated, for example, that in
the sixteenth and seventeenth centuries fully two-thirds of
labourers wealthy enough to leave an inventory had been
involved in by-industry, and it is evident that in very
many cases the by-industry had depended heavily on
female labour.[45] Women's work could make the marginal
difference between poverty and a modest prosperity. In
the proto-proletarian family, on the other hand, it might
make the difference between 'primary misery' (arising
from the conditions of the proto-capitalist system) and an
even worse 'secondary poverty' (brought on by the family
life-cycle). It was precisely because the wages of both

partners had fallen so low that the earnings of wife and daughters were every bit as essential as those of husband and sons, even where it was possible to differentiate them.[46] Moreover, it is worth pointing out that under this system, because they had to work so hard and for such long hours, the productiveness of both women and men may actually have increased if we take as our standard of measurement the value of their total output rather than the productive efficiency of their labour.

Conclusion

Historians are frequently heard to complain that sociologists are over-inclined to make generalisations that are insufficiently supported by evidence. Certainly, this is a risk of which we need to be aware but undue cautiousness in this matter would be equally regrettable. In the first place the results of historical research need to be made available to wider publics in an accessible and memorable form – and I am not simply referring to publics who become interested in history 'for its own sake'. Social groups invariably possess and act in the light of images of their own and others' past histories which are simplified and distorted. Historians should be concerned to make these myths more informed (though they will never cease to be myths in the anthropological sense). Negative responses to this challenge to the effect that we do not know enough about what happened in past times will simply leave those myths untouched. The excessive restraint of some (though by no means all) historians in this regard is based on a false sense of modesty (though one suspects that the veil of modesty may occasionally be designed to preserve a professional mystique as much as anything else). Historians are nearly always in a far better position than the public at large to make informed speculations and inferences about the social structures of the past, and this is so even in the case of the obscure histories of non-literate populations.

Moreover, generalising is not a sin of sociologists alone. Historians too make generalisations often of the most sweeping kind. This is not intended as a criticism, but rather to indicate an unavoidable quality of all historical interpretation. In the best, most stimulating, and certainly most memorable work these general propositions are brought into the open and laid bare for public scrutiny. But all historical commentary (as distinct from straight reporting) smuggles in sociological and even biological assumptions which are not properly articulated, yet are often of the most general kind imaginable. Nowhere, probably, has this been more true than in the

study of processes related to women: women's work, family
life, child-rearing, sexuality and so on. The possibilities
for a fruitful exchange of ideas between historians,
sociologists and anthropologists in this area are legion
especially in the light of recent feminist explorations of
the social relations of gender.

This article has therefore attempted to do two
things. It has argued that certain propositions concerning
changes in the sexual division of labour during the rise
of capitalism (generated by professional historians, but
now widely accepted by lay publics) are pitched at a
level of generality which involves an unnecessary degree
of simplification. It seems unhelpful, indeed positively
misleading, to conceive of capitalism as a monolithic
entity tending to have a uniform impact on the sexual
division of labour wherever it appeared. We now have
sufficient evidence to refine the model developed by the
'critical-pessimistic' tradition, without having to abandon
systematic generalisation (or the concept of capitalism)
altogether. Secondly, the article has attempted to expose
and clarify various unspoken and unanalysed assumptions
that have often passed for 'knowledge' in historical
accounts of women's work. It is in relation to these two
aims that I hope it will be judged.

Notes

1. I should like to thank Lindsey Charles for her many
   helpful suggestions for improving an earlier draft
   of this paper.
2. A. Clark, *Working Life of Women in the Seventeenth
   Century*, London, G. Routledge and Sons, 1919
   (Reissued by Frank Cass, 1968).
3. I. Pinchbeck, *Women Workers and the Industrial
   Revolution, 1750-1850*, London, Routledge and Kegan
   Paul, 1930 (Reissued in paperback London, Virago
   Press, 1981).
   L.A. Tilly and J.W. Scott, *Women, Work and Family*,
   New York, Holt, Rinehart and Winston, 1978.
4. R. Hamilton, *The Liberation of Women: A Study of
   Patriarchy and Capitalism*, London, George Allen &
   Unwin, 1978; A. Oakley, *Housewife*, Harmondsworth,
   Penguin, 1976, Ch. Two and Three; S. Lewenhak,
   Women and Work, London, Fontana, 1980;
   E. Zaretsky, *Capitalism, the Family and Personal
   Life*, London, Pluto, 1976.
5. Clark, pp.6-7. MacPherson's classification of
   models of society is unsatisfactory for a similar
   reason. His 'possessive market society' covers both
   proto- and full industrial capitalism, though his

stress on 'labour-power' (p.57) emphasises the latter. C.B. MacPherson, *The Political Theory of Possessive Individualism,* Oxford, University Press, 1964.

6.   The term 'family wage' has a different connotation in this context from that which it has subsequently acquired. It refers to a wage that covers the services of the whole family working together and belongs to the family as a whole.

7.   Clark, p.296.

8.   Ibid., pp.304-5.

9.   Pinchbeck, p.306. Likewise, Tilly and Scott trace a reduction in female productive activity from a relatively high level in the pre-industrial household economy to a lower level in the early stages of industrialisation.

10. Hamilton, pp.15-16.

11. It should be said, though, that in separating the rise of capitalism from the process of industrialisation we are making use of an analytical device that, while having implications of a chronological and causal kind, does not refer to any clear-cut sequence of stages of the kind suggested by Hamilton.

12. Hamilton, pp.18-19 and p.47.

13. It should be noted that the acquisition of an occupational identity does not automatically flow from the possession of skills. In particular, skills acquired by women may not receive full recognition precisely because they are female skills. Elson and Pearson have recently pointed out female skills are often viewed as natural attributes. D. Elson and R. Pearson, 'The Subordination of Women and the Internationalisation of Factory Production' in K. Young, C. Wolkowitz and R. McCullagh (eds), *Of Marriage and the Market,* London, CSE Books, 1981.

14. According to the classic Marxian analysis of capitalism, necessary labour is equivalent in value to the cost of hiring labour power and is performed entirely by the wage-labourer. Recently, of course, this claim has been challenged by some contributors to the 'domestic labour debate'. For a summary of this still unresolved debate, see M. Molyneux, 'Beyond the Domestic Labour Debate', *New Left Review,* No.116, July-August 1979.

15. Note, however, that the distinction between necessary and surplus labour cross-cuts that between domestic and non-domestic labour. The latter refers to a particular way of structuring the allocation of tasks.

16. C. Middleton, 'Peasants, Patriarchy and the Feudal Mode of Production in England: A Marxist Appraisal. Part I,' *Sociological Review*, 29 (1) New Series, 1981, pp.125–128.

17. 'Typically at home' because we should not forget workers such as spinners and handknitters of both sexes who worked as they walked along the road.

18. For agriculture, see M. Roberts, 'Sickles and Scythes: Women's Work and Men's Work at Harvest Time', *History Workshop*, 7, Spring 1979, pp.3–28. For household and other tasks, see C. Middleton, 'The Sexual Division of Labour in Feudal England', *New Left Review*, Nos. 113–114, Jan–April 1979, pp.147–168.

19. M.M. Postan, 'The Famulus: The Estate Labourer in the Twelfth and Thirteenth Centuries', *Economic History Review*, Supplement 2, 1954, Appendix II.

20. A. Everitt, 'Farm Labourers' in J. Thirsk (ed), *The Agrarian History of England and Wales, Vol.IV, 1500–1640*, Cambridge, University Press, 1967, pp.430ff.

21. *Ibid.*, p.433.

22. M. Roberts. The assumption that the male monopoly of ploughing can be explained in terms of superior strength has been challenged by, among others, L. Davidoff. See 'Power as an "essentially contested": Can it be of use to feminist historians?': paper delivered at International Women's History Conference, University of Maryland, 1977.

23. See, for example, M. Reich, D.M. Gordon and R.C. Edwards, 'A Theory of Labour Market Segmentation' in A.H. Amsden (ed.), *The Economics of Women and Work*, Harmondsworth, Penguin, 1980, pp.232–241.

24. See D.C. Coleman, *Industry in Tudor and Stuart England*, London, Macmillan, 1975, Ch.3.

25. P. Hudson, 'Proto-industrialisation: the case of the West Riding Wool Textile Industry in the Eighteenth and early Nineteenth Centuries', *History Workshop*, No.12, Autumn 1981, p.37.

26. F.F. Mendels, 'Proto-industrialisation: the first phase of the industrialisation process', *Journal of Economic History*, 1972, p.242.

27. J. Thirsk, 'Industries in the Countryside' in F.J. Fisker (ed.) *Essays in the Economic and Social History of Tudor and Stuart England*, Cambridge, University Press, 1961.

28. See, for example, J.D. Chambers, 'The Vale of Trent', *Economic History Review*, Supplement 3, 1957, p.13, n.8; A. Everitt, pp.425–29; E.L. Jones, 'Agriculture and Economic Growth in England, 1660–1750: Agric-

ultural Change', in W.E. Minchinton (ed.), *Essays in Agrarian History*, Vol. I, Newton Abbott, David and Charles, 1968, p.214; D. Levine, *Family Formation in an Age of Nascent Capitalism*, London, Academic Press, 1977.

29. D.C. Coleman, 'Labour in the English Economy of the Seventeenth Century', *Economic History Review*, 2nd Series, VIII, 1956, pp.280-95.

30. Thirsk, *Industries*, pp.73 and 81; Levine, Ch.2; R. Scott, *Women in the Stuart Economy*, M.Phil. (London), 1973, pp.57-8.

31. Levine, Ch.2.

32. Thirsk, *Industries*, pp.70 and 81-2. E. Shorter, 'Women's work: what difference did capitalism make?', *Theory and Society*, 3 (4), 1976, p.517.

33. H. Medick, 'The proto-industrial family economy: the structural function of household and family during the transition from peasant society to industrial capitalism', *Social History*, Vol.I, 1976, pp.311-13.

34. *Ibid.*, p.304.

35. *Ibid.*, p.302.

36. See for example, R. Scott, p.148 (and also p.134).

37. E. Power, 'The Position of women' in C.G. Crump and E.F. Jacob (eds.), *The Legacy of the Middle Ages*, Oxford, Clarendon Press, 1926, p.427.

38. Indeed, Everitt reports that 'In populous Pennine valleys like Garsdale and Dentdale, and in parts of Wales, both men and women knitted stockings as they walked from house to house, and village to village.' Everitt, p.426.

39. In view of this it would appear that most histories of changing attitudes towards work, especially those which depict the spread of a Protestant or similar 'work ethic' are probably inapplicable to women – another example of women's 'invisibility' in historical writing.

40. In a personal communication.

41. See n.37. Direct evidence for pre-industrial England is difficult to obtain, but for European examples see E. Shorter, *The Making of the Modern Family*, Glasgow, Fontana, 1977, pp.172-73. For a summary of some English evidence, see R. Fletcher, *The Family and Marriage in Britain*, Harmondsworth, Penguin, 1966.

42. Levine, p.1.

43. Clark, p.304.

44. Scott, ch.6.

45. Everitt, pp.425-29.

46. Medick, pp.304ff.

THE CONTRIBUTORS

Lindsey Charles did post-graduate research in women's history at Oxford and is now a History Editor for Thomas Nelson & Sons.

Lorna Duffin was a post-graduate at Oxford, a lecturer at Leicester University and now teaches for the Open University, South Region.

Kay Lacey is currently doing post-graduate research on medieval English silkwomen.

Diane Hutton teaches at Channing School, Highgate, and is doing post-graduate research on Shrewsbury in the Late Middle Ages.

Sue Wright is an ESRC research fellow at the Department of English Local History, University of Leicester.

Michael Roberts teaches in the Department of History, University College of Wales, Aberystwyth.

Chris Middleton teaches in the Department of Sociological Studies, University of Sheffield.